Ecclesiological Investigations

Series Editor

Gerard Mannion

Volume 5

Ecumenical Ecclesiology

Ecclesiological Investigations brings together quality research and inspiring debates in ecclesiology worldwide from a network of international scholars, research centres and projects in the field.

Other titles in the series:

Ecumenical Ecclesiology

UNITY, DIVERSITY AND OTHERNESS IN A FRAGMENTED WORLD

Edited by

Gesa Elsbeth Thiessen

t &t clark

Published by T&T Clark
A Continuum imprint
The Tower Building, 11 York Road, London SE1 7NX
80 Maiden Lane, Suite 704, New York, NY 10038

www.continuumbooks.com

British Library Cataloguing-in-Publication Data
A catalogue record for this book is available from the British Library

Typeset by Data Standards Limited, Frome, Somerset
Printed and bound in Great Britain by the MPG Books Group,
Bodmin and King's Lynn

ISBN: HB: 978-0-567-00913-5

CONTENTS

ACKNOWLEDGEMENTS

The idea for this volume emerged from the talks presented at the Unit of the Ecclesiological Investigations International Research Network at the American Academy of Religion annual meeting, 2007, in San Diego, and at a conference on contemporary ecclesiology held at Milltown Institute, Dublin, in 2008.

My sincere gratitude to Gerard Mannion for his encouragement to edit this volume and for his unfailing and kind support in the process. Thanks also to Paul M. Collins for his encouragement and to the members of the Steering Group of the Ecclesiological Investigations Network. Thanks are due to Milltown Institute, especially Rector Prof. Finbarr Clancy, SJ, for hosting the ecclesiology conference. My special thanks to Prof. Linda Hogan, Head of School, Irish School of Ecumenics, Trinity College, Dublin, for her preface and to all the contributors to this volume. Their wonderful collaboration made my task a very pleasant experience. To Thomas Kraft and T&T Clark/Continuum my thanks for their courteous cooperation. Last but not least, Declan Marmion mein herzlicher Dank.

List of Contributors

Travis E. Ables is a PhD candidate in Theological Studies and Philosophy at Vanderbilt University. His dissertation is a study on the pneumatological construction of subjectivity in the Western tradition, examining issues of ontology, analogy and apophaticism from Augustine to Rahner. He holds an MDiv from Trinity Evangelical Divinity School.

Radu Bordeianu is an Assistant Professor of Systematic Theology at Duquesne University, Pittsburgh, PA (USA). Born, raised and educated in Romania, he received his ThM from Duke University (2000) and PhD from Marquette University (2006). His research focuses on ecumenical ecclesiologies, especially Orthodox and Catholic. He is most interested in the ecumenical relevance of Dumitru Staniloae's trinitarian ecclesiology. He has published several articles and has presented various papers on ecumenical and environmental issues.

Eddy Van der Borght received his PhD from Leiden University in 2000. Associate Professor of Systematic Theology at Vrije Universiteit Amsterdam, he has published on the theology of ministry, on ecclesiology, and on faith and ethnicity. He recently published *Theology of Ministry: A Reformed Contribution to an Ecumenical Dialogue* (Brill, 2007). His next monograph will focus on church and ethnicity. He is editor-in-chief of the *Journal of Reformed Theology* (www.brill.nl/jrt) and of the series *Studies in Reformed Theology* (www.brill.nl/srt).

Julie Clague is a lecturer in Catholic theology at the University of Glasgow. She has written numerous articles and has been co-editor of the journal *Feminist Theology* since 1993 and the journal *Political Theology* since 2005. She serves on the steering committee of the American Academy of Religion: Ecclesiological Investigations Programme unit. She is a founder member of the International Association for Catholic Social Thought, and a member of the Theological Commission of the Catholic Bishops' Conference of England and Wales agency, Caritas-Social Action. Additionally, she works as a theologian with the Catholic international aid agencies CAFOD and SCIAF.

Paul M. Collins, PhD, is a priest in the Church of England, Reader in Theology at the University of Chichester, and a member of the coordinating group of the international Ecclesiological Investigations Research Network. Among his publications are: *Trinitarian Theology West and East: Karl Barth, the Cappadocian Fathers and John Zizioulas* (Oxford University Press, 2001), *Christian Inculturation in India* (Ashgate, 2007), *Receiving the Nature and Mission of the Church*, co-edited with Michael Fahey, SJ (T&T Clark, 2008), *Christian Community Now*, co-authored with Gerard Mannion, Gareth Powell and Kenneth Wilson (T&T Clark, 2008).

Wendy Dackson is Director of Studies for the Local Ministry Training Scheme in the Diocese of Canterbury. She has been a Research Fellow of the Oxford Centre for Ecclesiology and Practical Theology at Ripon College, Cuddesdon. Her doctoral dissertation on the ecclesiology of Archbishop William Temple was published by Edward Mellen Press. Her reviews and articles have appeared in *Anglican and Episcopal History*, *Journal of Church and State*, *Anglican Theological Review*, *Studies in Christian Ethics*, and *Journal of Anglican Studies*.

Edwin C. van Driel is assistant professor in theology at Pittsburgh Theological Seminary. A native of the Netherlands, he holds Masters degrees in theology and philosophy from Utrecht University and an MA, MPhil, and PhD in religious studies (theology) from Yale University. His book *Incarnation Anyway: Arguments for Supralapsarian Christology* is published by Oxford University Press (2008).

Madeline Duntley, PhD, is Director of Chapman Learning Community and Associate Professor of American Culture Studies and Sociology at Bowling Green State University in north-west Ohio where she teaches North American religions. She has published several articles on Japanese American Protestants, Catholics and Buddhists in Seattle, and she is writing a monograph on Japanese American Religion.

Brian P. Flanagan completed his PhD in theology at Boston College in 2007, with a dissertation entitled *Communion, Diversity, and Salvation: The Contribution of Jean-Marie Tillard, OP, to Systematic Ecclesiology*. He was a Visiting Assistant Professor in the Department of Religious Studies at the College of the Holy Cross, Worcester, Massachusetts and is now Assistant Professor of Christian Theology at Marymount University, Arlington, Virginia. His most recent publication is 'The Limits of Ecclesial Metaphors in Systematic Ecclesiology', in the journal *Horizons*.

Miriam Haar is a PhD Candidate in Ecumenical Theology at the Irish School of Ecumenics, Trinity College, Dublin. She received an MPhil in Ecumenics from Trinity College, Dublin, in 2007, having previously been awarded a *Diplom* in Protestant Theology from the University of Tübingen in 2006.

Evan F. Kuehn received his MA in historical and systematic theology at Wheaton College (IL), where he is currently the cataloguing associate at the Buswell Memorial Library. He is continuing graduate work in theology at the University of Chicago, and is the author of articles in *Theological Studies* and *The Ecclesiastical Law Journal.*

Hak Joon Lee is Associate Professor of Theology and Ethics at New Brunswick Theological Seminary, where he has taught since 1998. He also taught at Drew University and New York Theological Seminary. Lee received his MDiv (1990) and PhD (1997) from Princeton Theological Seminary. He has published *Covenant and Communication: A Christian Moral Conversation with Jürgen Habermas* (University Press of America, 2006), *We Will Get to the Promised Land: Martin Luther King, Jr.'s Communal-Political Spirituality* (Pilgrim Press, 2006), and *Public Theology for a Global Society*, co-edited with Scott Paeth and Deirdre Hainsworth (Eerdmans, 2008).

Gerard Mannion was educated at Cambridge and Oxford Universities. He has lectured at church colleges of the universities of Oxford and Leeds, and was previously Associate Professor of Ecclesiology and Ethics at Liverpool Hope University. Presently, he serves as Chair of the Ecclesiological Investigations International Research Network. He is a Senior Research Fellow of the Katholieke Universiteit Leuven, Belgium, and a Visiting Professor of the University of Chichester, UK. Recent publications include *Ecclesiology and Postmodernity – Questions for the Church in Our Times* (Liturgical Press, 2007), *The Routledge Companion to the Christian Church*, co-editor (Routledge, 2007), and *The Vision of John Paul II: Assessing his Thought and Influence*, editor (Liturgical Press, 2008).

Andrew Pierce, PhD, is Lecturer in Ecumenics at the Irish School of Ecumenics, Trinity College, Dublin, where he is involved in continuing research into the theological engagement with so-called religious fundamentalism. In 2008/9 he is a Government of Ireland Senior Research Fellow and a Visiting Scholar at University College Dublin International Centre for Newman Studies.

Gesa Elsbeth Thiessen, MPhil (Ecum), PhD, studied theology at Tübingen University, the Irish School of Ecumenics (Trinity College), and at Milltown Institute of Theology and Philosophy in Dublin. She lectures in systematic theology at Milltown Institute and is an Honorary Research Fellow of the Department of Theology and Religious Studies of the University of Wales, Lampeter. Her publications include *Theology and Modern Irish Art* (Columba, 1999), *Theological Aesthetics: A Reader* (SCM/Eerdmans, 2004), and, co-edited with Declan Marmion, *Theology in the Making: Biography, Methods, Contexts* (Veritas, 2005). She is a member of the Steering Group of the Ecclesiological Investigations International Research Network.

PREFACE

Linda Hogan

As we approach the centenary of the 1910 World Missionary Conference, which is widely recognized as the formative event in the emergence of the modern ecumenical movement, it is both opportune and necessary to consider the theological significance and impact of a century of ecumenism. Throughout that century a small number of themes have continued to be of critical concern to Christians worldwide, key among them being that of ecclesiology. Moreover, it is within the frame of ecclesiology that many Christians have encountered the pain of fragmentation and division most acutely. This collection, focused as it is on ecumenical ecclesiology, brings readers to the heart of one of the most enduring of concerns for Christians today and enables us to take an uncompromising look at the depths of division, the challenges of encounter and the prospects for reconciliation.

The volume gathers an impressive group of theologians, established and emerging, who together deliberate on themes of shared ecclesiological and ecumenical concern. The collection achieves a commendable balance, with essays that extend the scope of existing debates and those that introduce new perspectives and ideas into the discourse of ecumenical ecclesiology. The global nature of ecumenical dialogue is evident herein, too, with analyses from diverse countries including, e.g., the UK, Korea, Nigeria, USA and Japan, contextualizing the thematic considerations in illuminating ways. Intra-ecclesial debates are never far from the surface either, suggesting that many of the difficulties that arise in ecumenical dialogue also have a resonance within the different denominational contexts.

Much of what has been learned during the first century of the ecumenical movement has revolved around the difficulties of encounter. While unambiguous respect for the distinctive contours of denominational identity has not yet been achieved, nonetheless there is an evident commitment to the development of relationships of integrity, mutuality and cooperation. Moreover, as ecumenical encounter has continued we have come to appreciate how critical the ecclesiological domain is in this regard. This collection, ably edited by Gesa Thiessen, makes an important contribution to this most contested and vibrant aspect of ecumenical theology and deserves to have an impact where it matters most, in the churches.

INTRODUCTION

Gesa E. Thiessen

The present volume is a contribution to the ongoing task of developing ecumenical ecclesiology. The articles originate from papers which were presented at the Unit of the Ecclesiological Investigations International Research Network at the American Academy of Religion in San Diego, 2007, as well as at a conference on contemporary ecclesiology organized under the auspices of the EI Network and Milltown Institute of Theology and Philosophy in Dublin, 2008.

The 15 European, North American and Asian scholars, lay and ordained, represented in this book are of the Anglican, Lutheran, Orthodox, Reformed and Roman Catholic traditions. The book not only outlines and addresses a variety of concepts in ecumenical ecclesiology, but, as such, is a manifestation of a rapidly growing trend, namely of theologians from numerous denominational backgrounds working on themes that are of common ecclesiological and theological interest. In other words, doing ecclesiology ecumenically is becoming commonplace. This, indeed, is a hopeful sign that ecumenism – despite the lamentably slow progress in concrete steps towards ecclesial unity – is, in fact, working. Shared ecclesiological interests and an ease of relating to one another as theologians of different churches evidence the *actual* progress that has been made in theological and ecumenical circles, and it is, of course, also a sign of how theology, like other sciences, is nowadays conducted in a global fashion.

In a way this may also be indicative of the fact that today deep-running divisions tend to be at least as much *intra*-ecclesial – i.e. *within* a tradition – as they are inter-denominational. That creates a decisive change and challenge, yet equally opportunities not only between churches but also in their inner relations. The fundamental goal of church unity is thus faced with, and has to seek answers to, fragmentation in inter-ecclesial and intra-ecclesial domains as well as in the secular, multicultural and multifaith sphere.

In an age often described as promoting belief in God without the church, it is interesting to note that a good number of the papers have been authored by younger theologians. It shows that thinking about ecclesiology has become anything but meaningless or superfluous; rather it is at the centre of theological thinking today. Indeed, it is encouraging to realize that the Ecclesiological Investigations Research Network is itself supported by both junior and senior scholars.

The book is divided into three parts: I. various perspectives on contemporary ecumenical issues, in particular, reflections on ecumenical models and on methods in ecumenism; II. communion ecclesiology and otherness with reference, especially, to the ecclesiological contributions of Zizioulas and Volf; and III. ecclesiological themes in global contexts with articles relating to diverse ecclesiological developments in Europe, Africa and Asia.

In Chapter 1, 'Driving the Haywain: Where Stands the Church "Catholic" Today?', Gerard Mannion sets the scene not only for the issues discussed in this book but for any engagement with ecclesiology today, namely our context of globalization and its problematic implications for the world. This article could have been equally included in Parts II or III. However, as it spans a wide canvas, including social-analytical, ethical and ecclesiological considerations, it is a fitting opening chapter to this volume. In the light of the global credit crunch and talk of shifting economic and political paradigms, Mannion examines the ecumenical challenges posed by globalization in general and global capitalism in particular, so as to explore possible empowering contributions of the churches to human life in the twenty-first century. In envisioning the challenge of moving from an era where the dominant ideology is one of rampant exploitation to a more genuine global solidarity, Mannion focuses on resources from the Christian social tradition and, specifically, on a reconceptualization of the ecclesial mark of catholicity as a powerful social imaginary. He enters into hermeneutical considerations and notes how ecumenical thinking itself can offer resources towards a practical application of the notion of catholicity as a path from exploitation to solidarity. How we relate to the other and to otherness offers insights into the true 'mark' of a global church of the poor. Mannion concludes that ultimately catholicity is both an 'ecclesiological concept' and an 'ethical task'.

In the second chapter, I outline some methods and related matters in contemporary ecumenism, the point of departure being the common Christian confession that the church is one, holy, catholic and apostolic. The question is how such unity and apostolicity can be realized in a church that understands herself as, and aims to be, a unity in diversity. This leads us into the very heart of the ecumenical quest, i.e. a shared concept of church structures and the concurrent lack of reception of bi- and multilateral ecumenical statements. The fact that ecumenical dialogue in itself has become so multifaceted and is clearly lacking in a unified vision makes reception even more difficult. The article, then, considers the process and problems of reception, the idea and application of differentiated consensus statements, and pneumatological freedom in furthering ecumenical agreements and in shaping the apostolic church. Finally, the essay takes up and attempts to develop an idea first mooted by Karl Rahner about the factual faith of the people *vis-à-vis* church teaching. This factual faith and operative ecclesiology among the people of God is examined as potentially enabling progress and shedding significant light on the ecumenical vision of church unity.

Miriam Haar, in her chapter 'The Struggle for an Organic, Conciliar and Diverse Church: Models of Church Unity in Earlier Stages of the Ecumenical Dialogue', engages in a related topic as she investigates the significance of two models of church unity which emerged in the larger context of the World Council of Churches: 'Organic Unity' and 'Conciliar Fellowship'. While the visible unity of the church is the ultimate ecumenical aim, she points out that such unity is 'a reality of which the churches have as yet no previous experience'. Thus the final shape is as yet unknown and 'in the making'. On this road towards unity, various – and often closely related – models of unity have been envisaged. These models are not 'abstract constructs', but, rather, they express something of the 'real being of the church'. She also considers how recent ecumenical debate has focused on the concepts of *koinonia* and *communio*. Significantly, she notes that a real appreciation of these concepts must imply an awareness of their roots in earlier models of unity. Haar thus attempts to examine the 'synergy' of these two models, how they influenced each other, and how they play a role in more recent concepts of unity and in ecumenical ecclesiology. Finally, she asserts that as 'no final answer has been reached as to what full visible unity entails'; the ecumenical quest remains an 'ongoing transformative process'. Ultimately we are reminded that unity is not something which can emerge simply by human effort but does so through divine, eschatological grace.

A further reflection on how to imagine concepts of church unity is that of Edwin van Driel, who focuses on the idea of 'covenant'. This is another model of unity explored in recent ecclesiological discussion. He examines this concept through the perspective of his own church, the Netherlands Reformed Church (NRC). Driel briefly outlines this Church's somewhat turbulent history and examines the idea of covenant as adopted by the NRC. However, he emphasizes that while recent discussions conceive of 'covenant' as being of human making, he seeks to recommend the idea of a 'divine covenant' as a basis for the church. He proceeds by expounding this concept through five theses. Driel mentions that, as with other American mainline churches, the NRC counts among its members both liberals and conservatives, with substantial theological differences. Yet this concept of a divine covenant as the basis of the NRC's unity has enabled liberals and conservatives to accept each other still as members of the same church. Fundamentally, church membership of 'the other' is not at stake, because it does not rest on a human, but on a divine, choice, expressed in baptism: 'You did not choose me but I chose you' (Jn 15.16). Significantly, he observes that if God chooses 'the other' as a fellow member of the covenant, what right would one member have to separate her or himself from another? In a final outlook he relates this concept more broadly to the future of the American mainline churches and affirms that 'we do not belong to God's people based on our own willing, choosing, or acting, but on God's actions'.

In 'Comprehensive Vision: The Ecumenical Potential of a Lost Ideal', Andrew Pierce – from an Anglican historical and contemporary perspective – explores a further model of unity. He notes that in the internecine polemics of early Anglican theological self-understanding, the concept of 'comprehensiveness' was expounded and defended by a number of leading writers. However, in more recent Anglican conflicts this concept has been ignored. He thus considers whether a renewed engagement with compre-hensiveness may be beneficial to debates within Anglicanism and, more broadly, in working towards an ecumenical ecclesiology, e.g., in the Faith and Order Commission of the World Council of Churches. Historically, the Church of England and the Church of Ireland consciously defined themselves as national bodies which 'comprehended' both Reformed and Catholic theological traditions. Pierce notes that Elizabeth I self-con-sciously shaped a 'national' church to serve a particular nation's interest. However, the consolidation of parties within the Church of England – Evangelicals, Broadchurch, Anglo-Catholic – later effectively subverted comprehension. What these parties effectively achieved was a separation of the traditions that comprehension had held together. Pierce observes how each of these claimed classical status, and each disputed the other's Anglicanity. As Anglicanism moved into a post-colonial and post-*Book of Common Prayer* context, this party-based ecclesiality has impacted on attempts to understand Anglicanism's unity and identity. Pierce concludes by suggesting that Anglicanism might consider offering comprehension as an 'ecumenical gift' that could contribute to the quest for an ecumenical ecclesiology. He points out, however, that for such a gift to commend itself, Anglicans would have to provide some evidence of its theological value within Anglicanism.

In Chapter 6, Wendy Dackson also writes within the context of the Anglican Communion, focusing on the issue of impaired communion. In 2003 the General Convention of the Episcopal Church (USA) confirmed the election of Gene Robinson as Bishop of New Hampshire. Since then in Anglican circles much has been discussed in relation to 'impaired communion' and 'instruments of unity'. She notes how this debate has been mainly at 'the level of primates' meetings'. It 'presupposes that "communion" exists in, and is determined by, the relationships between primates, bishops and other senior officials in the Anglican Communion'. This in turn raises the question, 'whether the primates, or even all the bishops, constitute the "Communion"', or whether it, in fact, includes all the faithful belonging to the Communion. Moreover, she asks whether bishops and primates actually represent the people in their provinces and dioceses. She emphasizes that her essay is not about sexuality, but, rather, she wishes to address 'questionable processes of theological reasoning' which have led to the 'confused situation' in the Anglican Communion. In fact, she notes how the concept of 'theological integrity' (Rowan Williams) has suffered serious violations. She comments on how the behaviour of some primates and bishops 'bear[s] the marks of, and encourage[s] participation in, "alternative aggressions"'. Her article ends with a reflection on the question of what actually constitutes the 'Anglican Communion', while critically addressing 'the lack of an agreed-upon working definition of "impaired communion"', and pointing out that the use of language and metaphors, such as 'illness', as employed in *The Windsor Report*, ought to be more carefully chosen.

Part II, 'Communion Ecclesiology and Otherness', begins with Paul M. Collins' essay, 'The Church and the "Other": Questions of Ecclesial and Divine Communion'. Thinking about 'the Other' has emerged as an important theme in recent theological and philosophical discourse. Against the multicultural context in which the vast majority of people now live, at least in the West, against the horizon of breakdown of human relations in world wars, and in the context of ongoing ecclesial disunity, the theological engagement with the notion of 'the Other', the stranger, the one who does not belong and who yet needs to find identity and a home, does become rather urgent. How do the churches relate to 'the Other'? Collins has written extensively on the Trinity, and in this article he reflects on the connection between the church and God as Trinity, which has implications for the question of the church and 'the Other'. Collins thus asks where 'the other stands' in the 'conceptualization of a connection between ecclesial and divine communion'. His dialogue partners include a range of thinkers: Boff, Küng, Volf, Caputo, Barth and Zizioulas. Collins finally asserts that – in the face of the church's 'ongoing exclusion' of 'the schismatic', 'the

heretic', 'the excommunicate' and 'the [Non-] Religious Other' – it
remains a concrete task for the churches to seriously reflect on how 'to
respond to demands for tolerance and/or hospitality'.

Travis Ables, in his chapter, offers a critique of John Zizioulas'
communion ecclesiology. His aim is to 'examine and test the attempt to
ground communion ecclesiology in the doctrine of the Trinity'. Zizioulas'
theology has been an important resource in constructing an ecumenical
ecclesiology on the basis of a trinitarian ontology of person-in-relation.
While Zizioulas has been challenged on the historical accuracy of his
reading of the Cappadocian Fathers, Ables argues that Zizioulas' systematic
proposal has not often been given serious scrutiny on its own terms. He
critically examines 'the ambiguity of analogy in Zizioulas' theology', the
dialectic between uncreated and created being. Ables finds the central
problem in the very heart of Zizioulas' proposal: 'a proffering of an *ontology*
of communion, authorized by the analogy between the event of
communion of persons that is the Trinity, and the event of communion
in the church, where communion is an ontological category of the ekstasis
of the hypostasis'. Ables seeks to interrogate the very idea of ontology as a
basis for ecclesiology, pointing out, finally, that the construction of
ontology may function 'as the evasion of the truly difficult task of being
with the other'. He concludes by presenting an alternative account of the
relationship of trinitarian theology and ecclesiology as an attempt to answer
the problems raised by Zizioulas' proposal.

In Chapter 9, Radu Bordeianu concerns himself with the quest for
retrieving a eucharistic ecclesiology, and he focuses on Nicholas Afanassieff,
John Zizioulas and Dumitru Staniloae. Bordeianu notes how twentieth-
century Orthodox theologian Nicholas Afanassieff contended that the local
eucharistic assembly is fully autonomous and that it represents the church
in its fullness. Moreover, Afanassieff maintained that the Catholic and
Orthodox Churches celebrate the same Eucharist, which is a sign of their
already-existing unity despite canonical disunity. Therefore he suggested
the possibility of practising intercommunion. Afanassieff's position was
critiqued by Zizioulas and Staniloae as 'unsatisfactory'. Bordeianu analyses
and compares each of the latter two theologians' communion ecclesiologies
in their response to Afanassieff. Zizioulas criticizes intercommunion as he
maintains that the Eucharist is inseparable from sharing the same teaching
and from communion among the bishops. Staniloae contends, among
other things, that although the Orthodox and Catholic Churches both have
a valid Eucharist, intercommunion was to be rejected, as eucharistic
communion ought to be based on the 'unity of faith', especially in relation
to papal primacy. Bordeianu analyses the strengths of each of these three
thinkers and proposes a communion ecclesiology that includes elements

from Afanassieff, Zizioulas, Staniloae, and Vatican II theology, thus aiming to advance Orthodox–Catholic dialogue.

The theme of communion ecclesiology and inner-denominational otherness is explored by Brian Flanagan. Aware that inner-denominational problems – 'internal "otherness"' – can be as divisive as inter-denominational divisions, Flanagan's central argument is that the use of the concept of communion in ecclesiology and in ecumenical dialogue to address questions of ecumenical otherness provides theoretical and practical resources for dealing with issues of inner-denominational diversity today. He thus expounds the need for a 'unified theory of communion' which asserts that there should not be 'separate theories of Christian communion for extra-denominational and intra-denominational ecclesial relationships'. This theory was developed by Jean-Marie Tillard, OP, who used it as a theoretical tool for analysing ecclesial diversity, both ecumenically and within the Roman Catholic Church. Flanagan provides an in-depth account of Tillard's thought. The second part of his article follows the trajectory of Tillard's communion theory in an exploration of how the 'skills, structures and values' developed in the ecumenical movement can be utilized in assisting the churches in their internal negotiation of communion in difference, particularly within the North American Roman Catholic context. Flanagan finally proffers a simple but important fact – that communion among those who are 'others' is a 'mark of the church, [and] not a mere concession to a situation of imperfection'. Working towards inner-denominational communion and reconciliation thus remains an imperative in all churches.

The second section of this volume concludes with Eddy Van der Borght's 'Evangelical Ecclesiology as an Answer to Ethnic Impaired Christian Community? An Inquiry into the Theology of Miroslav Volf'. Van der Borght points out that ethnicity has been 'a challenge for the identity of the church' throughout its history. The recent reshaping of Europe and the subsequent resurgence of diaspora and migrant churches urges theologians to think again about the issue of ethnicity *vis-à-vis* ecclesiology and church identity. Ethnic differences may become church divisive; a community based on ethnic identity 'runs the risk of building communion by excluding otherness'. Migrant churches, not without coincidence, often encounter problems in trying to integrate into local churches of the same confessional tradition. Van der Borght maintains – with reference to Zizioulas – that 'the ethnic factor is a non-legitimate form of otherness within the Christian Community'. In particular, he analyses the ethnic factors which can be damaging to churches, and he examines whether Volf's evangelical ecclesiology 'is able to overcome the church-dividing potential of ethnic differences'. 'Not really', he concludes. In a

Free Church perspective, the church is considered an assembly of individual faithful whereby the new relationship with Christ simultaneously links them to other believers. Thus cultural identities are not erased, but they do not influence the identity of the church. But, Van der Borght notes, this evangelical ecclesiology built on the individual believers and the local congregation is at the same time rather vulnerable, as the local church is in reality – although often not officially – a very locally culturally determined church.

The final part of the book, 'Ecclesiology in Global Contexts', presents four quite diverse articles. Julie Clague's 'On Being a European Catholic' deals with 'the politics of inclusion' in the context of the vision of the European Union and the 'ecclesiology of exclusion' encountered in Roman Catholicism, in particular towards the presence of the 'Islamic other' (Turkey) in Europe, and the Church's stance towards gays and lesbians. The growth of Christendom, centred on Rome, was intricately linked to the emergence of Europe as a centre of political power, intellectual life and cultural expression. As Clague notes, European Christian identity today is less secure, and Catholicism's relationship with Europe is more ambivalent, as evident, for example, in some of the statements by Popes John Paul II and Benedict XVI, such as John Paul's *Ecclesia in Europa* (2003). The demise of Europe's Christian identity is seen by official Catholicism to go hand in hand with a crisis of moral values. Both are said to have their source in the European Enlightenment. Clague comments that as the European Union seeks to forge a community of nations united by common interests and shared values that transcend religious particularity, the Roman Catholic Church tries to retain the idea of a Christian Europe whose values coincide with religious conservatism. She explores these issues through an examination of recent debates over the wording of the EU Constitution, Turkey's admission to membership of the EU, and the legalization of civil unions for same-sex couples. She concludes that instead of applying 'ecclesiologies of exclusion' the church must emphasize the building of community, an inclusive ecclesiology that anticipates 'the community of God's Holy Polity'.

Serious ecclesiological and ecumenical questions about the future of global Anglicanism have resulted from the current crisis in the Anglican Communion over issues of human sexuality and ecclesiastical authority. Evan Kuehn sets out to examine the structural reforms in the Church of Nigeria's canon law revision of 14 September 2005, which constitutes a significant attempt at responding to the crisis. The revision redefined the terms of inter-provincial Anglican unity from a focus on communion with the Archbishop of Canterbury to communion based explicitly upon the authority of scripture and historic doctrinal statements. Kuehn's article analyses the revision as an ecclesiastical reform connected to, yet independent from, the current controversy over human sexuality. He discusses pertinent issues of episcopal structure and ecclesial communion as they are affected by the canon law change. The ecumenical implications of the revision are examined with particular reference to the Anglican–Roman Catholic dialogue and the 'continuing' churches of North America which have broken away from the Episcopal Church. Finally he opines that while the Church of Nigeria canon law revision of 2005 'has remained controversial as a response to current structures of Anglican unity, it should be recognized as a legitimate revision of ecclesiastical law'.

A very different theme is expounded in Hak Joon Lee's chapter 'Sacral Authority and Pastoral Ministry: A Shamanistic Inculturation of the Protestant Church in Korea'. Lee points out how Protestant churches in Korea are hugely active churches, well known for their 'spiritual fervour' and 'evangelical passion'. Yet, despite their success, they are in a situation of crisis, occasioned by public distrust due to the church's 'negligence of public responsibility and the underdevelopment of Christian social ethics'. Lee argues that the Korean Protestant Churches, regardless of their denominational variations, demonstrate unique characteristics that are distinctive from their Western counterparts: a sacral nature that is exhibited in the numinous concepts of time, space and person. He contends that this sacral nature is the consequence of the Korean Protestant Churches' long assimilation of indigenous shamanism. This assimilation, according to Lee, has gradually transformed what was once a vibrant prophetic form of Korean Protestantism into a religion that is mostly apolitical, sacral and utilitarian in nature. Although this sacralization has contributed to the churches' explosive growth by providing necessary pastoral care for lay Christians living in a highly transitional society, Korean Protestants now face a profound challenge as Korean society has become more open-minded, progressive and democratic. This new situation demands critical ecclesiological rethinking and a revision of ministerial church practices. Lee affirms that Korean Protestantism needs to respond to the demand for ecclesiastical democracy, transparency, public engagement, and, in particular, an ecclesiology that maintains a balance of pastoral and prophetic ministries in the new Korean social context.

The final chapter, by Madeline Duntley, concerns itself with the specific situation of the Japanese diaspora in the USA. From 1890 to 1935 Japanese Christian leaders advocated a missionary model of 'internationalist ecclesiology'. Duntley notes that Japanese Christians were critical of both materialist and imperialist Americanist Christian nationalism. The leaders' ecclesiology sought to merge ideas from the East and the West. Japanese Christian missionary activists created an ecclesiological model which was ecumenically oriented; the Church of the 'Pacific Era' intended to break down racial, national, class, denominational, gender and even inter-religious borders and barriers. Duntley employs the Japan/Seattle, Washington connection as a case study, utilizing the *Shiatoru Nihonjin Kirisuto Kyokai Domei* (a little-known Japanese-language mission history of a six-church inter-denominational confederation known as the 'Domei' or league established in 1912 and continuing to this day). The article demonstrates that 'the Japanese diaspora in Seattle did not merely recreate ethnic versions of American denominations, but implemented a uniquely Japanese Christian vision that set the stage for twentieth-century ecumenism and activism in future Pan-Asian Civil Rights activism in Seattle's Japanese American community'.

These 15 essays, then, offer a variety of themes and perspectives on contemporary ecclesiological concerns. They make evident that the way of being church in the (post)modern world continues to be of interest, even urgency, among theologians of diverse ecclesial backgrounds. Each chapter will hopefully contribute in a small way to further thinking about ecumenical ecclesiology, to ecumenical progress, and to offering some responses regarding the inclusion and cherishing of the other in multicultural and multifaith societies in a global context.

The church of Christ is called to be one. If these essays shed some light on how the one, holy, catholic and apostolic church can be envisioned in a fragmented, divided and suffering world, then the book will have served its task.

PART I

PERSPECTIVES ON CONTEMPORARY
ECUMENICAL ECCLESIOLOGY

Chapter 1

DRIVING THE HAYWAIN: WHERE STANDS THE CHURCH 'CATHOLIC' TODAY?

Gerard Mannion

Introductory remarks

The Haywain by Hieronymus Bosch (1450–1516) is a striking triptych. In its centre panel, an enormous haycart is depicted as it moves forward relentlessly, with a mass of characters in the scene being engaged in channelling all their efforts into grabbing handfuls of the hay from the cart before it passes them by, oblivious to the fact that what they are devoting their time and energies to is the pursuit of something ultimately worthless and ephemeral, compared with more edifying and noble pursuits. Significantly, the so-called leaders and people of power and influence of the world are seen to be following the haycart. Yet, as with the Emperor's new clothes, no one seems able or willing to desist from doing so or to point out not only that all these people are throwing away their time, but also that alternatives present themselves – there are better and more fulfilling pursuits than the seemingly deterministic grasping after the worthless hay in which the characters are fatalistically embroiled. Above all else, the painting illustrates sin taking over humanity as its primary motivating force. The sin which encapsulates this in the painting is unchecked and mindless avarice. The art historian, Walter S. Gibson, points out that, although Bosch's painting (c. 1485–90) no doubt influenced later Flemish allegorical art, the symbol of hay had a long history in low countries folklore:

> A Netherlandish song of about 1470 tells us that God has heaped up good things of the earth like a stack of hay for the benefit of all men, but that each man wants to keep it all to himself. But since hay is of little value, it also symbolizes the worthlessness of all worldly gain. This is certainly the meaning of the allegorical haycarts which appeared in several Flemish engravings after 1550. A haycart also formed part of a religious procession at Antwerp in 1563; according to a contemporary description, it was ridden by a devil

named Deceitful, and followed by all sorts of men plucking the hay, so as to show that worldly possessions are *al hoy* (all hay). 'In the end it is *al hoy*' echoes a song of the same period.[1]

Bosch's paintings, of course, have a quality that speaks out far beyond their time. It has struck me for some years now how well this painting might serve as a most vivid picture of the depressing cycle of materialism and exploitation that blights our world today. Such constitute the antithesis of community. Indeed, the painting captures in so evocative a way what we today refer to as global capitalism. The latter, in turn, is in numerous ways the driving force behind globalization and so might in some sense be deemed synonymous with globalization. The thought of Bosch's painting returned to me recently because of further resonance between Bosch's image and our contemporary world in 2008. Globalization in general, and global capitalism in particular, have been the subject of an enormous amount of discussion and literature. They have formed an increasing topic of concern and debate for the Christian churches, as well as for other faiths and, of course, secular institutions, NGOs and the like. In this chapter I wish to explore a few issues illustrating how these are themes that should preoccupy ecclesiological as much as ethical concern.

'Fool's gold' and the social gospel today: challenges for ecumenism in mission

From an ecclesiological perspective, the Christian gospel seeks to spread a message of love, peace, justice and community that has universal relevance across the globe. Fundamental to this message, as it was termed in the 1960s, is the 'preferential option for the poor'. What is detrimental to the furtherance of the ends of such a message is obviously something the churches must collectively challenge. Other world religions have similar missions and hence concerns. Of course, some of those religions have experienced (been party to) previous versions of what we today term globalization. Christianity especially so, as it was born in the midst of and became the official religion of the Roman Imperial version of global expansionism in terms of the then known world.

A few years ago,[2] I wrote about the dehumanizing forces of global capitalism and globalization as being in many ways the antithesis of the gospel itself. I suggested that we must try to counter the evils of globalization and might do so with imaginative employment of some familiar images from the Christian tradition such as *oikoumene* and, in particular, catholicity. But, just as 'catholicity' was once allowed to mutate away from its original gospel-inspired meaning into a more exclusivistic notion of a homogeneous and rigid set of doctrines, so, too, has global capitalism – ostensibly about the 'freedom' of markets and trade and commerce – been taken over by rabid protectionism, cartels, the acquisition of more and more companies by fewer and fewer, and the invention of ever more mechanisms whereby those companies and market-states, and hence individuals, who are already rich and powerful can maintain their wealth, position and hence power through the continued exploitation of others – from the workers in their own societies to those far across the globe.

Indeed, the Bosch painting in recent times seems more poignant than ever as, according to one report from the BBC, a quarter of global GDP in 2008 was spent on bailing out irresponsible banks and financial institutions in the form of loans, guarantees and investment. We saw in 2008 the hitherto ridiculous situation whereby the most liberally capitalistic and monetarist economies in the world suddenly adopted certain mechanisms and tools of socialist collectivism. But they did so not to protect the poor and the vulnerable, but rather to safeguard the future of those rich and powerful corporations and nation-states themselves. So the hard-earned income of workers was taken from them and allowed to shore up failing banks and companies that had for years behaved in an utterly irresponsible way by gambling with their own resources and that of their workers' pensions in investments that were eventually doomed to failure in a pathetically obvious fashion.

In other words, betting on debt and moving debt around has kept the world's economy afloat for many years now. Again Bosch's painting and epoch are brought to mind as '[i]n the sixteenth century, hay also possessed connotations of falsehood and deceit, and to "drive the haywain" with someone was to mock or cheat him'.[3] Entire economies built upon wealth and resources that do not exist? Some might say there is no greater example of the triumph of deceit in the age of 'spin'. Once word got out that, actually, even the markets were now beginning to think this was unsustainable, as some major US investment banks had been particularly excessive in overstretching themselves in such gambling, then the domino-effect of the momentum of failing confidence across the whole house of cards of global capitalism was bound to follow. And it did so with a vengeance. There is a superb irony in all of this. Finally, world leaders grasped the bull by the horns to try and stop the once deemed omnipotent 'market' from running rampage through their societies. But they did not do so from the starting point of a preferential option for the poor and vulnerable, but rather from a preference to protect those that have much already and to preserve their own power.

There has been much rhetoric in recent times of a 'new capitalism' but really people should be speaking about the need for the dawn of a new collectivism. In this the world's religions, of course, have a long-standing store of rich traditions. Speaking from a Christian starting point but wishing also to encourage further 'community in mission' with those of other faiths, traditions and ideologies, in this chapter I wish to offer some food for thought about perceiving how we relate to one another differently so that constructive practical consequences might follow.

Beware the ship of fools ... Ecclesial failings vis-à-vis globalization

The challenge for churches today is not simply to lecture the governments, bankers and financial personnel as if the beam in their own eye had disappeared. For, of course, churches also played and continue to play that market.[4] Only relatively recently have some churches sought to address issues such as their investing in arms manufacturers. And churches continue to hold shares in (and/or do business with) corporations that deal in morally questionable practices and even practices that fly in the face of the same teachings of those churches themselves. Financial experts and financial expediency seem to have as much a priority in the churches as elsewhere. Witness, for example, how in parts of Europe and North America just how many church buildings are closed and thus parish communities are extinguished due to these decisions taken, *primarily*, for financial reasons. The churches' critique of global capitalism is all too often made with a forked tongue.

Returning to Bosch's painting, one notes that among those grasping after the tufts of hay are nuns, monks and clergy, just as even a pope is seen to be following the cart. And might that be a theologian or two one can detect as well? In the painting, Bosch has Christ above the scene of grasping and untrammelled greed and desperation, almost anonymously, save for an angel atop the cart who notices him. And, as Gibson remarks, 'no one notices the Divine Presence; and, above all, no one notices that the wagon is being pulled by devils towards hell and damnation'.[5] And, of course, numerous parallels have been drawn between this painting and Bosch's *Ship of Fools*.[6] It is well rehearsed, also, how frequently Bosch sought to critique ecclesial and clerical hypocrisy. *The Haywain* is no exception. It also offers a lament for the decline of those great institutions of mutuality and solidarity, the guilds. Individualistic greed triumphs over collectivism. The church is seen to be complicit in this as opposed to doing all it can to oppose it. *The Haywain*, then, depicts a situation which is a consequence of a breakdown in collectivism and a selfish failure of people to relate to the other in a right way.

It is important, therefore, to acknowledge that the church and other faith communities frequently have the highest aspirations in terms of service and equality, yet – in practice – all too often fail to live up to their lofty principles. However, much can be learned from such failings, and perhaps it is time today to take stock once again in the light of how the social gospel and 'preferential option for the poor' have been allowed to have their radical edges blunted by decades of reactionary ecclesial agendas and ecclesiological perceptions.

Globalization and the church: background and parameters of the debate

Here, by way of clarification, let us recall a definition of globalization that helps offer some tentative steps towards a 'genealogy' of the state of our current world. The former secretary of the World Council of Churches, Konrad Raiser, offered the following definition of globalization some years ago:

> There is no accepted definition of globalization, and even the question since when globalization has begun to manifest itself elicits different responses. In a very general way, globalization refers to the process of increasingly closer integration of societies, economies, political systems, cultures and media of communication into one worldwide framework. The immediate precursors of the present manifestation of globalization have been the formation of multinational business corporations and the transnationalization of economic and financial activity. In that sense, globalization as it has begun to develop after the collapse of the communist bloc and the dismantling of the systems of state socialism, can be interpreted as the extension of the previous system of transnational business to all parts of the world. Globalization, therefore, is being interpreted as the result of the final victory of global capitalism.[7]

But Raiser acknowledges that globalization has also come to mean much more than this, and he identifies the new ecological threats to the planet, the implications of the electronic revolution and the end of the Cold War as further defining factors. He likewise mentions the predominance of often confusing 'plurality' throughout the world and the 'spread of the values of postmodernity', along with 'growing fragmentation and fundamental changes in the religious fields, including the Christian churches'.[8] He believes the period of 1989–90 was a historical turning point in this process and he holds that the increase in *religious* plurality is fundamentally bound up with the trends associated with globalization itself.

Although some of the reductivistic and deconstructionist postmodern theorists have sought to suggest that our era marks a shift from an emphasis upon the universal to a greater attention being paid to the local and the particular, globalization demonstrates that, in many respects, the exact opposite has actually been the case. Although more recent accounts acknowledge that it is a case of both/and – the globalizing and localizing tendencies have emerged in tandem and frequently because of one another – that we now live in an era of 'globalization' is taken as a given. That it has for a long time functioned, in a variety of ways, as a new 'grand narrative', and what the full implications of this fact, socially, morally and politically, actually are, is less universally agreed upon. But few will deny that the local and particular are now directly affected by events and decisions that may originate, literally, across the other side of the globe. Social, economic, cultural and political realities are interlinked and interdependent to an intensity hitherto unparalleled. Technology and the communications revolution have facilitated the development of this phenomenon. Howland Sanks states that: 'For theologians, our growing awareness and analysis of this phenomenon [i.e. globalization] is part of the ongoing reading of the signs of the times ... We are faced with a new situation that calls for new analysis and conceptualisation.'[9] However, Sanks' words are as true today at the end of globalization's 'second decade' as they were when written at the end of the first. The phenomenon of globalization and its attendant social and economic consequences have continued to bring about a decline in social networks, cooperation and social 'capital' in a number of communities and societies. These changes represent a real and immensely powerful counter-force to the gospel ethos and mission. As, once again, rampant individualism, driven by materialism, has been seen to triumph over community (only now on an unprecedented scale), many places have witnessed developments little short of the very *death* of community.

None of this is to presume that globalization is simply about homogenization – there are the attendant dynamics of glocalization (which some also call heterogenization) and the related 'deterritorialization'.[10] However, much discourse concerning global capitalism and globalization operates on different levels. Much recent talk in theological circles, particularly in the Roman Catholic tradition, speaks about trying to 'redeem' globalization or to create a form of 'solidaristic globalization'. So, notwithstanding the complexity of the dynamics at work, much confusion can enter the fray here.

Many today do, indeed, assume that globalization constitutes a coherent system and many who believe it to be a good thing would argue that it is, indeed, an end in itself (being the 'triumph' of the market). And this is not simply *Laissez Faire* anew, it is a manifestation of the quasi and/or civil 'religious' status that global capitalism has acquired in the minds and lives of so many. Indeed, for many, globalization – with the omnipotent 'market' itself at its centre – has served as a new 'religion' with numerous evangelists, ministers, missionaries and even analogous institutions to the 'Holy' Inquisition.

To my mind, it appears questionable whether one can conceptually 'have it both ways', by retaining some 'good' umbrella concept of globalization that will effectively facilitate discourse to counter the effects of 'bad' globalization. Attempts to do so would appear to veer towards making the mistake of applying 'misplaced concreteness' to the notion of globalization itself. The term 'misplaced concreteness' (coined by Alfred North Whitehead[11]), has been aptly applied to the debate on globalization by William Schweiker:

> We have to avoid mistaking an abstract idea, like globalization, for an actual concrete thing. And we should avoid other forms of reductionism, as well, say, believing that one form of analysis – economic, political, cultural, theological or ethical – alone says it all. Like many phenomena so too with globalization: miss the complexity and you have missed the thing. When I use the term 'globalization' I mean a description of specific, interlocking social and cultural processes and structures.[12]

Schweiker, indeed, prefers to speak of 'global dynamics' more than globalization, following Roland Robertson in identifying such as the extension of modernity to social life in general ('modernity on a global scale'), typified by 'reflexive relations among societies and culture'.[13]

But, as diverse a range of subjects as the term embraces, it might serve collective ethical undertakings all the better to counter the negative effects of globalization by confronting it with terms and concepts including, if possible, empowering new umbrella concepts, which encapsulate all that stands in sharp contrast to the evils of globalization. In what follows, I wish to explore a few parameters of such a task.

'All is hay': discerning key challenges

But what of the precise nature of the broader challenges facing the churches today, then? Bosch's painting captures the sheer alienation and rampant anti-ethic of exploitation that too often dominates human social existence. The gospel itself is a radical ethic of love which deconstructs such forms of social being. The challenge that global capitalism presents to the churches today is aptly summed up by Paul Lakeland, in a passage written before the 2008 crash, but prescient in its wisdom in how it anticipates the challenge that the churches are now faced with:

> Today we have to confront directly the flawed picture of human fulfilment that is promoted by our market-driven capitalist vision of reality. Because this vision is powerful and so incomplete, the mission of the Christian community today will be deeply involved in challenging the largely unquestioned sway that the capitalist vision seems to have over the world. It is, in important respects, after the end of the cold war, the only remaining antihuman ideology.[14]

But what, in particular, has globalization to do with the *gospel* and the vision of ethics and community it inspires? Well, put simply, globalization poses a serious threat to community and, *therefore*, to the *ecclesia* and its vision of community and the moral life. Furthermore, there is an obvious linkage between social ethics in general and the mission of the church *vis-à-vis* globalization, in particular. Lakeland has further suggested that '... mission in the postmodern world is in large part about dealing with the challenges of global capitalism, since this is the biggest force at the root of antihuman impulses today'.[15] Hence Jesus' *universal* message of love, community and salvation, encapsulated somewhat definitively by the term 'catholicity', itself poses an alternative to the negativities of the phenomenon of globalization. T. Howland Sanks has also ably summarized the challenge that globalization puts to the church thus:

> For Christians, committed as they have always been to the promotion of the common good and of justice and peace for all, this new context poses challenges and opportunities. It challenges us to rethink the place and function of nation-states in the pursuit of justice. It challenges us to promote and preserve cultural particularity while enabling diverse cultures to participate in the global marketplace. It challenges us to promote individual freedom without that becoming an isolating individualism. It challenges us to foster new international structures to deal with issues and problems that exceed the capabilities of sovereign nation-states. It challenges us to communicate Christian principles of social justice in a form that is persuasive and that leads to the conversion of human hearts. It challenges us to exemplify in the life of the institutional Church the justice we preach.[16]

Given the sentiments expressed in such commentaries, and the vast amount of literature and indeed practice engaged in terms of Christian social ethics in recent decades, we might reflect that the current global credit crisis demonstrates that the churches have not been very successful in crying out in the wilderness of the rampant global capitalism of recent times. Various reasons might be offered as to why this has been the case – from getting embroiled in ideological and political and cultural debates to wasting energies on internecine and inter-ecclesial and interfaith disputes, to prioritizing rigid forms of dogma and/or doxology over and against acknowledging and praising God through actually living the gospel and feeding Christ's sheep.

Indeed, there are numerous ways in which the church in the past and present alike has, despite its best intentions, actually assisted the spread of the negative effects of what we now refer to as globalization. Sometimes it has been that failure to live out the gospel fully enough. Sometimes it has been preoccupations with still further, less pressing questions and adiaphora.

But I would also contend that today the church risks committing similar failings for four further reasons. First, because of certain ambiguities in church teaching with regard to the understanding of globalization currently employed in the institutional churches. Second, aspects of the *methodology* employed in the formation of such teachings are actually ill-suited to countering the very same negative effects of globalization that these teachings correctly identify as requiring opposition. Third, I also suggest that the church must counter its own 'globalizing' tendencies if it is to speak with true moral authority against other forms of negative globalizing forces.

The fourth reason, linked to the third, is that the forces of globalization have impacted upon the church as much as anywhere else. Miller suggests that, in particular, the forces of heterogenization and deterritorialization result in the reactionary situation whereby 'Religious communities cease to image the diverse unity of the Body of Christ and become instead enclaves of the likeminded.'[17] To my mind Miller is here simply describing further trends of that process which I have elsewhere described as neo-exclusivism. One of the effects of globalization and the other trends of a postmodern age has been to transform the manner in which we relate to, understand and tolerate others – or our failure to do any of these appropriately. It is in this sense that catholicity is narrowed into a badge of identity rather than an affirmation of the unity in plurality of the world. But, of course, this latter trend had begun long before this present era of globalization, starting rather in an earlier wave of an analogous cultural phenomenon following the period of European reformations when the main Christian denominations began to harden their belief and identity systems into an increasingly dogmatic and rigid orthodoxy.

And the alternative? In an address to the General Chapter of the Dominican Order, Robert Schreiter has stated that 'a task of our ministry is to create the social spaces where people can find themselves and one another, and take hold of their own lives'. Hence, as we near the end of the 'second decade' where the challenges of globalization cry out for more collective responses, Schreiter believes that we must engage in finding

> ... ways of contributing to and linking global and local discourses. Those connections [for Christians] entail both being faithful to living out the Gospel in local life and remaining critical of global (and local) discourses and practices that distort and degrade the dignity of the human person ... Put more theologically, the second decade of globalization prompts us to find new forms of solidarity at both the global and local levels. Solidarity has to be more than a battle cry or a general notion of intellectual agreement; it must translate into concrete forms of action.[18]

Central to such a task will be, Schreiter believes, the theological development of this concept of solidarity – including its recent formulations within Catholic Social Teaching which, of course, has analogous and complementary forms across the broader spectrum of Christian social ethics. In his now famous work, *The New Catholicity*, Schreiter explores the twin challenges of finding a new understanding of the term for today that does full justice to traditional meanings that described the globality on the one hand and the fullness of faith on the other.[19] For Christians, catholicity is the conceptualization of such solidarity – understood in theological as much as geographical, social and moral terms.

Thus we to turn to explore but a few examples of the conceptual, methodological and hermeneutical challenges involved in undertaking such tasks.

From vicious to virtuous circle: ecclesial methods and resources for opposing dehumanizing globalization

The Christian church itself already has, of course, many rich conceptual resources at its disposal in the fight against globalization. For example, we have a model and a science for transcending divisions and encouraging greater mutuality which is also global in character. That framework and science is, of course, ecumenics or ecumenism. The ancient world, in Greek, spoke of *oikoumene* – meaning the entire (then known) world. Christians from early times saw a need to reinterpret this concept so that, instead of an imperial model, they developed a communitarian model whereby there could be unity with tolerance of diversity among very different communities in very different places (that is, at least, until the conversion of Constantine, when the church became the religion of the empire). Their understanding of *oikoumene* looked towards the establishment of the kingdom of justice and righteousness to which Christ called humanity. In turn, this called for them to share common values to fight what is unjust, dehumanizing and evil.

Hence ecumenism, which was revived in the nineteenth century, in particular, by different Christian denominations seeking closer unity, is actually a model for our search for global alternatives and dialogue. Ecumenism is the science of bridge-building – a science of dialogue across different groups. It is now a concept which relates to all attempts concerned with bringing together different people and communities. It obviously became very evident that there are wider questions relating to the divisions between all human communities, and today the term 'ecumenism' can also mean dialogue and efforts at bringing about greater unity throughout the whole human family – i.e. the unity of peoples of all faiths and none. As Paul A. Crow states: 'It seeks to overcome all things that divide the church as well as the human community; that isolate people, nations, and cultures; that break fellowship or separate persons from God and from each other.'[20] This ecumenism thus must be concerned with global alternatives and hence necessitates a framework that allows people to unite and work together to realize common values without dissolving real differences into forced consensus.

The concept of *koinonia* or *communio*, for the church of the late twentieth century, as it was for church of the early centuries, is obviously fundamental to this quest which is at one and the same time a task, an 'imperative', a sacramental worldview, and ethical aspiration alike. And also of fundamental importance to ecumenical conversations has been the notion of catholicity. The quality or otherwise of the koinonia enjoyed throughout the oikoumene consists in the presence of catholicity and its own qualitative development. In fact, catholicity is one of the driving energies behind all ecumenical endeavour.

Of course, in much of the recent literature, globalization has been juxtaposed with catholicity, many commentators perceiving them as polar alternatives. Such literature, exploring the links between the two notions, has grown to enormous proportions. Let us turn to consider but a few indicative elements of these recent debates about catholicity.

What does catholicity consist of in the twenty-first century?

Why has catholicity preoccupied much of this literature? Well, in relation to the challenges facing the world in the light of the global economic crisis today, I believe catholicity is an enormously powerful 'social imaginary' which can inform how churches come together to act as a leaven in the future policies of countries and trans-national institutions into moving away from self-destructive and dehumanizing capitalism (and the attendant power games and conflicts that engenders) towards a more federal, pluralist and happily differentiated form of peaceful coexistence, whereby the resources of the world are not exploited for the benefit of the few but might truly be further enabled to enrich the existence of all. True catholicity is also a pluralistic as opposed to a rigidly universalizing (or globalizing) social imaginary.

So much of the literature, as noted, speaks of a solidaristic globalization and of attempts to 'redeem' the latter. But in the current world a *via media* is not what is needed. Global capitalism is beyond redemption. Unless the churches can see and acknowledge this they will remain doomed to follow in the haywain's futile path for another generation or more, with the human, animal and ecological cost being too great to contemplate.

If we are first to ponder what catholicity is not, then our attention is turned towards considerations of the emergence of those retreatist forces of neo-exclusivism whereby difference is hardened into the materials with which to build walls around isolationist enclaves and to demonize and persecute both the 'other' and the 'world' beyond such confines.

We might also reflect upon a fact that must also be acknowledged: that the notion of catholicity, itself, has also fallen prey to the various forces of globalization, as Miller has recently illustrated, 'one frequently hears "catholicity" used as a less onerous noun for "catholicness" ... Catholicity is defined in terms of the contested issues that can be used to project a distinct identity ... the term "catholicity" is now merely a label of shallow particularity'.[21] Yet it would not be too churlish to point out that Miller in parts of his own analysis not only aptly illustrates this trend, but is also in danger of offering another example of it, as the way in which he himself employs the term catholicity reflects that North American equation of the term with *Roman* Catholic identity (just as he above speaks of 'religious communities' and then immediately refers to the body of Christ as if all relate to such in the same fashion). The macro-ecumenical context must not only be attended to but also involved in the conversation processes necessary.

Of course, we must equally avoid pretending that catholicity has not been utilized as a concept to deny the rights of the other and to accentuate otherness or to demand such be subordinated to power and unity in past eras of the church.[22] Catholicity has been confused with the imposition of universalizing tendencies at various stages of the church's history.

But, in a more constructive sense (and that which concerns us more here), in so much of the recent literature, and in many differing ways, the mark of 'catholicity' has been proposed and commended as the theological conceptualization of what the solidarity necessary to oppose globalization might entail.

Certainly, much of what we have been here discussing involves questions of a hermeneutical nature. If the assertion be granted that many of the more promising treatments of the ethical implications of globalization are those which are trans-communitarian (both in inter- and intra-religious terms as well as those beyond the confines of faith-based communities and religious traditions alone), then it is obvious that of paramount importance are further hermeneutical questions. For if there is to be something of a successful ethical alliance against the negative impact of globalization upon human communities, then we must also ask about how we engage, literally, with those 'others', beyond our own respective communities, cultures and traditions (hence existential and ontological hermeneutical engagements are relevant here). Any rigid or overtly insular ethical methodology, then, will not assist such undertakings. Catholicity is a means by which Christians can begin such tasks.

Schweiker perceives the global dynamics of globalization in three particular forms. First, in terms of 'proximity', which, for Schweiker, is the problem of 'how to live with others amid powerful forces shaping one's own society and identity'.[23] Second, 'the expansion of consciousness in terms of media and markets so that we increasingly picture the world as one but in doing so relativize our lives',[24] and, third, the 'dynamic of reflexivity' in economic, as well as cultural, terms, leading to transformed social identities. But the cultural, economic and political dynamics which typify the globalizing trends and so must be the subject of hermeneutical thinking need to be supplemented by *ethical* hermeneutical endeavours as well. As Schweiker states:

> These global social and cultural 'dynamics' must be grasped as forming a moral space if we are to understand the force of the religions in the worldwide scene ... Most simply put, a moral space is any context in which persons or communities must orient their lives with respect to some ideas about what are higher and lower, better and worse, ways of conducting life ... [I]n this 'space' we are concerned about reason for actions rather than causes of events; one wants to explicate human conduct, not simply explain natural phenomena. So defined, every culture, and globality itself, is a moral space; it is an arena of normative reasons.[25]

Today we see so much ethical and hermeneutical debate alike concerned with our understanding of and, in turn our relations with, the 'other' and this is increasingly so, also across debates concerning global capitalism, globalization, social ethics and ecumenism. The question is, how might we best go about understanding and improving how we relate to the other?

This, perhaps, is the most pressing *theoretical* question confronting us today which has, in turn, numerous practical implications. As Schweiker states, 'hatred is becoming globalized as well as access to weapons that continue the suffering',[26] while Christopher Duraisingh believes that the totalizing tendency in Western culture bears much of the blame for our fear of the other and so of pluralism: '[t]he colonial and Euro-centric definitions of other cultures and traditions arise out of the same philosophical mind-set where "the other," that which is "strange" is to be conquered, or suppressed, converted and civilised.'[27]

But we must also ask how we engage in meaningful shared discourse with those others – assuming we do not take the neo-exclusivistic line of Milbank, Hauerwas, *et al* that we need no such common mode of discourse.[28] And all of this we now do against the backdrop of the painstaking efforts of those engaged not just in the quest for a global ethic, but also through drawing upon the efforts of many ecumenists in Christianity to engage in social ethics that transcend the boundaries of respective traditions (for such are tasks in which Christians must engage long before they can ever dream of aspiring towards something like a global ethic). Schweiker captures this need for an ethical-hermeneutical under-taking with regard to globalization in the following terms, locating the moral significance of globalization firmly in the realm of discourse concerning the 'titanic power of human beings':[29]

> Come what may, the global scene is one in which agents of various sorts (corporations, ethnic groups, nations, individuals) act and orient themselves in ways that further or destroy life. To understand this scene requires exploring reasons used to explicate behavior. Insofar as the dynamics of globalization are intrinsically bound to representational, evaluative, and motivational forces working on and in these agents, then globality is a moral space, a space of perception, motives, reasons, and choice.[30]

All of the foregoing, then, helps reinforce our initial concern to argue that the church catholic needs to decide where it stands. It cannot have it both ways; it cannot be part of global capitalism and its systems and benefits while at the same time preaching against its excesses and evil implications and outcomes.

Let us consider some brief examples of how a reappropriation of catholicity for these times might help the churches confront the challenges of globalization, postmodernity and pluralistic belonging alike.

Catholicity and the path from exploitation to solidarity: the true mark of a global church

When we accentuate the otherness of others in negative ways and exaggerate their distance from ourselves by suppressing their common existential bonds to ourselves, then it becomes much easier either to ignore their exploitation or to become complicit in their exploitation ourselves. The challenges of globalization – particularly of the exploitation driven by global capitalism – are essentially challenges of how we perceive and relate to otherness and others. These same challenges are, not by coincidence, the core challenges of the postmodern era as well. So, too, are they the key challenges for people of faith today and this is seen in an especially poignant fashion in the ecclesiological and ecclesial debates and struggles of recent times.[31]

Again helping to discern the complexities of such challenges, Miller admirably captures the profound potential of a reappropriation of the notion of catholicity contra the negative forces of globalization:

> The mark of catholicity provides both measure and means for engaging these cultural dynamics: an ideal of unity as a harmony of difference that challenges the dominant sectarianism, and a call to the fullness of salvation that cannot settle for purity abstracted from concrete engagement with the world ... [C]atholicity is a theological ideal, joined to the structures and practices of the church.

In this sense, then, Miller believes catholicity constitutes a form

> ... of what Roland Robertson terms 'the particularization of the universal' – a particular cultural understanding of the global whole that guides action within it. By fostering relationships and exchanges not happening elsewhere, the church, as a global community with a global infrastructure of its own, can foster a better form of globalization than the one promoted by the forces of advanced capitalism.[32]

Miller also rightly points out that a retrieval of the notion of catholicity would need to focus more on the fullness of the gifts of God on the one hand, and not be subordinated to the mark of unity on the other hand. Catholicity is better understood in a qualitative (*pace* Tillard)[33] and not quantitative sense and also 'in a more complementary sense as adding "dimensions of plurality and integration" to unity, [it entails that] locality appears not as a threat to the unity of the church, but as its realization'.[34] Thus the mark of catholicity retains its distinctiveness. Echoing the debates about neo-exclusivism once again, Miller believes such would constitute an analogical as opposed to a dialectical approach driven by a negative 'Augustinianism' whereby cultures are perceived to be fallen and requiring the 'redemption' offered through conformity to 'truth' contained in faithfully adhering to the demands of unity.[35]

We might say that, in a complementary model of catholicity, following the 'more optimistic anthropology of the analogical tradition', and this is what I think Miller is driving at, the realm of activity for God's grace extends across all the world as opposed to being confined to mere pockets or enclaves. Thus, '[t]he spread of the church is not the expansion of a cultural boundary, but the embrace of new cultures that provide greater insights into the gospel message'.[36] For Miller, the alternative dialectical approach in the end only accentuates the trends it seeks to oppose; fearing for orthodoxy and unity, it ultimately encourages a 'smaller, purer church' and hence sectarianism.[37]

For Miller, a complementary understanding of catholicity helps the church confront the challenges of heterogenization, deterritorialization and the retreat into enclaves whereby culture becomes but a tool for identity politics. Catholicity thus remains a task and challenge – unity without engagement with difference is not an option.[38] The qualitative model affirms breadth (the universal and geographical extension), harmony amidst differentiation (and riches of communion in diversity) and depth (of local and particular cultures) alike.[39] It is in the local church that catholicity as fullness in diversity itself is actually concretized. Such also affirms a more sacramental understanding of the church.[40] For, of course, suffering is experienced first hand in the local and particular, something the Church Fathers knew well as Miller (again following Tillard) further reminds us.[41] Thus, 'catholicity provides an idea of the universal that embraces global diversity, an imperative of unity that must reach into the local, and an ideal of wholeness that embraces difference'.[42]

Yet Miller, again, appears to address, in the main, the idea of Roman catholicity or at least intra-Christian concerns at best. The core challenges in an age of globalization, as he would no doubt acknowledge, of course have much wider relevance. In this sense, catholicity itself must not fall prey to the tendency of 'misplaced concreteness', just as we must resist the concretization of globalization itself. Catholicity is a hermeneutical tool – a powerful one when applied as a social imaginary and one that draws together so many theological, particularly sacramental, as well as existential, social and moral concerns for Christians. But our relations with the other and the ground of our being, whom we Christians call God, as opposed to any particular conception of such relations are what really count.

Writing some years before Miller, but almost as if in response to his analysis, and a further excellent and wider example of how we can glean new insights and conceptual resources from a reappropriation of catholicity, Christopher Duraisingh (a South Indian and Anglican Christian), noting that 'Christianity has become truly polycentric',[43] has argued that due attention to *contextuality* as well as catholicity can allow us to forge effective 'conditions for Cross-Cultural Hermeneutics', the latter, of course, being a key challenge in today's world. What is particularly valuable about Duraisingh's analysis is that he begins the engagement with the other by acknowledging that not only must we begin where we are at, but also we must allow others to do the same. And, of course, he adds a more ecumenical dimension to those many recent intra-Roman-Catholic-focused discussions (including that of Miller). Hence Duraisingh's suggestions serve Christians very well in their attempts to draw upon the wealth of conceptual, mythological and symbolic resources at their disposal in their various traditions.

Duraisingh, therefore, calls for 'serious cross-cultural conversation and the use of a critical hermeneutics of difference' and, in a telling assessment of the failures of Christian communions genuinely to engage in such, he believes that unless 'the diverse cultural expressions of the Christian story everywhere are received as central elements in the tradition-ing process, we will not be liberated from a past which remains essentially European. Nor can we receive the stories of the good news in Christ in ever new and multifaceted ways relevant to our times'.[44]

For Duraisingh, the call to the praxis of mutual recognition and cross-cultural conversation can be understood best by reference to what he considers to be the two inseparable concepts of context *and* catholicity. These both unite into a 'cross-cultural hermeneutics of our pluralist traditions'.[45] And, we might add, there is no reason that such undertakings cannot spread out beyond the confines of the Christian family. The call to contextuality and catholicity means 'both to witness to a gospel that frees and affirms authentic identities of cultures in all their diversity and irrevocably to call them into a mutually challenging and enriching community'.[46] For the story and encounter of Jesus of Nazareth is one which both 'frees and unites'. Echoing Schweiker's appropriation of the biblical account of creation in many ways, Duraisingh continues by affirming 'the good news about God's mission in the world, which is both liberative and community-constituting. Christian mission is to point to God's purpose and action toward a *domination*- and *fragmentation*-free human community through the Church's own practice of a "reconciled diversity" in Christ within its life'.[47]

Hence Duraisingh suggests that we should counter the 'hermeneutics of domination', which, as I have suggested elsewhere, characterizes globaliza-tion best, with the 'hermeneutics of solidarity'. Instead of singularity of

tradition and meaning, along with uniformity, reducing the other into the
same, the familiar, Duraisingh believes that 'the hermeneutics of solidarity
is committed to "being-with" the other in solidarity and dialogue even in
the midst of difference, tension or conflict. It is to hold that the truth in its
fullness is not found in any single tradition . . .'[48] This leads us to appreciate
that the negative forces which globalization unleashes can be countered by
solidaristic practices where the 'other' is respected 'as other'.

Taking – in tandem with our earlier considerations – Duraisingh's
vision, Miller's affirmation of the complementary and qualitative understanding of catholicity and, finally, Schweiker's 'hermeneutical ethics' as
applied to globalization, we may thus begin to steer a way through the
impasse illustrated by the ineffectiveness generated by the ambivalence in
present church and theological attitudes towards, and practices in relation
to, globalization.

All such efforts and methodologies are directed towards those tasks of
understanding the other and engaging with and fostering better relations
with all others. Of course, this flies in the face of the thinking prevalent in
many Christian denominations and the works of numerous scholars today,
just as it goes against the grain of much thinking among proponents of
other world faiths, political and economic ideologies (especially neo-
liberalism and neo-imperialism). Above all, it challenges the quasi-religion
of globalization itself, for the default approach to the 'other' in that
'religion' is to ensure that the other becomes as much like 'us' as possible so
as no longer to be deemed an-other (and so a threat) at all. So, although
Miller is right to draw attention to other forces of globalization, this should
never entail that the homogenizing forces be played down in any sense.

Christians must draw upon the resources to counter these 'levelling' and
totalizing tendencies. As Duraisingh argues, we can and we must engage in
a 'praxis of mutual recognition across traditions' because the gospel itself

> . . . is always an imperative for a permanent openness to the other, the
> stranger, the alien. Hospitality to strangers and mutuality of recognition of
> 'the other' is intrinsic to the Christian story of God's love in Christ . . . The
> central purpose of the Church in the economy of God in an increasingly
> diversified world is 'to cooperate with God in making the *oikoumene* an *oikos*,
> a home, a family of men and women of varied gifts, cultures, possibilities,
> where openness, trust, love and justice reign'.[49]

Only by engaging in such a praxis can we counter the twin forces of
fragmentation in the numerous struggles for particular identities as well as
the seemingly paradoxical presence of such globalizing forces to turn the
world into 'one large consumerist collective'.[50]

Concluding remarks

In conclusion, I suggest that hermeneutical and ethical reflections upon, and dialogue concerning the challenges posed by, globalization are better informed through the employment of more openly dialogical methodologies and strategies throughout the Christian community and with other religious communities and other peoples of good will across the human family. In other words, due attention to how we perceive, understand and relate to the 'other' (whether in individual or collective terms) is a necessary prerequisite to any attempt to form a collective moral approach to counter the negative effects of globalization.

Ecclesial efforts today are best focused upon how we might, from our starting point within our Christian communities, appropriate anew our rich conceptual, mythological, liturgical and pastoral resources in the collective battle against the evils of globalization. In particular, the notions of ecumenism and, most of all, *catholicity* can (again) be commended and reappropriated as two concepts that can serve as counter-concepts to deterministic and fatalistic notions of globalization itself. Otherness is fundamental to catholicity.

The two sides of the balance between ethics and ecclesiology are united by the proposition that we need to shape a 'public ecclesiology' for these postmodern times. By 'public ecclesiology' I mean a self-understanding of the church that envisions the church as being an affirming member of the wider human family – playing its full part in open dialogue and collaboration with other members of that family and communities towards common constructive, moral and social ends. In contradistinction to the 'neo-exclusivist' approach, here we argue in favour of a method that might allow the church and individual Christians to form part of what Lewis Mudge calls a coalition of 'Traditioned Cosmopolitans'[51] who, affirming multiple-belonging in their daily lives, collectively seek to respond to the moral and social challenges of our times. I wish to suggest that the churches, along with various other influential 'players' in public life today, can all form part of a wider 'community of moral discourse', a community that listens to all voices and which privileges no particular interest group save the vulnerable.

Such approaches would help provide encouragement to those who would reject any deterministic and even fatalistic attitude towards the 'march' of the haywain of global capitalism and hence globalization – i.e. the default position (or at least feigned position) of so many involved in governmental and economic policymaking until the most recent of times.

The churches already have so many of the resources necessary to confront and defeat the dehumanizing forces of global capitalism. The Christian socialist tradition, the marvels of liberation theology – these powerful dynamics have often been perceived to be long *passé*. In fact, I believe their time has yet to come in its fullness, and perhaps the twenty-first century is the age when they will come to the forefront and bear fruition in the fashion their founding theorists and practitioners envisaged. If the churches can collectively, in a catholic fashion one might say, engage more earnestly and fervently in attending to such tasks – not being distracted by the trappings of global capitalism and power itself, by debates of lesser concern, or retreating into a 'purifying' mentality – then a twenty-first-century Bosch might be able to paint Christians, including church leaders, engaged in a struggle against the relentless, yet futile, onward march of the haywain, as opposed to merely following in its wake or being distracted by its empty allure as it passes by. Catholicity, then, in the final analysis, is as much an ethical task as an ecclesiological concept: to be catholic is to be open to, supportive of, and in communion with the other.

Notes

1. Walter S. Gibson, *Hieronymus Bosch* (London/New York: Thames and Hudson, 1973 and 2005), 70. There are echoes here, of course, of Aquinas' words towards the end of his life that all he had written now seemed to him 'as straw'. See also Lynn F. Jacobs, 'The Triptychs of Hieronymus Bosch', *The Sixteenth Century Journal* 31, 4 (Winter 2000), 1009–41; Jacobs also notes (p. 1016) that the inspiration for Bosch may have been the Dutch proverb 'all the world is a haystack and each man plucks from it what he can'.
2. Gerard Mannion, 'What's in a Name? Hermeneutical Questions on "Globalisation", Catholicity and Ecumenism', *New Blackfriars* 86, 1002 (March 2005), 204–15.
3. Walter S. Gibson, *Hieronymus Bosch*, 73.
4. One noted with further irony how some Catholic bishops in England and Wales were preaching sermons in the wake of the credit crisis which included statements such as 'the false "god" of the market is dead', *The Tablet* (12 December 2008).
5. Gibson, *Hieronymus Bosch*, 69.
6. Ibid., 44, 69, 86.
7. Konrad Raiser, 'Opening Space for a Culture of Dialogue and Solidarity – The Missionary Objectives of the WCC in an Age of Globalization and Religious Plurality', Lecture at the *SEDOS* Seminar, Ariccia, 19 May 1999, 1. See www.sedos.org/english/raiser_2.html (accessed 30 November 2008).
8. Ibid.
9. T. Howland Sanks, 'Globalization and the Church's Social Mission', in *Theological Studies* 60 (1999), 625.
10. Vincent Miller has recently offered an insightful and succinct discussion of these various dynamics, which is discussed further, below. Vincent J. Miller, 'Where is

the Church? Globalization and Catholicity', *Theological Studies* 69 (2008), 412–32. On the latter two forces he states: 'The same economic and technological forces that make globalization possible also encourage people to think of themselves as members of distinct cultures and to join together in ever purer, smaller cultural units.' So 'heterogenization' means that '[g]lobalization reifies difference as much as it homogenizes it'. The latter is intensified by deterritorialization, which means that [m]ediated culture, easy travel and migration, and choice of community unbind culture from geographical space … These two dynamisms combine to give rise to a certain 'cultural ecology' which fosters communities that focus on their own identities. Religious communities are diminished as they ignore elements of their traditions that ground a complex form of life in favor of those that project a clear identity. (Ibid., 412–13)

11. Alfred North Whitehead, *Science and the Modern World* (New York: Macmillan, 1948).
12. William Schweiker, 'A Preface to Ethics: Global Dynamics and the Integrity of Life', *Journal of Religious Ethics* 32, 1 (2004), 17.
13. Ibid.
14. Paul Lakeland, *The Liberation of the Laity* (New York: Continuum, 2003), 230.
15. Ibid., 281.
16. T. Howland Sanks, 'Globalization and the Church's Social Mission', *Theological Studies* 60 (1999), 650.
17. Miller, 'Where is the Church?', 420.
18. Robert Schreiter, 'Globalization's Second Decade', an excerpt from his address to the General Chapter of the Dominican Order at Providence College, Providence, USA (10 July–8 August 2001), entitled 'Major Currents of Our Times: What They Mean for the Church', also published in *Origins*, 16 August 2001.
19. Robert Schreiter, *The New Catholicity: Theology between the Global and the Local*, (Maryknoll: Orbis, 1997).
20. Paul A. Crow, Jr, 'The Ecumenical Movement', in vol. 2 of *Encyclopedia of the American Religious Experience*, ed. Charles H. Lippy and Peter W. Williams (New York: Charles Scribner's Sons, 1988), 978.
21. Miller, 'Where is the Church?', 419.
22. Here and with reference to the related theme of 'classical conceptions of universality' and how we should conceive of tradition in a postmodern age, cf. John Thiel, 'Pluralism in Theological Truth', *Concilium* 6 (1994), 57–69.
23. Ibid., 17.
24. Ibid., 21.
25. Ibid., 22. Schweiker is here drawing upon Charles Taylor's *Sources of the Self*, (Cambridge: Cambridge University Press, 1990) and his own *Power, Value and Conviction: Theological Ethics in the Postmodern Age* (Cleveland, OH: Pilgrim Press, 1998).
26. Schweiker, 'A Preface to Ethics', 25.
27. Christopher Duraisingh, 'Contextual and Catholic: Conditions for Cross-Cultural Hermeneutics', *Anglican Theological Review* 82, 4 (Fall 2000), 681.
28. Cf., similar rejections of such approaches in Schweiker's, 'A Preface to Ethics' itself, and Nicholas Healy, 'Practices and the New Ecclesiology: Misplaced Concreteness', *International Journal of Systematic Theology* 5, 3 (November 2003), 287–308.
29. Schweiker, 'A Preface to Ethics', 24.

30. Ibid., 23.

31. Cf. Gerard Mannion, 'Church and the Grace of Otherness: Exploring Questions of Truth, Unity and Diversity', Chapter 1 in *Church and Religious Other: Essays on Truth, Unity and Diversity*, ed. G. Mannion (London and New York: T&T Clark, 2008), 1–22.

32. Miller, 'Where is the Church?', 421, citing Roland Robertson, *Globalization: Social Theory and Global Culture* (London: Sage, 1992), 100.

33. Ibid., 422, 424.

34. Ibid., 422, utilizing the thought of Joseph A. Komonchak, 'The Local Church and the Church Catholic: The Contemporary Theological Problematic,' *Jurist* 52 (1992), 416–47, at 445.

35. Ibid., 422.

36. Ibid., 423.

37. Ibid., 423.

38. Ibid., 424.

39. Ibid., 424–30.

40. Ibid., 427–8. Miller cites the example of the Central American Solidarity Movement of the 1980s.

41. Ibid., 430.

42. Ibid., 432.

43. Christopher Duraisingh, 'Contextual and Catholic: Conditions for Cross-Cultural Hermeneutics', 679.

44. Ibid., 682.

45. Ibid., 685.

46. Ibid., 685.

47. Ibid., 685.

48. Ibid., 687.

49. Ibid., 683, citing Philip Potter, *Report of the General Secretary, WCC Central Committee*, Geneva, July/August 1977, Doc. 18.9.

50. Ibid., 684.

51. As proposed in Lewis Mudge, 'Covenanting for a Renewing of Our Minds: A Way Together for the Abrahamic Faiths', Chapter 8, in *Beyond Idealism: A Way Ahead for Ecumenical Social Ethics*, ed. Julio De Santa Ana, Robin Gurney and Heidi Hadsell (Grand Rapids and Cambridge, UK: Eerdmans, 2006), 163–208.

Chapter 2

SEEKING UNITY: REFLECTING ON METHODS IN CONTEMPORARY ECUMENICAL DIALOGUE

Gesa E. Thiessen

Remarkable progress has been made in ecumenical dialogue over the last forty years. This includes topics such as the search for a shared understanding of apostolicity, catholicity and unity, and, in particular, the thorny questions regarding church structures and ministry. In bi- and multilateral dialogues between the Lutheran, Anglican and Roman Catholic Churches, much agreement has been achieved in ecumenical statements such as the *Joint Declaration* (JD), *The Church as Koinonia of Salvation* (CKS), *The Gift of Authority* and the *Porvoo Common Statement*. Yet, despite such advancement, the slow progress in the reception of these statements into the churches is keenly felt among those who have dedicated themselves to ecumenism, and above all among the many believers whose ecumenism of life is often far more advanced than what has been officially agreed.

In the following I will consider several issues pertaining to contemporary ecclesiology and ecumenical dialogue: the process of reception and its problems; the method of a differentiated consensus; comparative ecclesiology; the notion of pneumatological freedom as essential to ecumenical progress; and, finally, an idea first mooted by Karl Rahner about the normativity of the factual faith of the people of God *vis-à-vis* official church teaching.

Reception

One of the most difficult concerns in ecumenical dialogue is the question of reception. As Harald Goertz has shown, reception is a multilayered process; it can mean full, partial, or non-reception.[1] It involves a church's reception of bi- or multilateral ecumenical documents into its own life, its dogmas and structures. It includes a reception process in which documents are put into practice on all theological, ecclesial and ecumenical levels. It entails a reception procedure whereby a church must decide on a document's binding and legal authority, and it requires an official response with a preliminary commentary on, and evaluation of, the document. Finally, it demands the implementation, i.e. the continued application, of the theological and spiritual contents of the document on all levels of church life. This is obviously a long drawn-out process, stretched over years, and often churches simply do not seem to consider it imperative to act on reception.[2] In short, the problem is that the many documents worked out in painstaking fashion are not put into practice in the churches.

In his survey of texts, mainly from the Lutheran–Roman Catholic dialogue, Udo Hahn speaks of the sobering fact that a number of documents – from the *Malta Report* (1972) to *Church and Justification* (1994) – have not been received,[3] even if some efforts were undertaken, mostly by the Vereinigte Evangelisch-Lutherische Kirche Deutschlands (VELKD).[4] Not only is this an entirely frustrating situation for ecumenists, it also actively prevents progress in ecumenical ecclesiology and thus progress in church praxis. In fact, one could go so far as to suggest that such non-reception and lack of interest in reception is an offence against, and serious omission in, the apostolic task of teaching, proclamation and pastoral service in the church. One cannot reiterate that there is no alternative to ecumenism, as numerous church officials have done, and ignore decisive theological-ecclesiological work undertaken towards church unity. Apostolicity and catholicity today, as in the earliest centuries of the church, demand attention to any work that aims to further the goal of visible unity in the one church of Christ. This applies to bi- and multilateral documents as well as to other ecclesiological studies. This implies also that a genuine willingness towards the possibility and, in parts, necessity, of change in each church is involved in the path to unity. If such willingness is not genuinely sought, work in ecumenism has little value.[5] It also means to recognize and grapple with the very fact that our churches and our world are shaped by plurality, where, as Roger Haight, Gerard Mannion and others have argued, retreat into neo-exclusivism or into total relativism will do little to foster the vision of the one church of Christ.[6] On the contrary, in this situation truthful dialogue with an attitude of humility and respect is doctrinally, ecclesially and morally necessary.[7]

It is clear that this situation has direct repercussions for the apostolicity of the whole church (e.g., proclamation, prayer, pastoral activities, etc.), on ecclesial structures and *episcope*, and on systematic theology and ethics. The lack of reception hinders and limits striving towards unity and catholicity, towards a greater understanding of, and life in, apostolicity, in particular the notion of the primacy of the apostolicity of the whole church as

favoured among ecumenists today. In this way, possibilities for transformation and progress through listening to and acting upon the signs of the
times are lacking in enthusiasm at best or, at worst, result in cynicism and
resignation.

Differentiated consensus

The method of a differentiated consensus has had a significant impact on
recent documents, notably the *Joint Declaration*, as well as on *The Church
as Koinonia of Salvation* and the Porvoo agreement, even if the method
features less explicitly in the latter two. A differentiated consensus allows for
and even welcomes difference on the level of ecclesial perceptions and
church life, while at the same time it can transcend and accept difference in
a larger consensus. Different views can be compatible with and even
complementary to one another and thus integrate into a more comprehensive picture.

One of the dangers in ecumenical dialogue has been, on the one hand,
the denial of differences in an – often genuine – enthusiasm for ecumenical
progress. On the other hand, there are those who are only too keen to dwell
on and dissect ever more differences, which, in fact, do not create any
significant obstacles to agreement on essentials. The method of a
differentiated consensus can contribute to some extent to solving this
problem. This type of consensus reflects something of our postmodern
mindset in the best sense as it allows for pluralism, historicity, the
limitations of narratives and concepts, while at the same time enabling a
common ground for agreement.[8] As the Catholic Church with Vatican II
advocates a legitimate diversity even amongst its own local churches, such
recognition and cherishing of diversity will be as essential in the unity of
different denominations. Hence this method in ecumenical dialogue
manifestly fosters the notion of unity in diversity. It thereby can enrich our
understanding of the church and its structures, and lends to the marks of
the church possibilities, vibrancy and freedom in theological expression and
in church life. It can also be instrumental and advantageous in accelerating
ecumenical progress as essential aspects are distinguished from those that
need less attention or can simply be left as they are. Some ecumenists today
point out that the method of differentiated consensus may be the only way
forward in the ecumenical arena. Others hold that it might be a way of
circumventing thorny issues.

Comparative ecclesiology

In the second volume of his *Christian Community in History*,[9] Roger Haight expounds the idea of comparative ecclesiology. This method, which is likely to become of increasing relevance to ecumenical ecclesiologists, also has direct implications on apostolicity and catholicity. Haight comments that 'the church has become a multi-coloured tapestry of ecclesiologies ... so that it is simply no longer possible to think that a single church could carry the full flow of Christian life in a single organizational form'.[10] This statement, with its acknowledgement of a plurality of organizational structures, might lead one to imagine that Haight advocates merely diversity and difference rather than unity. However, he proceeds with a rigorous comparative template in his examination of ecclesiologies from the Reformation to our day, and asserts that the 'theoretical goal' in his study is not a stress on differences, but 'rather, after having displayed them [the ecclesiologies] in their difference, to see each one as part of the one tradition of the whole church'.[11]

In a way Haight is working from a future premise, i.e. as if the actual unity in diversity of the one church of Christ had already happened. Haight analyses ecclesiologies from Luther and Calvin to the present, and acknowledges all of these as being part of the whole tradition of the church. Thus he is able to throw light on how we can comprehend the apostolic church; one church made up of various churches all of whom offer ecclesiological insights that contribute to and make up our understanding of the church. With his method there is a genuine balance between the local and the universal church; neither attains dominance over the other. Churches can retain their own confessional identities, yet they belong to the one church. Haight therefore appears to be taking *Lumen Gentium* one step further: not only are there local churches within the Roman Catholic tradition but all churches are local, and all churches belong to the universal church. His may be an idealistic perspective and certainly belongs to our hopes for the future, but it does offer ways forward also in ecumenical ecclesiology.

Comparative ecclesiology, then, takes seriously the pluralist situation in which we find ourselves today. It emphasizes respectful dialogue as an imperative in the face of such pluralism. Moreover, it acknowledges the pluralism of theologies that has always existed in the church, as Rahner already observed decades ago. Thus, in Haight's opinion, all true theology must be ecumenical, a fact that becomes ever more urgent in our day of denominational and, above all, religious pluralism. Comparative theology, Haight argues, 'consists in analyzing and portraying in an organized or systematic way two or more different ecclesiologies so that they can be compared'.[12] It is exactly this which he undertakes in his book. As the church is divided into a plurality of churches, this comparative method for him is the 'only way to understand the whole church'. Haight therefore, unlike official Roman Catholic teaching but like many other Catholic ecclesiologists, acknowledges other churches, i.e. Protestant churches, as *church* and in this way, implicitly, the pre-eminent ecumenical concept of the apostolicity of the whole church.

However, one would suggest that, as with all methods, there are strengths and limitations within this method. Even with the best of intentions, one's own horizon may colour one's hermeneutic, and therefore one might lack in objectivity on occasion. Any theologian who acknowledges personal adherence to a particular denomination will be in 'danger' of prejudice or preferences, even if these are minor. On the other hand, a truly ecumenical author can at times supply a more objective reading on another denomination than a member of that church. Anyone who applies this method must necessarily be aware of such problems from the outset.

Related to this development is the more basic fact that today there are not only differences in ecclesiology *between* churches but, emphatically, *within* churches. Theological spectra in postmodernity are now so diverse that it is no longer possible to say 'a Catholic holds ...', or 'a Lutheran believes ...' One hundred years ago such statements, by and large, were still possible. Today, however, many Catholics have given up adherence to a number of official teachings of their church and have adopted, as one might put it, 'Protestant views' on certain matters. Many Protestants have become more open to sacramentality, high church liturgy and celebration, pilgrimages, sacred images, etc., and even to the positive aspects of the papacy, especially in the light of the more recent ones, starting with John XXIII, and notably John Paul II and Benedict XVI, who could not but impress many Christians, even if they do not share all the views expressed by these popes.

Further, while for some Christians eucharistic hospitality and intercommunion are not to be realized until full unity is achieved, for others it has become part and parcel of their faith life. Thus ecclesial parameters and thinking have become more fluid. In itself much of this is a positive sign that ecumenism *is*, in fact, working. However, against the background of postmodern pluralism, it is a fact to be reckoned with in ecumenical dialogue. It provides both difficulties and opportunities as the gap between lived ecumenism, theological ideas, and official teaching is increasing.

Theology today then is increasingly becoming an ecumenical discipline frequently undertaken in joint research projects by theologians of different confessions with mutual concerns. Thus the believer's and, in particular, the theologian's point of reference will transcend the teaching of her or his own church and will be open to and integrate doctrinal aspects from traditions other than their own.[13] This can create genuine tensions and, for a minority, such a way of operating may seem threatening or even unorthodox. Yet what other way forward can there be? Ecumenism without openness to new ways of doing theology and new ways of being church is an impossibility, even perhaps a contradiction in terms.

The freedom of the Spirit in ecumenical dialogue

The pneumatological dimension is a central but sometimes undervalued reality in the search for a comprehensive ecumenical ecclesiology. Fundamentally, we are aware that neither the New Testament nor the theologians in the early church provide us with a definitive set of church structures. What is definite is that offices in the earliest years of the church were not completely new but rather developed from the model of the synagogue communities. Offices in the church arose earlier than a unified understanding of these, i.e. there was no cohesive development of offices in the church communities. Most importantly, Jesus himself did not give us any instructions as to how his church should operate. Thus, from hierarchical episcopal churches to non-episcopal churches and to demo-cratically run fellowships, a variety of forms of church or ecclesial communities are possible and have existed and survived throughout Christian history. Certainly it is an ironic truth that often small fellowships which do not have the traditional bishop-presbyter-deacon ministry have led committed, humble and wholly convincing Christian lives, a fact that is little acknowledged in ecumenical documents, and which might well be a point to be explored in discussions about church structures. The fact that Jesus did *not* tell us how his group of followers should be organized, as well as the fact that other writers, especially Paul, reiterate the importance of the various gifts of equal worth which make up the one body, and, moreover, the supreme idea of God as Trinity, i.e. God who in Godself is relationship and love, give us some important clues about the church's apostolicity, catholicity and unity. Essentially this implies openness, relationality, respect and concern for the other.

From the origins of Christianity we witness a variety of accentuations in ecclesiology. This is further underscored by the fact that the Church Fathers differed in their notions about church organization. Based on numerous biblical sources, some of the foremost early theologians emphasized the role of the Holy Spirit in the notion of apostolicity, notably Origen, Clement of Alexandria, the *Traditio Apostolica* (Hippolytus) and Augustine. This surely needs further exploration. The pneumatic-charismatic criterion offers considerable possibilities, as it is fundamentally based in the freedom of the divine *ruah* who blows where She wills, and it respects the gift of individuals and groups within the people of God. Naturally this can also imply dangers, namely those of extreme individualism and even arbitrariness. Yet, one must trust that church leaders and the faithful will discern what belongs to genuine apostolicity, catholicity and unity and what does not. If it is the divine will that the Spirit should reign among the people of God, it is the task of overseers to try and facilitate the Spirit's floating in the body of Christ and not unnecessarily to hinder the Spirit's power. The recognition of the dominion of the divine Spirit fosters a certain openness, freedom and respect for otherness which in itself constitutes a healthy antidote to any attempts to constrict dialogue and to explore untrodden paths in ecumenism, in interfaith dialogue and in the theology of religions. It should contribute to a certain freedom in the ongoing task of reflecting on the role and content of appropriate church structures, offices and ministry.

In this context let us make an excursion and consider one ecumenical document, the *Porvoo Common Statement* (1992), as an example in which the sense of the freedom of the Holy Spirit was instrumental in bringing about significant progress. Twelve Lutheran and Anglican churches from the British, Irish, Nordic and Baltic countries were involved in issuing this document.[14] There are a number of strengths and a novel dimension in this statement.

It is of particular interest what Porvoo says about the threefold ministry and how it has solved the problem of apostolic succession. 'The threefold ministry of bishop, priest and deacon became the general pattern in the Church of the early centuries and is still retained by many churches, though often in partial form. "The threefold ministry of bishop, presbyter and deacon may serve today as an expression of the unity we seek and also as a means for achieving it" '(#32). The agreement here takes up the Meissen Statement and intensifies it:

> We believe that a ministry of pastoral oversight (episcope), exercised in personal, collegial and communal ways, is necessary as witness to and safeguard of the unity and apostolicity of the Church. Further, we retain and employ the episcopal office as a sign of our intention, under God, to ensure the continuity of the Church in apostolic life and witness. For these reasons, all our churches have a personally exercised episcopal office. (#32)

John J. Burkhard has noted that this text 'has offered the most concentrated theological focus' on apostolicity.[15] As in the other documents, Porvoo asserts that apostolicity pertains above all to the whole church: 'Thus the whole Church, and every member, participates in and contributes to the communication of the gospel ... [T]he primary manifestation of apostolic succession is to be found in the apostolic tradition of the Church ...'(#38, #39).

One of the most difficult and sensitive matters in view of apostolic succession, namely the question how episcopal churches can accept those churches that have genuine forms of *episcope* but have not kept the historical episcopate, is addressed, and, further, how these divergent positions can find reconciliation.[16] It reads:

> Faithfulness to the apostolic calling of the whole Church is carried by more than one means of continuity. Therefore a church which has preserved the sign of historic episcopal succession is *free to acknowledge* an authentic episcopal ministry in a church which has preserved continuity in the episcopal office by an occasional priestly/presbyterial ordination at the time of the Reformation.[17] Similarly a church which has preserved continuity through such a succession is free to enter a relationship of mutual participation in episcopal ordinations with a church which has retained the historical episcopal succession, and to embrace this sign, without denying its past apostolic continuity. (#52)

This paragraph constitutes one of the most remarkable and 'innovative' passages in the text, and a milestone in ecumenical relations. What so far seems impossible to affirm between the Lutheran and Roman Catholic Church is here solved in one paragraph. The key words are 'free' and 'to accept'. The churches have the *freedom* to accept each other's *episcope* as genuine, historical and adequate. Freedom is always associated with the Holy Spirit and one cannot but sense that this paragraph has been *in-spired* and may be inspiring for methods in ecumenical dialogue. What appeared impossible is transcended with unexpected, disarming simplicity: the dynamic freedom of the Christian, the *freedom* of one church to accept another. And this is no 'flippant' freedom; it comes out of a *humility* of recognizing that

> ... to the degree to which our ministries have been separated all our churches have lacked something of that fullness which God desires for his people (Eph 1.23 and 3.17-19). By moving together, and by being served by a reconciled and mutually recognized episcopal ministry, our churches will be both more faithful to their calling and also more conscious of their need for renewal. (#54)

There is no question here of one church imposing its ecclesiological understanding on another, or considering itself superior; rather the focus is on what is *lacking* when separation is upheld and what can be gained when separation is overcome. It is not a quick reconciliation whereby differences are denied. Rather the concrete desire to realize reconciliation for the greater good of the churches, out of a sense of lacking something if one does not, drives the partners. In this way the Anglican and Lutheran churches have made visible progress by dealing with one another as sister churches, by acknowledging differences, and transcending them at the same time through an approach underpinned by freedom and humility.

In this way, too, as the Franciscan theologian Henrik Roelvink has noted, the agreement, although it does not consider universal *episcope*, 'opens the way for a new analysis of the catholicity of the Church'.[18] The consensus in this agreement is more than substantial, and it is clearly more advanced than the dialogue between Roman Catholics and Lutherans, or between Roman Catholics and Anglicans. With the affirmation of apostolic succession as embedded in the apostolicity of the whole church, it is possible for both churches to affirm the sign of succession as of 'value and use'. At the same time it contains a differentiated consensus regarding the valuation of episcopacy. I agree with Harding Meyer when he asserts, in the context of the Porvoo statement, that a 'valid solution' to the problem of episcope can only be brought about 'in the direction of a new common sharing in the ecclesial reality of the episcopal office' while accepting a 'partial, though clearly perceptible difference in the valuation of this office and its exercise'.[19] What has been achieved with this agreement is a unity in diversity 'transposed from the level of doctrines to the level of structures and ecclesial realities'.[20] In this way it leads the way for further dialogues and agreements between churches and enriches the Christian notion of the marks of the church.

The operative ecclesiology of the people of God

Already in the 1970s Karl Rahner prophetically claimed that, from a dogmatic point of view, church unity was possible; yet he lamented the stagnancy in ecumenical development.[21] His observations are entirely, almost uncannily, up to date. This confirms, on the positive side, his status as one of the great theologians in history and, on the negative side, the snail's pace in ecumenical progress.

Rahner offered some pertinent reflections, which have hardly been seriously expounded upon in ecumenical dialogue, namely on the difference between what is actually believed among the people of God in a church, and what is officially taught in that church. In the context of our theme one could say that there is a considerable difference between what the people of God consider as constitutive for the one, holy, catholic and apostolic church and what is officially taught in this regard. Rahner noted that what the believer *actually* receives in his or her own church is basically to be found in all churches: belief in God, the acknowledgement of Jesus Christ as Saviour, forgiveness of sins, prayer and hope for eternal life. One might add sacraments, community, and consolation. These aspects have essentially shaped the faith of people in all churches, even if in varying forms and emphases. Unless church members have a decidedly propositional understanding of their faith in their respective denominations, for most the awareness and concern about actual differences between Christian affiliations are therefore much smaller than for theologians and office holders who work on the level of theology, dogma, and ecclesial history. In general the faithful have little precise knowledge about differences between the churches and, frequently, such differences are not their uppermost concerns, probably because they simply do not carry enough importance for them. This is why church members often do not perceive ecclesiological problems in the same way (for example, with regard to intercommunion) as do theologians and church officials.

Prophetically, Rahner noted that in the church of the future, the traditional points of controversy will still play some role, but what would essentially matter to people are *existential* questions about the very substance and foundations of faith. In this situation, he opined, it would be possible to discuss the traditional dividing issues in a much more 'relaxed manner', and always in the greater context about the innermost meaning of the Christian faith.[22] At the same time he was far from advocating a relativist stance, a difference-denying ecumenism, and he was wholly aware that there must be room for those who fully live by the rules and dogmas of their church, in particular, the Catholic Church. Yet he raises a crucial point by advocating the 'normative meaning of factual faith', the operative theology of the faithful, as one might put it, as a point of reference in our search for unity. Significantly, Rahner remarked that an exploration of this difference between what is factually believed and what is officially taught hardly seems to matter in ecumenical dialogue.[23]

This state of affairs has implications for ecumenical ecclesiology. One look at the countless documents published over the last fifty years generally confirms Rahner's observations. Yet the texts manage to express *something* of his hopes. In the various ecumenical documents mention is made repeatedly of the apostolicity of the whole church; this includes foremost the people of God and then the tiny percentage of theologians and church leaders. However, while the people of God are referred to in all the documents, their actual life of faith – hence their *factual apostolicity* – is neither examined nor taken seriously as a contributing factor in dialogues. Theological-sociological studies and surveys among denominations would be of revelatory significance concerning how *de facto* apostolicity, catholicity, holiness and unity are lived and understood among contemporary believers. In short, it would be significant to find out how the people of God understand their faith and the role that the church plays in and for their faith life.

As theologians, we may not like to admit what appears to be true: namely that most theologians and *episcopoi* would not consider it worthwhile undertaking such investigations, given that bishops and theologians – and not the people – are theologically trained and thus, as one might put it, basically 'know more and know better'. Naturally such analyses would be large-scale undertakings, for such studies would have to be conducted in local churches.[24] But it would indicate that those who engage in dialogues and those who are responsible for reception are serious about the apostolicity of the *whole* church, and that 'the people of God' does not simply connote a politically correct theological term. With insights gained from such studies – which could be started in local, national contexts – ecumenical dialogue in general, and a commonly worked-out understanding of the marks of the church in particular, would become a more holistic enterprise, in which church dogma, contemporary theological discourse and the actual faith of the people of God could be integrated into a credible, solid systematic and practical ecclesiology.

In order to reach new perspectives ecumenical bilaterals and multilaterals could take into account the hermeneutical principles that liberation theology set out over thirty years ago: (1) to be guided by and investigate the actual faith contexts of the people; (2) to confront these results with church dogma, creeds, confessions and academic theology; and (3) to draw some comprehensive, synthetic and hopefully inspiring conclusions.

Realistically, such studies cannot always be undertaken, nor are they essential or even to be recommended in relation to every issue. Official dialogues need to be continued, as they have built on one another. Yet this kind of method might be employed on certain, mutually agreed themes – especially those where dialogues have reached an impasse – and it would definitely offer new insights. Not only would the results be interesting in themselves, but they could instil renewed life into the ecumenical movement at large. Most importantly, such a method would transcend the lip service so often paid to the importance of the people of God. Moreover, it could also further collaboration by theologians of various denominations, as advocated in the *Charta Oecumenica*.

Conclusion

Dialogues which have occasioned actual progress – i.e. reception, to a
smaller or larger extent – are also those which inspire, precisely because of
their new methods, dynamism and courage. Notable examples are the
Porvoo Common Statement (1992), as mentioned earlier, and the *Joint
Declaration* (1999). In each case the dialogue partners dared to set out on a
genuinely new stage. This can be prophetic, yet it is often accompanied by
obstacles, especially with regard to the partial and/or full practical
realization of the agreement's stated aims. Why is it, for example, that,
after the *Joint Declaration* – which addressed and largely worked out the
question of justification, i.e. *the* central issue of the Reformation – the
Roman Catholic and the Lutheran Church have not yet managed to reach
any closer links between them? Indeed, Rahner's voice again rings true
when he noted – over thirty years ago! – that church leaders should not
pretend they cannot do anything because theologians are unable to find
agreement.[25]

To seek visible unity in true diversity is an urgent aim for the churches in
order to give common witness to our faith in Christ and to face together the
gravity and expanse of the world's problems. This endeavour presents for
the churches in postmodern Europe as well as for churches in other parts of
the world enormous challenges but also an opportunity to find ways in
which unity, holiness, catholicity and apostolicity will continue to be the
fundamental marks of church life. In an age characterized, on the one hand,
by materialism, cynicism and apathy, and, on the other hand, by
monumental poverty, injustice and an endangered natural environment,
this is an almost overwhelming task. It is a task, however, that is required of
the churches as long as divisions exist.

Notes

1. Harald Goertz, *Dialog und Rezeption, Die Rezeption evangelisch-lutherisch/römisch-
katholischer Dialogdokumente in der VELKD und der römisch-katholischen Kirche*
(Hannover: Lutherisches Verlagshaus, 2002), 40–1.
2. Given the proliferation of ecumenical statements over the last decades, it is not
even surprising that those churches, which are at first willing to engage in
reception, do not bother in the end, when they realize that sister churches are not
willing to do likewise.
3. Also *Church Unity in Word and Sacrament* (1984) and *Lehrveruteilungen –
kirchentrennend?* (1986) have not been officially received.
4. Cf. Udo Hahn, *Das kleine 1 × 1 der Ökumene, Das Wichtigste über den Dialog der
Kirchen* (Neukirchen-Vluyn: Neukirchener Verlagshaus, 2003), 106–17. H.
Goertz, *Dialog und Rezeption*, 193–6. 'Mit einer Ausnahme stammen sämtliche

Voten von Seiten der VELKD bzw. der evangelischen Kirchen. Die römisch-katholische Kirche hat sich bisher zu keinem der bilateralen Dokumente verbindlich geäussert. Lediglich zum Lima-Dokument liegt eine offizielle Stellungnahme von 1987 vor.'

5. Notable exceptions are the *Joint Declaration* and the Porvoo agreement, which have been officially received by the respective Churches.

6. Cf. Gerard Mannion, *Ecclesiology and Postmodernity: Questions for the Church in Our Time* (Collegeville, MS: Liturgical Press, 2007), 164.

7. Gerard Mannion, *Ecclesiology and Postmodernity*, 132–3, 138–9.

8. Cf. John J. Burkhard, *Apostolicity Then and Now: An Ecumenical Church in a Postmodern World* (Collegeville, MS: Liturgical Press, 2004), 159–64, 249–50. Burkhard's book is an excellent study of apostolicity through history and its relevance in a postmodern context for an ecumenical church.

9. Roger Haight, *Christian Community in History*, vol. 2: *Comparative Ecclesiology* (New York and London: Continuum, 2005), 7.

10. Ibid., 7.

11. Ibid., 6.

12. Ibid., 4.

13. Cf. G. Mannion, *Ecclesiology and Postmodernity*, 162–5. Cf. Roger Haight, 'The Church as Locus of Theology', *Concilium* 6 (1994), 16–18, 22. Haight notes: 'The great church, in its long history and especially in its united future, is theology's primary context.' An important contribution which deals with the related notions of evangelical catholicity and with 'the great tradition of the church' as a way forward in ecumenical dialogue has been developed by Ola Tjørhom, *Visible Church – Visible Unity: Ecumenical Ecclesiology and 'The Great Tradition of the Church'* (Collegeville: Liturgical Press, 2004), see, in particular, Chapter 2.

14. The Church of Denmark, the Church of England, the Estonian Evangelical-Lutheran Church, the Evangelical-Lutheran Church of Finland, the Evangelical-Lutheran Church of Iceland, the Church of Ireland, the Evangelical-Lutheran Church of Latvia, the Evangelical-Lutheran Church of Lithuania, the Church of Norway, the Scottish Episcopal Church, the Church of Sweden and the Church in Wales.

15. Burkhard, *Apostolicity Then and Now*, 193–6, at 193.

16. Ibid., 195.

17. My italics.

18. Henrik Roelvink, OFM, 'The Apostolic Succession in the Porvoo Statement', in *One in Christ* 30, 4 (1994), 344–54, at 353. Cf. also Burkhard, *Apostolicity Then and Now*, 195–6.

19. Harding Meyer, 'Apostolic Continuity, Apostolic Succession and Ministry from a Reformation Perspective', *Louvain Studies* 21, 2 (1996), 169–82, at 181–2. See also Mary Tanner for a fine analysis of the document. She has noted the 'holistic' manner in which the Porvoo statement treats apostolicity. M. Tanner, 'The Anglican Position on Apostolic Continuity and Apostolic Succession in the Porvoo Statement', *Louvain Studies* 21, 2 (1996), 114–25.

20. H. Meyer, 'Apostolic Continuity', 181.

21. Cf. Karl Rahner, 'Ist Kircheneinigung dogmatisch möglich?', *Karl Rahner Sämtliche Werke*, vol. 27: *Einheit in Vielfalt*, ed. Karl Rahner Stiftung unter Leitung von K. Lehmann, J. B. Metz, K.-H. Neufeld, A. Raffelt, H. Vorgrimler (Freiburg: Herder, 2002), 119–34 (orig. publ. in *Schriften zur Theologie* 10,

Einsiedeln (1972), 503–19). K. Rahner, 'Die eine Kirche und die vielen Kirchen', *Karl Rahner Sämtliche Werke*, vol. 27: *Einheit in Vielfalt*, 93–104. See also Richard Lennan's article on Rahner's ecclesiology and ecumenical perspective in Declan Marmion and Mary E. Hines (eds), *The Cambridge Companion to Karl Rahner* (Cambridge: Cambridge University Press, 2005), 128–43, esp. 139–40.

22. Rahner, 'Die eine Kirche und die vielen Kirchen', *Karl Rahner Sämtliche Werke*, vol. 27, 96–102.

23. Rahner, 'Ist Kircheneinigung dogmatisch möglich?', *Karl Rahner Sämtliche Werke*, vol. 27, 121.

24. Some work in this area, although mainly with the focus on worship, has been undertaken by Martin D. Stringer, *On the Perception of Worship: The Ethnography of Worship in Four Christian Congregations in Manchester* (Birmingham: Birmingham University Press, 1999) and *A Sociological History of Christian Worship* (Cambridge: Cambridge University Press, 2005).

25. Rahner, 'Ist Kircheneinigung dogmatisch möglich?', *Karl Rahner Sämtliche Werke*, vol. 27, 134.

Chapter 3

THE STRUGGLE FOR AN ORGANIC, CONCILIAR AND DIVERSE
CHURCH: MODELS OF CHURCH UNITY IN EARLIER STAGES OF
THE ECUMENICAL DIALOGUE

Miriam Haar

Models of church unity – introductory reflections

The visible unity of the churches is the ultimate aim of the ecumenical
endeavour. The continuous process of approaching visible unity and
formulating corresponding models of unity comes from the realization of
the churches that their separation contradicts God's will both for the unity
of the church as well as for the unity of humankind. The question was then,
and is now, how the aim of ecumenicity can be determined in a manner
that takes account of existing ecclesiological differences while still being
sufficiently compelling to provide a point of orientation for the *common*
ecumenical struggle. The full reality of visible unity of the churches is a
reality of which the churches have no previous experience; the final
outcome and shape are unknown and in the making. It is far greater than
any single model can describe. Provisionality is therefore a key characteristic. Consequently, full unity cannot be conceptualized into a rigid model,
but requires the flexibility to integrate emerging theologies as well as
multifaceted ecumenical experiences. Models of unity serve as focal points
for the elaboration of full visible unity and are preceded by theological
reflections and deliberations. Their formulation marks both the apex, a
point of synthesis which serves as a stepping stone, and the end of the
development process. It is not a linear process, one model following
another, but rather an organic process, one model emerging from another.
Models of unity are not mere abstract constructs, they address and express
the real being of the church, and as such they are concerned with the reality
of the churches both intrinsic and extrinsic. The quest for unity and its
expression in models of unity is therefore characterized by an ecclesiological
quality. It is decisively influenced by the understanding of church and of

ecclesiastical unity that Christians and churches bring with them from their particular tradition.

The unity the churches seek is more than an organizational and formal matter, though full visible unity has to entail some form of mutual recognition or union.[1] It is a costly commitment to each other and to a *concordia* of the being, life, and witness of the churches. Recent debate on ecumenical ecclesiology and models of unity has centred on two concepts: *koinonia* and *communio*. Although often regarded as the latest developments in ecumenical dialogue, closer analysis of earlier periods of ecumenism reveals that these concepts were already part of the ecumenical discussion and that a real appreciation of these two models must imply an awareness of the ecumenical tradition from which they stem – the preface of their emergence.

The World Council of Churches (WCC) and the Commission on Faith and Order (F&O)[2] have provided throughout the history of the modern ecumenical movement a forum of discussion from which many unity models emerged. Two models gained singular significance, Organic Unity and Conciliar Fellowship. It must be remembered that these two models originated at a time when ecumenical theology was in its infancy and when F&O constituted a unique opportunity for exchange for leading theologians in the field. Subsequent debate on those models of unity within the wider context of the WCC created an interface for the concrete reality of ecumenism and the being of the churches in the world. The prominence some models gained for a certain period of time was not exclusivist but rather focal. Organic Unity and Conciliar Fellowship represented perspectives, summaries of past insights and experiences under which the concept of unity could further unfold. Models of unity in themselves are synergetic; one could speak of a growth from one unity model to another.

This essay thus investigates the theological significance and synergy of Organic Unity and Conciliar Fellowship. It applies an historical sequence for the methodological reason that each of these models of unity formed the centre of discussion at their respective time. In the process of ecumenical reflection the formulation of unity models are times when past, present and future coincide. Inasmuch as a model holds the memory of a previous learning experience, it must likewise envision the future of the ecumenical movement to provide guidance for further reflections. It is hoped that this critical appraisal of early models of church unity will provide an insight into the theological considerations and tenets that facilitated the elaboration of *koinonia* and *communio* and a re-evaluation in light of the present state of ecumenical debate.

Organic unity

To this day, the most compelling image of unity is Paul's description of the church as the body of Christ (cf. 1 Cor. 12). This is the guiding imagery of Organic Unity. Two stages in the development of this model can be distinguished: reflection within the Commission on F&O prior to the Second World War and reflection within F&O as a part of the WCC. The imperative during both periods was clearer determination as to what the ecumenical engagement of the churches entailed. It can be summarized in the words of the report from the First World Conference of F&O in Lausanne (1927): 'The Unity of Christendom and the Relation Thereto of Existing Churches'.[3]

As early as 1927, delegates in Lausanne spoke of the visible unity the churches seek as 'a church so united [that] the ultimate loyalty of every member would be given to the whole body and not to any part of it'.[4] It was this solid and much-needed image that formed the theological foundation upon which continuing reflection on unity built. It provided a base conceptualization of what the churches aimed to achieve.

An extended elaboration of visible unity as an organic body was presented at the Second World Conference of F&O in Edinburgh (1937) in the report 'The Meanings of Unity'.[5] Unity was described, integrating the Lausanne notion, as 'the unity of a living organism, with the diversity characteristic of the members of a healthy body … a church so united the ultimate loyalty of every member would be given to the whole body and not to any part of it'.[6] The Edinburgh conference concluded: 'Our task is to find in God, to receive from God as His gift, a unity which can take up and preserve in one beloved community all the varied spiritual gifts which He has given to us in our separations.'[7] These examples from the first decades of the ecumenical movement contain some central tenets that provide the foundation for present debate on models of unity.

Unity is more than the monolithic event of church union; it is a dynamic living reality.[8] Furthermore, diversity is not only accepted but viewed within the context of spiritual gifts. It can be argued that the absence of representatives from many Orthodox churches as well as the Roman Catholic Church facilitated such agreement among a Protestant majority. It can be nevertheless contended that the theologians who developed the reports and the delegates who discussed and approved them touched upon some fundamental qualities of unity.

With the formation of the WCC in 1948 the main focus of reflection was on forming and giving shape to this new ecumenical body. By 1952, when F&O gathered for its Third World Conference in Lund, it had become an integral part of the WCC. Consequently, F&O had to reflect on its mission and purpose. It was a reaffirmation of its primary function to proclaim the essential oneness of the church of Christ and the subsequent query which asks what kind of unity God demands of His church.[9] Delegates at Lund, furthermore, when addressing the divisions of the churches, stated for the first time the importance of non-theological factors that still contribute to the divisions of the churches.

The report from Lund marked a first apex of reflection on unity as an organic unity. It served as the foundation for the report of F&O, 'Our Oneness in Christ and our Disunity as Churches',[10] at the Second Assembly of the WCC in Evanston (1954), containing a profound theological overview of the image of the body of Christ and oneness in Christ. The Lund report and Evanston report, read side by side, bear witness to how reflection on unity had evolved since the previous World Conference on F&O in 1937. It was stated that the churches are not creating a unity but are striving to retrieve a unity which never ceases to exist through Christ in his Holy Spirit. It is the Holy Spirit who binds all that constitutes the body of Christ into an organic unity. The churches which are in fellowship with each other are perceived to form a *communio sanctorum*, 'a fellowship in the Holy Spirit'.[11] Furthermore, it was clarified that, contrary to idealized perceptions of the apostolic time, 'the Church has never realized the fullness of that unity'.[12] Disagreement and controversy have dogged the Church from its beginning. F&O applied the concept of 'growth from unity to unity',[13] a unity which had been given when Christ was among his disciples and a unity into which the churches grow.

The work of the WCC, especially in matters of Life and Work (L&W),[14] deeply affected the work of F&O concurrently to theological reflection within the commission. The World Conference in Lund developed one of the key paradigms and imperatives of ecumenism, acknowledging the singular importance of the churches' mission in the world albeit formulated as a question, 'whether [the churches] should not act together in all matters except those in which deep differences of conviction compel them to act separately'.[15] The Lund principle evidences the continuous efforts within F&O to integrate matters of L&W inasmuch as the theological outlook of F&O was widened from a rather systematic theological focus to incorporate also ethics and pastoral issues. This internal development within F&O found wider audience at the Second Assembly of the WCC in Evanston (1954) with the theme 'Christ – the hope of the world'. This brought a new perspective to the discussion on unity, the kingdom of God and its relation to the state of humankind. The acknowledgement of the singular importance of the churches' mission in the world was made an imperative.

The elaboration of Organic Unity reached its peak and its conclusion at the Third Assembly of the WCC in New Delhi (1961). Here, the WCC had to accommodate deep-reaching changes both within the Council and the wider ecumenical movement. Delegates at this assembly witnessed to the greatest denominational and geographical expansion in the history of the modern ecumenical movement, bringing the ecumenical movement closer to truly representing the *oikoumene*. A wider spectrum of theological traditions was voiced, facilitating a more varied appraisal of, for example, organic unity, adding new perspectives and aspects to be taken into consideration. Consequently, New Delhi presented an opportune time for a critical re-evaluation of the aim of ecumenism. Delegates at this assembly expressed the need to state more clearly 'the nature of our common goal ... the vision of the one church [which] has become the inspiration of our ecumenical endeavour'.[16] This vision of unity was formulated in one of the longest and most crucial sentences ever written in ecumenical history, remaining the definitive expression of organic unity:

> We believe that the unity which is both God's will and his gift to his Church is being made visible as all in each place who are baptized into Jesus Christ and confess him as Lord and Saviour are brought by the Holy Spirit into one fully committed fellowship, holding the one apostolic faith, preaching the one Gospel, breaking the one bread, joining in common prayer, and having a corporate life reaching out in witness and service to all and who at the same time are united with the whole Christian fellowship in all places and all ages in such wise that ministry and members are accepted by all, and that all can act and speak together as occasion requires for the tasks to which God calls his people.[17]

The delegates were aware that a commitment to such a unity is costly: '[t]he achievement of unity will involve nothing less than a death or rebirth of many forms of church life as we have known them. We believe that nothing less costly can finally suffice.'[18] The question as to what degree member churches would be willing to pay this price has been an ecumenical issue ever since.

Organic Unity, as given in the New Delhi statement, builds on the central impetus for the ecumenical endeavour: the unity of the churches is God's will. Consequently, the question as to what being church signifies was raised in a new context. The connotation 'organic' marked a paradigm shift in ecclesiology. After monolithic, isolated and, at times, adversary concepts of each church tradition had dominated for centuries, a paradigm of interdependence began to emerge which set each church in relation to each other and to the one church. The churches perceived themselves to be part of the one church; a unity which has always been but has never been fully realized. Furthermore, this unity was perceived not as being restricted to the churches but as extending also to the unity of all of humankind. This dual conception of church unity and unity of humankind reflects an envisioned symbiosis of L&W and F&O as they both constitute the being of the church.

Organic Unity enunciates a unity that is visible and whose form is expressed 'in all places and ages'.[19] This aspect remained a major point of theological reflection and debate in the years following the assembly in New Delhi, acting as a catalyst to venture in new theological areas and directions.

Another issue pursued was the description of unity as 'one fully committed fellowship'.[20] Signs of this unity are the one apostolic faith, participating in common praise and prayer, celebrating one baptism, sharing a corporate life which allows the church to be engaged in a common mission in the name of Christ. Here we find a wide array of topics that became focal points of ecumenical research to this day. Organic Unity constitutes a commitment to the discovery of a form of unity which represents unity in diversity, and to achieving a fellowship in which authentic diversity is honoured and encouraged and in which authentic unity and communion are experienced. The delegates in New Delhi, for example, sought a transformation of divisive aspects between traditions within a wider experience of catholicity. This vision of unity incorporates both an act and a state of being by which previously separated church entities come together in faith, worship and sacramental life, ministry and mission. Organic Unity is a dynamic concept which became the central model of unity for the future work of F&O and still remains a viable option for many Christians.

Conciliar fellowship

Compared to Organic Unity, Conciliar Fellowship emerged over a much shorter period. Organic Unity provided a solid foundation from which theologians could aim to integrate further aspects pertaining to unity. Individual theologians, discussions within bilateral dialogues as well as the continuous work of the WCC provided a wide spectrum of reflection on unity and unity models which could be synthesized. This is not to be taken in the sense of a formal process, but rather via careful observation and analysis of emerging theologies and conceptualizations of unity. Meetings and studies of F&O as well as WCC assemblies served as intermediate points of consolidation, both summarizing latest findings and setting directions for future studies. In the following, one central aspect, catholicity, which facilitated the elaboration of Conciliar Fellowship, will be examined, as it provided the theological framework for the development of Conciliar Fellowship.

Critics of Organic Unity saw a major deficiency with this unity model. Many contended that it overemphasized the institutional aspect of the churches, churches as denominational bodies, and thus neglected the local reality. The brief characterization of visible unity as visible 'in all places and ages'[21] in New Delhi opened the way to develop an ecclesiological concept which gave greater weight to the local church. An initial step was the work of the section ' "All in each place": the process of growing together'.[22] The report from the section 'The Church in the Purpose of God',[23] in which the delegates at the Fourth World Conference on F&O in Montreal (1963) attempted to clarify the relation between the church, the churches as denominational bodies and the local churches is ecclesiologically significant. Contrary to prior world conferences, the reports from Montreal did not represent polished and elaborate documents and, as a result, the Montreal report was described as 'a most promising chaos'.[24] Clear-cut results were impossible due to the task of addressing the diverse and complex issues of a rapidly changing geopolitical environment. Furthermore, increased Orthodox presence and the attendance of Roman Catholic observers contributed to a much wider debate, which in itself posed a challenge. Yet, these reports, as fragmented and preliminary as they are, provide a unique insight into the growth of the churches' understanding of unity.

The concept of catholicity, which gained prominence at the Fourth General Assembly of the WCC in Uppsala (1968), provided a theological and ecclesiological foundation for reflection on the local reality of the churches as catholicity universally rests on catholicity locally. Each local church lives in fellowship with the others and is dependent on the others, together forming a cosmically united body, while retaining its individuality.[25] The theological expression of 'in all places and ages' turns the focus to the horizontal dimension of the unity the churches seek. Under an ecclesiological perspective, the effort to develop a shared notion of catholicity is part of a less apparent, yet continuous ecumenical project. For centuries the *notae ecclesiae* – oneness, holiness, catholicity and apostolicity – served as exclusivist categories to determine the ecclesial being of other church traditions. Ecumenical reflection on the visible unity of the one church has inevitably to entail the elaboration of shared concepts of these ecclesiological attributes. There cannot be a concept of the visible united church which does not describe it as one, holy, catholic and apostolic. At the outset of the Organic Unity discussion catholicity stood for the bond of unity the churches share through Jesus Christ in the Holy Spirit; that which ties them together in the body of Christ. In Uppsala the visible unity was interpreted as a dynamic catholicity which expresses a deeper internal dimension of unity. 'It is the quality by which the Church expresses the fullness, the integrity, and the totality of life in Christ.'[26]

Catholicity was perceived as a gift of God and the Holy Spirit: 'Since it has been given this gift, the Church *is* catholic, but at the same time, no church can claim to *be* catholic. The Church is constantly on the way to *becoming* catholic. Catholicity is a task yet to be fulfilled and it can be fulfilled only if the churches together engage in a movement of renewal.'[27] Catholicity is an essential, dynamic calling for the churches which cannot be achieved quickly, but 'reaches its completion when what God has already begun in history is finally disclosed and fulfilled'.[28] Four key areas of the quest for catholicity were determined: diversity, continuity, unity of the whole church, and unity of humankind with the aim being 'to make visible the bonds which unite Christians in universal fellowship'.[29]

The focus on the local realities of the churches called for a new appraisal of diversity. The focus on unity always carries the danger of devaluing diversity among the church traditions. Since the Second Assembly of the WCC in Evanston (1954), which stated that '[t]here is diversity which is not sinful but good',[30] continuous attempts were made to transform pejorative views into an appreciation of the diversity of the gifts of the Holy Spirit. The acknowledgement of legitimate diversity in the context of the development of Organic Unity proved to be too general to suffice. In the reports from Uppsala a dual approach is taken. Vertically, the Christocentric emphasis which had prevailed in earlier decades is widened to a trinitarian outlook.

> It is because the unity of the Church is grounded in the divine triunity that we can speak of diversity in the Church as something to be not only admitted but actively desired ... [I]t follows that, in order to be faithful to our calling to unity, we must consider this calling within the wider context of the unity and diversity of humankind.[31]

This provides diversity with a trinitarian foundation and legitimization. Horizontally, diversity is set in relation to the community of believers.

This was more clearly formulated in the aftermath of Uppsala: 'Since each part is committed to accountability to the whole fellowship, it needs neither to be afraid of diversity nor even conflict. As long as the segments are open to the guidance of the Spirit, they will be held together in "reconciled diversity".'[32] Such a concept requires appropriate fora of discussion, an aspect which was not addressed in Uppsala. The concept of conciliarity continued to emerge until the following WCC General Assembly in Nairobi (1975). It originated from one area of interest at the Fourth World Conference on F&O in Montreal (1963), 'Scripture and Tradition', which was pursued in three separate studies, one of which focused on the Councils of the early church.[33] This study served over time as a catalyst for the retrieval of conciliarity. Conciliarity also further explicated the aspect 'that all can act and speak together as occasion requires for the tasks to which God calls his people'[34] from the New Delhi Statement.

The reports from Uppsala unfolded what catholicity also entailed in regard to the being and life of the church in a broken world. There, the term catholicity was not only taken as a theological concept but also as a concept for the being of the church in the world and thus for the whole of humankind. The delegates in Uppsala concluded that a united church is a universal community where people of different traditions, cultures and races are brought into 'an organic and living unity in Christ'.[35] In its witness to catholicity, the church 'is bold in speaking of itself as the sign of the coming unity of mankind'.[36] True catholicity involves a quest for diversity in unity and continuity. True unity is the gift of companionship with God's people who are struggling for peace and justice. F&O's contribution, 'The Holy Spirit and the Catholicity of the Church',[37] offered one lasting statement on the essential unity of the churches' witness in the world and their quest for unity:

> We cannot be isolated from the shocks and turmoil of our time, as conflicts between races and nations tear apart the fabric of our common life, as developed and developing countries become more and more alienated, and ideologies and crusades clash in deadly struggle for survival. The miseries of man multiply. In such a time it is the Holy Spirit who calls us to share Christ's unlimited love, to accept his condemnation, of our fears and treasons and for his sake to endure shame, oppression, and apparent defeat. In the agonising arena of contemporary history – and very often among the members of the Churches – we see the work of demonic forces that battle against the rights and liberties of man, but we also see the activity of the life-giving Spirit of God. We have come to view this world of man as the place where God is already at work to make all things new, and where he summons us to work with him.[38]

In the aftermath of the assembly in Uppsala, Conciliar Fellowship emerged as a concept that included the latest developments in reflection on unity. Conciliar Fellowship could be called the first dual model of church unity, equally visualizing both church unity and the church's being in the world.

It further elucidates the concept of catholicity by developing the theme of interdependence within the body of Christ; a mutual relationship that entails mutual responsibility and accountability. This was complemented by the ongoing reflection on the issue of diversity and its integration into the concepts of unity,[39] which was further emphasized at the Fifth General Assembly in Nairobi (1975) where it was clarified that conciliarity also signifies that the life of the church is not 'monolithic'.[40]

Several meetings of F&O furthered the development of the concept of Conciliar Fellowship. The definite conceptualization as approved in Nairobi was essentially the text that was drafted at the F&O consultation on 'Concepts of Unity and Models of Union' in Salamanca (1973). Less than one year after the Salamanca consultation the F&O Commission met in Accra where discussion centred on the relation of Organic Unity to Conciliar Fellowship. It was clarified that the Church can only be truly and organically one at *all* levels of its life as a Conciliar Fellowship; thus its congruence with Organic Unity and consistency in reflections on unity was preserved.[41]

Although the emphasis in Nairobi was on the context of unity, matters of L&W, a landmark was reached in defining Conciliar Fellowship. The New Delhi statement, as amended by Uppsala with the term of catholicity, was reaffirmed and the goal of unity was restated in new language using the imagery of Conciliar Fellowship, quoting the draft description of Salamanca:[42]

> The one church is to be envisioned as a conciliar fellowship of local churches which are themselves truly united. In this fellowship each church possesses, in communion with the others, the fullness of catholicity, witnesses to the same apostolic faith, and therefore recognizes the others as belonging to the same church of Christ and guided by the same Spirit ... [T]hey are bound together because they have received the same baptism and share in the same eucharist; they recognize each other's members and ministries. They are one in their common commitment to confess the Gospel of Christ by proclamation and service to the world. To this end, each church aims at maintaining sustained and sustaining relationships with her sister churches, expressed in conciliar gatherings whenever required for the fulfilment of their common calling.[43]

One of the characteristics of this model is its trans-confessional nature, i.e. it proposes a union of previously divided congregations and local churches and a reconciling of the rich diversity of previously divided denominations or confessions. The vision of the one church as a Conciliar Fellowship is an expression of the inclusive participation of the people of God from their many cultures, races, and nationalities, deeply touching the ways and various levels in which the churches relate to each other and respond together to their mission and environment. Such visible unity would reconcile the divisions between these confessions, which obscure their witness to Christ's mission to all humankind. This understanding of fellowship explicates the concept of a unity that is given and has to be realized in the context of the reality of the churches. 'Each local church lives in fellowship with the others, each depending on the others, each responsible for the others. Though each retains its individuality, they together form one body throughout the world.'[44] The fellowship between the local churches is in itself a sign of the one, holy, catholic and apostolic church and is constitutional to the church's witness in the world.

> True conciliarity is the reflection in the life of the Church of the triune being of God ... The source of the Church's unity ... is the meeting of the Apostles with the risen Christ who bears the marks of his cross, and the continued encounter with the disciples today with his living presence in the midst of the eucharistic fellowship.[45]

Conclusion

The development of recent models of unity, *koinonia* and *communio*, was only possible because of the difficult and strenuous foundational work to which many theologians of various church traditions committed themselves over more than 50 years. It was a journey marked by tension between the simplicity of the aim and the complexity of the task involved. From evaluation of the two models, three guiding principles emerge as scarlet threads intertwining them. (1) The basic ecumenical conviction: unity belongs to the nature of the Church. (2) The ecumenical indicative: the essential unity of the Church is presupposed in every effort for unity. (3) The ecumenical imperative: the essential unity of the Church must be lived and made visible.[46] The indicative pushes towards the imperative: 'If we live in the Spirit, let us also walk in the Spirit. If we are one, then let us live and act in unity' (Gal. 5.25). The unity that is a gift to the churches also becomes a unity that is a task and responsibility for the churches.

No final answer has been reached as to what full visible unity entails. It is, as it always was, an ongoing transformative process. Ecclesiology was rarely explicitly addressed, being one of the most contentious theological areas. Preliminary work was necessary. The development of Organic Unity and Conciliar Fellowship provides a horizontal and vertical orientation, creating a space in which the churches can aim to probe deeper. The insights gained from these early times of the modern ecumenical movement are cornerstones for ecumenical theology today.

Models of church unity are built on the common agreement that the churches strive towards a unity that is already given in Jesus Christ as well as the awareness that their interdependence is rooted in the body of Christ which transcends and permeates the reality of this world. As Christian churches they are called both in and out of the world to a unifying fellowship in their responsibility for the unity of all humankind. The mission of catholicity compels churches to witness in the world and partake in struggles for justice and peace, holding them in a bond of mutual accountability as the proper expression of God's will. In a world determined by pluralism, the churches' ecumenical vocation manifests a reconciled diversity which is not indifferent towards the other but regards difference in another tradition as complementary, an aid to understand more deeply God's will for the whole of creation. This costly commitment to visible unity is made with the awareness that the unity the churches seek is ultimately a gift of God which will come to its full fruition at the end of time. In this eschatological perspective, all human divisions are provisional.[47]

Notes

1. In this chapter, unity refers to the overall unity the churches seek and which they regard to be a divine imperative, whereas union refers to the merger of churches into a larger ecclesial body.

2. Faith and Order is taken representatively for all doctrinal issues in the work of the WCC.

3. *Faith and Order: Proceedings of the World Conference Lausanne 1927*, ed. H. N. Bate (London: SCM, 1927), 398 (first draft), 436 (second draft).

4. Ibid., 10.

5. Cf. *The Meanings of Unity*, Faith and Order Paper No. 82 (Geneva: WCC Publications, first series, 1978).

6. *The Second World Conference on Faith and Order held at Edinburgh 1937*, ed. Leonard Hodgson (London: SCM, 1938), 252.

7. Ibid., 252.

8. Cf. *Faith and Order: Proceedings of the World Conference Lausanne*, 460f.

9. Cf. *Evanston to New Delhi 1954–1961: Report of the Central Committee to the Third Assembly of the World Council of Churches*, ed. n.a. (Geneva: World Council of Churches, 1961), 42.

10. Cf. ibid., 72–98.

11. *Faith and Order: The Report of the Third World Conference at Lund 1952*, Faith and Order Paper No. 15, ed. O. S. Tomkins (London: SCM, 1953), 23. Cf. 'The Report to the Churches', 11–68.

12. Ibid., 84.

13. Ibid., 84.

14. Life and Work stands here representatively for all matters pertaining to the being of the church in the world.

15. *The Evanston Report: The Second Assembly of the World Council of Churches 1954*, ed. W. A. Visser't Hooft (London: SCM, 1955), 90.
16. *The New Delhi Report: The Third Assembly of the World Council of Churches 1961*, ed. W. A. Visser't Hooft (London: SCM, 1962), 117.
17. Ibid., 116.
18. Ibid., 122.
19. Ibid., 118.
20. Ibid., 119.
21. Ibid., 118.
22. *Faith and Order: The Fourth World Conference on Faith and Order Montreal 1963*, Faith and Order Paper No. 42, ed. P. C. Rodger and L. Vischer (London: SCM, 1964), 80–90.
23. Cf. ibid., 41–49.
24. Ibid., 7.
25. Cf. *Uppsala to Nairobi 1968–1975: Report of the Central Committee to the Fifth Assembly of the World Council of Churches*, ed. D. Enderton Johnson (New York: Friendship Press and London: SPCK, 1975), 79.
26. *The Uppsala Report 1968. Official Report of the Fourth Assembly of the World Council of Churches Uppsala 1968*, ed. N. Goodall (Zürich: CVB-Druck, 1968), 13f.
27. Ibid., 13.
28. Ibid., 13.
29. Ibid., 17.
30. *The Evanston Report*, 87.
31. *The Uppsala Report*, 61.
32. *Uppsala to Nairobi*, 79. This qualification of reconciled diversity was further elaborated by the Lutheran World Federation as 'Unity in Reconciled Diversity' and is regarded by many as a complementary model of unity.
33. Cf. *New Delhi to Uppsala 1961–1968. Report of the Central Committee to the Fourth Assembly of the World Council of Churches*, ed. n.a. (Geneva: WCC, 1968), 76.
34. Ibid., 116.
35. *The Uppsala Report*, 224.
36. Ibid., 17.
37. Cf. ibid., 7–20.
38. Ibid., 12 .
39. *Uppsala to Nairobi*, 79.
40. *Breaking Barriers Nairobi 1975. The Official Report of the Fifth Assembly of the World Council of Churches, Nairobi 1975*, ed. D. M. Paton (London: SPCK and Grand Rapids, MI: Eerdmans, 1976), 60.
41. Cf. *Uppsala to Nairobi*, 80.
42. Cf. ibid., 59–61.
43. Ibid., 79.
44. Ibid.
45. Ibid., 60.
46. Cf. Harding Meyer, *That All May Be One: Perceptions and Models of Ecumenicity* (Grand Rapids, MI and Cambridge, UK: Eerdmans, 1999), 8.
47. Cf. *The Evanston Report*, 89.

Chapter 4

CHURCH AND COVENANT: THEOLOGICAL RESOURCES FOR DIVIDED DENOMINATIONS[1]

Edwin C. van Driel

In the face of growing divisions between their conservative and liberal wings, how should mainline churches think about the unity of the church? In recent years, proposed solutions to mainline crises have invoked the idea of 'covenant'. For example, the PCUSA Task Force on Peace, Unity and Purity of the Church started its work with covenanting that, amidst all their differences, they would hold together in prayer, worship, reading of scripture and intense listening.[2] More prominently, in 2006 the Archbishop of Canterbury proposed a covenant for the members of the Anglican Communion, in an attempt to restore unity and trust after the ordination of Gene Robinson as Bishop of New Hampshire.[3]

I, too, suggest the notion of 'covenant' as basis for the church's unity. However, in contrast to the 'covenants' I mentioned above, I will interpret this 'covenant' not as a human concept, a covenant made between church members, congregations, or, as in the case of the Anglican covenant, national churches, but as of divine making. I will explore 'covenant' from the perspective of the ecclesiology of the church in which I grew up, the Netherlands Reformed Church (NRC), the national church of the Netherlands. Like many other mainline churches, the NRC counted among its members both liberals and conservatives, with serious theological differences.[4] Even the topics under discussion over the past few decades were similar – homosexuality and the interpretation of scripture. However, given the concept of a divine covenant as basis of the church's unity, liberals and conservatives still accepted each other as members of the same church. The church membership of the other was not at stake, because this membership does not rest on a human, but on a divine choice, expressed in baptism: 'You did not choose me but I chose you' (Jn 15.16). If God chooses the other as fellow member of the covenant, what right do we have to separate 'us' from 'them'?[5]

In the following essay I will first examine the history of the Netherlands Reformed Church's ecclesiology. Thereafter, I will expound this ecclesiology's principles in five theses. With these five theses I hope to trigger our theological imagination. I am not going to give a fully fledged defence of each thesis, although I tend to think a good case can be made for each. I am also not going to suggest that this ecclesiology is the cure-all to all mainline ecclesial diseases, although I do think it would be a good start. My goal is more modest: I am inviting you to step into this different ecclesial world, to see how it fits together; and then, enriched with the new theological concepts and moves you encounter there, to return to your own situation, and to see for yourself if and how any of these could help us with our own struggles and divisions.

The origins of the ecclesiology of the Netherlands Reformed Church

What makes the Netherlands Reformed Church (NRC)'s understanding of the church based on 'divine covenant' all the more interesting is that it was itself the result of ecclesial strife. In the nineteenth century, the NRC seemed to be in the process of losing its theological identity. While some ministers denied the resurrection or the divinity of Christ and another famously came out as a follower of Buddha, the leadership of the church, to whom disciplinary means were available, refused to uphold the church's confessional standards. In this situation the conservative minority found itself divided into two camps on how to respond. One camp thought the church's traditional character should be restored by its members appealing to the church's courts and synod. If this did not help, the members would leave the church. This became known as the *juridical way*. For several decades, the juridical camp made its appeals, and when they did not succeed, members indeed dissented and formed the Reformed Churches in the Netherlands (RCN).

Meanwhile, the other half of the conservative minority followed what was called the *medical way*: its members believed that as long as one was not prevented from preaching the gospel, one should never leave the church. They believed that the medicine of the gospel itself can heal a sick church and, although they were weakened by the loss of their conservative allies, members of this group continued to focus on preaching the gospel.

The result seemed predictable. The dissenter RCN could be expected to become a conservative bulwark, its identity firmly protected by its juridical structure. The larger NRC would grow more and more liberal, with a slim but powerless conservative minority. However, things turned out differently. One hundred years later the dissenter RCN found itself at the far left of the theological spectrum, with its international daughter churches, including the Christian Reformed Church in the USA, declaring themselves in impaired communion with their mother church. Meanwhile, a spirit of renewal began to stir the larger NRC in the 1930s and 1940s. Liberals, middle-of-the-roaders and conservatives grew discontent with the perceived theological 'wishy-washiness' of the church. None of these groups gave up their particular approach to the gospel, but all came to realize that a church, to be true to its calling, needs to confess boldly its obedience to the gospel of Christ. They found one another in a notion of 'covenant' as developed by the people of the *medical way*. In 1951 an overwhelming majority of the national synod accepted a new, Christ-centred church order and restored the church's ties to its confessional documents. The preaching of the gospel – and that alone – had healed the church.[6]

What then was the notion of covenant developed by the medical way theologians? I will expound this notion in five theses:

Thesis one: the church and its unity are constituted by God's covenantal actions, not by human confessions, covenants, agreements, or practices

The decisive theological premise of the ecclesiology-of-the-medical-way theologians was that the church and its unity are constituted by God's covenantal actions, not by human confessions, covenants, agreements, or, as many contemporary ecclesiologies have it, practices.[7] God's covenant invites a response, that is certainly true – a response of faithful confessing, faithful practising, and so forth. But confessions are no more than that: they are acts of response, of acknowledgement, of acceptance, of gratitude and obedience to God's prior act. Yet that act is not dependent on human response. The covenant is not annulled even when faithful confessing or practice is absent. By contrast, when the covenant is absent, no confessing or practising is possible.

In interpreting the divine covenant the advocates of the medical way were strongly influenced by their reading of the Old Testament. The Old Testament is full of stories of Israel's disobedience to the covenant, and of God's response of anger, threats and judgement. And yet, nowhere does God's judgement on human disobedience amount to an end to the covenant; on the contrary, God's judgements always come *within* the context of the covenant. God judges to entice and implore God's people to return, and God's *Lo-ammi*, 'you are not my people and I am not your

God' (Hosea 1.9), is always immediately followed by the covenantal promises: 'Yet the number of the people of Israel shall be like the sand of the sea, which can be neither measured nor numbered; and in the same place where it was said to them, "You are not my people", it shall be said to them: "Children of the living God"' (Hosea 1.10).

What holds for God's actions under the old covenant, the people of the medical way believed, holds no less for God's actions under the new covenant. Where God does not treat human disobedience as an annulment of the covenant, neither can we.

Thesis two: the confessing nature of the church is not well safeguarded by a church of the confessions, but only by a confessing church

If the church is constituted by divine covenant, and not by human confession, what does this mean for the status of the church's confessional documents? The people of the medical way were no less attached to a central place for these documents in the church's life than the people of the juridical way. After all, both groups were theologically conservative. However, the medical-way theologians believed that juridical strategies could never lead to the desired outcome. To make their point, they introduced a distinction between 'a confessing church' and 'a church of the confessions'.[8] The strategies of the juridical way could only lead to the latter, a church of the confessions; that is, a church which by majority of vote is bound to its confessional documents. But that does not mean that the church as a body, the church as a whole, confesses the gospel. It only means that a group of church members who is attached to the traditional confessional documents has mustered enough votes to establish a majority. A *confessing church*, on the other hand, is more than a church that has some confessional capital in the bank. A confessing church is a church which as a whole, as a body, binds itself gratefully to the gospel and commits itself to confessing this gospel in the face of all powers and principalities of our age. Such confessing is not the outcome of a majority of votes. It is the outcome of a spiritual process in which the church as a whole – left and right, old and young – wrestles for the truth.[9]

Where wrestling for the truth will lead is not certain, of course. After all, the truth of God's revelation is larger than the formulations of our historical confessional documents; and only God knows what new, undiscovered insights we may receive in our common discernment. It might be something different, something richer, something of greater truth than any of the positions now proposed. Trying to get a majority of votes, however well meaning, is therefore taking a shortcut. It avoids the risk that God may lead us where we do not want to go. As Hoedemaker, one of the leaders of the medical way, exclaimed: 'May God protect us against an orthodox synod.'[10]

For a contemporary example of what this wrestling for the truth looks like, I refer to two articles published in 2004 by the American journal *Christian Century*. In these articles Richard Mouw of Fuller Theological Seminary and Barbara Wheeler of Auburn Theological Seminary explore the current divide in the American mainline. Mouw, an evangelical, answers the question: 'Why do conservatives need liberals?' and Wheeler, theologically liberal, tackled the reverse: 'Why do liberals need conservatives?'[11] Both authors, rather than simply holding their party line, speak movingly of how they were challenged by the other side. Wheeler reflects on how her encounters with the evangelical culture strengthened her faith:

Early on in my relationships with evangelicals there was a moment when I knew, and knew that the other knew, that we were hearing the same gospel. I am not proud of the fact that my evangelical friends spoke first, affirming my faith before I affirmed theirs. I'm not proud that I failed to take the initiative, but I'm grateful that they did.[12]

Mouw recalls a visit of his friend Virginia Mollenkott to Calvin College after her coming out, where she reminded the audience that:

You may disagree with everything I have said thus far, but I hope we can at least agree on this: Whatever your sexual orientation, there is nothing – absolutely nothing – that you have to do or agree to before coming to the foot of the cross of Jesus. The only thing any of us has to say as we come to Calvary is this: 'Just as I am without one plea, but that thy blood was shed for me, and that thou bidst me come to thee, O Lamb of God, I come.'

And Mouw reflects:

I believe that in that plea she was expressing good Reformed doctrine. We do not have to have either our theology or our ethics well worked out before we can come together to Calvary. All we need to know is that we are lost apart from the sovereign grace that was made available through us through the atoning work of Jesus Christ.[13]

Both authors acknowledge that these experiences in themselves do not bridge the theological divide. But they do allow them, as Mouw writes, '[to] journey on as friends – no longer strangers to each other – who are eager to talk to each other, and even to argue passionately with each other about crucial issues'.[14] They cannot let go of one another, because they have met one another at the foot of the cross of Christ. Leaving the other, turning one's back to the other, would mean turning one's back to the crucified Jesus. And therefore they hold on to one another, however uneasy it is in the moment, and however unclear where their path is going to lead. That is wrestling for God's truth.[15]

Thesis three: church discipline is eschatological

The topic of 'confessions' invariably goes hand in hand with another issue: that of church discipline. The theologians of the medical way believed in the need for church discipline; but at the same time they believed that, as much as confessing is not the result of juridical procedures but an act wrought by the Spirit, the same should be said about church discipline. This leads to the third thesis: *church discipline is eschatological.*[16]

By this slogan the medical-way theologians meant at least three things. First, the *criterion* for church discipline is eschatological. After all, there never was a time that the church's teaching was infallible; there was never a time that the church's life was impeccable. In determining whether someone's life or teaching is in conflict with the church's position, we have no gold standard in the past against which we can measure the life or teaching that is under consideration. The golden age is rather in the future: the kingdom of God. We can only speak provisionally, however, about the eschaton; therefore, if this is the criterion for our disciplinary actions, these actions also need to be provisional. The medical-way people liked to refer here to Jesus's parable about the kingdom of heaven as a field in which an enemy sowed weeds, and the master of the field does not allow his servants to gather the weeds for fear that they might also uproot the wheat: 'Let both of them grow together until the harvest; and at harvest time I will tell the reapers, Collect the weeds first and bind them in bundles to be burned, but gather the wheat into my barn' (Mt. 13.30).

Second, because the kingdom is not the outcome of our actions, but a gift to us from God, so also the real actor in church discipline is God. The church is only the instrument. Therefore, in our disciplinary actions we need to make use of those means God gives to the church in which God expresses judgements – and that is the preaching of the gospel. Church discipline is to take place not in the church court but in the pulpit. As another famous slogan of the medical-way people went: 'Throw in the Word, and you will see miracles.'

A third comment finally qualifies the preceding two: the church's disciplinary actions can be more firm and decisive the more immediately they concern the church's confession concerning the embodied Word, Jesus Christ. Even while the eschaton has not been realized yet, it has been inaugurated; and even while church discipline happens primarily by way of the preaching of the word, that Word has become flesh and has lived among us. Here we speak of a reality that is not eschatologically beyond us, but that, in the words of the first letter of John, 'we have looked at and touched with our own hands' (1 John 1.1). That most Christians can share the creeds of the early church is precisely because these creeds concern this reality. Here the truth has come to us the most closely, the most concretely present, with a human face and a human voice. Therefore, here the church can also speak and confess and judge the most clearly.[17] In other words – if there has to be a disciplinary action, or, even, if there ever has to be a church-dividing conflict, let it be disciplinary action or let it be a church-dividing conflict concerning the confession of Jesus Christ!

Thesis four: God's covenant constitutes the church in its invisible as well as visible nature, and in its organic as well as in its institutional nature

The medical-way people rejected a strong distinction between the visible and the invisible church; or between the church as institution and the church as body of Christ. When they spoke of the divine covenant as the basis of the church they did not mean by the latter an invisible church, a gathering of true believers, distinct from the crowd one sees in the church building on Sunday morning: instead, they meant the visible community. That community, including its institutional aspects of officers, church order, congregational meetings, assemblies and so on, is in its essence not a human association based on human decision or assent, but is constituted by a divine act: the covenant.[18]

Here again, the medical-way advocates were deeply influenced by their reading of the Old Testament. God's covenant with Israel did not apply to only an inner circle of believers, but to all the children of Israel. And within that covenant, God laid claim on the institutional life of Israel no less than on their hearts and minds. So, too, with the church, the medical-way theologians believed.

The belief that the church in all its visible and institutional aspects is not of human, but of divine, origin has powerful implications for our understanding of church membership. For the medical-way people, one is not a member of a church because one *decided* to join, but because one was either born in the church, or one was found by it.[19] In this, the medical-way theologians reflected a strong Augustinian understanding of faith: faith is not a human act, it is a divine gift. The same holds, they believed, for church membership. This implies, however, that one cannot leave the church if one no longer agrees with some of its members. If the church were of human origin, a human club or association, its members could leave at will. Human associations are based on the agreement of its members, but not so the church. If you and I are members of the same church, our common membership is not rooted in some agreement you and I have made, but is rooted in the fact that God placed both of us there together. And therefore, if you and I at some point come to disagree, you or I cannot take leave, because the church of which we both are a member is not mine or yours or ours, but God's.

Speaking from my current American context I have to conclude that on this point American and European sensibilities most strongly clash. American church life is based on a distinction between the invisible and the visible church; between the Church with a capital 'C', which can be said to have such lofty divine origin, and churches with a lower 'c', the actual institutional expressions of the church, what Americans call 'denominations'. As the German theologian Dietrich Bonhoeffer remarked on his visit to the United States about seventy years ago: American churches 'do not dare to claim for itself [sic] the name of the church of Jesus Christ because this name is too great, too dangerous. The church is something beyond the denominations.'[20]

The issue is that 'denomination' is not a theological, but a sociological, concept. And defining itself sociologically, rather than theologically, has very important consequences for the praxis of American church life. I want to point out two.

The first consequence is that, because American churches define themselves sociologically, they have no theological resources that can help them in a time of disagreement and ecclesial strife. The very fact that Christian communities define themselves as 'denominations', that is, as gatherings based on human assent and agreement, means that once that assent and agreement is undermined by dissent and disagreement, there really is no reason – no theological reason – to stay together. A reference to a recent article in a mainline church magazine, *The Presbyterian Outlook*, illustrates this. In the article a Presbyterian minister argued that one should not be upset about congregations and ministers who leave the denomination for other places of service. After all, the argument goes: 'Denominations are not the same thing as the Church. They are human constructs that have served us well, but we should not confuse any of them with the Church Proper.'[21] Based on this premise, the writer is of course right. If we are just *denominations*, why stick together? But on the other hand: why buy the premise? Why believe we are just denominations? What is the *theological* argument for saying so?

The second consequence of the sociological self-understanding of American church life comes in the form of a paradox: by making church communities theologically less important, they become more important in practice; while by making them theologically more important, in practice they become more disputable. For example: I live in a small north-eastern American town of 30,000 residents, most of which are Roman Catholic. In this town there are also, on the latest count, no fewer than 16 Protestant denominations represented. If people like the above-mentioned writer in *The Presbyterian Outlook* have their way, there may soon be a few more, and, on his argument, we should not find a theological problem with that. However, the practical result of all this is that each of these 16 represented denominations struggles to maintain a physical plant, pay a pastor and support staff, organize a Sunday school programme, do effective outreach, and so on. Although we say denominations are theologically not important, because they are not the Church Proper, in practice they consume a disproportionate amount of the church's – or should I say God's? – money, time, and energy. As I said: by making our church communities theologically less important, in practice they become more important. On the other hand, if we were to accept God's covenantal claim on the institutional aspects of our churches, if we no longer were to see these institutional expressions as just sociological, but of theological importance, at that very moment we will see their multitude not as a justified expression of our diversity, but as foreign to the unity of the covenant, as a sin against the body of Christ. By making them theologically more important, in practice we make them more disputable.[22]

Thesis five: church shopping is 'verboten'

When churches define themselves sociologically, as denominations, they have very little inbuilt theological resistance against the prevailing norms of the surrounding culture, which in the North American context means that very soon they start behaving economically, as corporations looking for one another's market share. After all, the church building must be maintained, the minister needs to be paid, and we need members to pay these bills. Valued economically rather than theologically, church members respond in kind, as consumers: they go church shopping.

However, if church membership is based on covenant rather than choice, church membership of local congregations should not be decided on individual preferences. This is why the new Netherlands Reformed Church order of 1951, in which the theological principles of the medical-way people got organizational hands and feet, adhered to the geographical principle of church membership: the whole country was divided up in small geographical areas, each one connected to a local congregation; and to which congregation one belonged was determined by the geographical area in which one lived. When one moved, membership was automatically transferred to the congregation of the new place of residence. Local church membership was thus not an expression of individual preference, but of the practice (!) of learning to live together as children of the same divine covenant.[23] As a principle, church shopping is *verboten*.

How would it look if we adopted a similar attitude towards membership of the local congregation? Obviously, the geographical principle would be very hard to apply to all contexts – for example, in the USA no Protestant church has the nationwide presence that would make this workable. But what American churches would be able to do is to apply the underlying theological ideas to our attitudes towards transferring and receiving members.

The article I mentioned earlier from *The Presbyterian Outlook* starts with the following story:

> During Faith Presbyterian Church's stated monthly Session meeting, the clerk notes that a letter has been received from Trinity Community Church, requesting that Tom and June Wilson's membership be transferred to Trinity. Session members anxiously eye one another without saying a word. Finally one elder speaks: 'I deeply regret that Tom and June have left the faith. You all know what we must do. I move that we deny this request and that we write a letter to Trinity, informing it of this decision and inquiring as to why it is so busy proselytizing Presbyterians.'[24]

The author of the article expects his readers to respond in outrage about the elder's proposal – after all, 'in real life, we gladly transfer members from any legitimate Christian body, regardless of our perceived doctrinal differences with them' – and uses this outrage then to suggest that, just as much as we have no trouble with members transferring out of our denomination, we should not worry about whole congregations leaving.[25] If we are members of a church by choice, all of this is indeed true. But if our membership is based on divine covenant, the elders of Faith Presbyterian Church are actually correct.

How would it be if church bodies would respond to requests to transfer out, as in the one described above, by saying: 'We are sorry, but we cannot do this. Obviously there is something that bothers you about our church. We are committed to working with you on this, however difficult and painful this might be for all of us. But we all are called to be together as members of the body of Christ; and just as much as the eye cannot say to the hand: I have no need of you (1 Cor. 12.21), we cannot let you go'? And how would it be if our churches would similarly say the following to members who want to transfer in, because they have conflicts with their parishes of origin, or simply because they prefer our youth programme, or Bible study, or the preaching of our pastor? 'We are sorry, but we cannot do this. Obviously there is something that bothers you about your own church. We are fully committed to helping you with that. If your church is lacking some of the resources we have, we would be interested in seeing whether we can share. If you have a conflict with your pastor, or church leaders, we would like to devote our time and energy to sit down with you and see if we can facilitate a process of reconciliation. But we cannot allow you to take the shortcut of leaving, and to avoid the risk to go where God might lead your church – including you! – as a whole.'

The least such polity would do is to ensure that, in order to sustain and grow the economy of our programmes and ministries, we would not look to our neighbour churches for new members, but to the place where our attention should be directed in the first place: the unchurched. And the most it would do, if we are serious about sharing resources and the ministry of reconciliation, would be to help us discover exactly what the author of *The Presbyterian Outlook* article wanted to say: that we do not make up the church on our own – but, in contrast to the article's implied theology, we will do so not without, but by underscoring, the church's visible, institutional nature.

The future of the American mainline

What would it look like if the churches I mentioned at the beginning of this chapter – the Anglican Communion and the American mainline – would heed some lessons of the Netherlands Reformed ecclesiology? Speaking for the latter, the mainline church seems to be the weakest link in American Christianity. Ageing, internally divided, and with a sharply dwindling membership, many predict that in the next twenty or thirty years we will see its end. The internal differences are simply too serious, the divisions too wide to be bridged. Maybe these voices are correct. If they are, I certainly do not believe what some optimistically add: that while we will see the current mainline churches break apart, we will then see a realignment along conservative and liberal rather than denominational lines. This prediction ignores the fact that, for example, conservative Presbyterians are as much *Presbyterians* as they are conservative; and the same holds for the Lutherans, or Episcopalians, of conservative or liberal stripe.

Nonetheless, I believe we need to be open to another possibility. How would it be if God called these dwindling, powerless and deeply divided churches to teach American Christianity something that it never seems to have internalized: that being church is not dependent on human agreements, covenants or confessions, but only on God's gracious covenanting actions towards us? Certainly, the theological differences within the mainline are serious; the divides are wide. They are indeed so serious and wide that no ecclesial 'compromise' will smooth them over; no ecclesial 'agreements' may bridge them. But what if, from God's perspective, these differences and divisions are not at all about what we take them to be – homosexuality, ordination, scripture? What if they are rather God's instruments to bring us to the point where all our attempts to save the church will run out, and we will finally turn to the one whose church we are trying to save – Christ? Maybe this is God's future for the American mainline: to embody, in all its divisions, in all its powerlessness, in all its inability to solve its own problems, what goes to the heart of the gospel: that we do not belong to God's people based on our own willing, choosing or acting, but on God's actions.

If this is what the mainline is called to embody, it would move the church away from the *main street* of American culture. The idea that churches are based on human confessions, agreements or covenants perfectly matches the American emphasis on freedom and choice. But could this be the place where, more than anywhere else, God is calling the American mainline to go against the cultural grain and embody in all its concreteness the real freedom that is in Christ – the freedom of being chosen; the gift of grace? If so, the 'mainline' could become an unexpected blessing for American Christianity.

Notes

1. An earlier version of this essay was published in *Theology Today* 66 (2009). Reprinted with permission.
2. *A Season of Discernment: The Final Report of the Task Force on Peace, Unity and Purity of the Church, as approved by the 217th General Assembly (2006)* (Louisville, KY: Presbyterian Church, USA), 51.
3. Rowan Williams, 'The Challenge and Hope of Being an Anglican Today: A Reflection for the Bishops, Clergy and Faithful of the Anglican Communion', a statement by the Archbishop of Canterbury, released by the Archbishop's Office on 27 June 2006.
4. In this essay I use the terms 'liberal' and 'conservative' in a technical sense, not as terms of praise or critique: descriptive, not evaluative.

5. I am using the past sentence for the Netherlands Reformed Church to mean the Church united in 2004 with the Reformed Churches in the Netherlands and the Evangelical-Lutheran Church in the Kingdom of the Netherlands to form the Protestant Church in the Netherlands.

6. Virtually all literature on the modern history of the Netherlands Reformed Church is in Dutch. Good sources for the period under discussion are: A. J. Rasker, *De Nederlandse Hervormde Kerk vanaf 1795*, 7th edn (Kampen: J. H. Kok, 2004); Th. L. Haitjema, *De richtingen in de Nederlandse Hervormde Kerk*, 2nd edn (Wageningen: H. Veenman en Zonen, 1953); Th. L. Haitjema, *De nieuwere geschiedenis van Neerlands Kerk der Hervorming* (Wageningen: H. Veenman en Zonen, 1964); H. Bartels, *Tien jaren strijd om een belijdende kerk* (Den Haag: Stockum en Zoon, 1946).

   The theologians most influential in shaping *medical-way* ecclesiology are: Daniël Chantepie de la Saussaye (1818–74), J. H. Gunning (1829–1905), Ph. J. Hoedemaker (1839–1910), Hermann Friedrich Kohlbrugge (1803–75), O. Noordmans (1871–1956), G. Oorthuys (1876–1959), P. J. Kromsigt (1866–1941), and Th. L. Haitjema (1888–1972). All these theologians wrote in Dutch; most of their works are brochures and articles written within the context of church debates. None of them wrote a systematic ecclesiology – what follows is therefore a rational reconstruction of their ecclesiology as implied by these occasional writings.

   Interestingly, the twenty-first century saw a repeat of the debate between the juridical and the medical way: when in 2004 the Netherlands Reformed Church united with the Reformed Churches in the Netherlands and the Evangelical-Lutheran Church in the Kingdom of the Netherlands, a small group of conservative congregations and pastors refused to participate, arguing that reuniting with the more liberal RCN would undermine the confessional nature of the NRC. Other conservative congregations and pastors did join the newly formed Protestant Church in the Netherlands, explicitly referring to the arguments of the nineteenth-century medical-way theologians. See: W. J. op 't Hof (ed.), *Belijdenis en verbond: Ecclesiologie in de gereformeerde traditie* (Zoetermeer: Boekencentrum, 2003); W. Verboom, *Om het verbond. Een persoonlijk getuigenis in het zicht van de Protestantse Kerk in Nederland* (Zoetermeer: Boekencentrum, 2003); Wim Verboom and Chiel van den Berg, 'De Protestantse Kerk in Nederland: een dispuut', in *Theologie in Dispuut*, ed. Gerrit de Kruijf (Zoetermeer: Meinema, 2004), 111–40.

7. Cf. Reinhard Hütter in his essay 'The Church', in *Knowing the Triune God: The Work of the Spirit in the Practices of the Church*, ed. James J. Buckley and David S. Yeago (Grand Rapids: Eerdmans, 2001), 35: '. . . the church is to be understood as a web of core practices which at the same time mark and constitute the church'.

8. See Th. L. Haitjema, *Gebondenheid en vrijheid in een belijdende kerk* (Wageningen: H. Veenman en Zonen, 1929).

9. For a similar position defended by a contemporary theologian see John Webster, 'Confession and Confessions', in *Confessing God: Essays in Christian Dogmatics II* (London and New York: Continuum, 2005), 69–70, 73 (69–83).

10. Quoted in W. Balke, 'De kerk bij Hoedemaker, Gunning, Kraemer en Van Ruler', in *De Kerk: Wezen, weg en werk van de kerk naar reformatorische opvatting*, ed. W. Van 't Spijker, W. Balke, K. Exalto and L. Van Driel (Kampen: De Groot Goudriaan, 1990), 208 (202–30).

11. Barbara G. Wheeler, 'Strange Company: Why Liberals need Conservatives', and Richard J. Mouw, 'Hanging in There: Why Conservatives need Liberals', *The Christian Century* 121, 1 (13 January 2004), 18–25.
12. Wheeler, 'Strange Company', 18–19.
13. Mouw, 'Hanging in There', 25.
14. Ibid., 25.
15. Another example of such contemporary wrestling is the position that the evangelical ethicist Oliver O'Donovan stakes out in his 'Sermons on the Subjects of the Day', especially sermons two and seven, written in response to the discussions about homosexuality in the Anglican Communion. The sermons are available at http://www.fulcrum-anglican.org.uk.
16. See O. Noordmans, 'Het eschatologisch karakter van kerkelijke tucht', in *Verzamelde Werken* 5 (Kampen: J. H. Kok, 1984), 82–7.
17. See Th. L. Haitjema, *Reorganisatie en Leertucht* (Wageningen: H. Veenman en Zonen, 1929), 23.
18. See P. J. Kromsigt, 'Het wezen der kerk', in G. Oorthuys and P. J. Kromsigt, *Grondslag en wezen der kerk* (Wageningen: H. Veenman en Zonen, 1933), 81–135.
19. See especially Ph. J. Hoedemaker, *De kerk en het moderne staatsrecht I: De kerk naar goddelijk recht* (Amsterdam: Hollandsch-Afrikaanse Uitgevers Maatschappij, 1904).
20. Dietrich Bonhoeffer, *No Rusty Swords: Letters, Lectures and Notes 1929–1936* (New York and Evanston: Harper and Row, 1970), 95.
21. Clay J. Brown, 'On Unity: Changing our Language ... Matching our Rhetoric with our Real Beliefs', *The Presbyterian Outlook* 189, 35 (29 October 2007), 32 (28, 32–3).
22. See here the important 'Princeton Proposal for Christian Unity', in Carl E. Braaten and Robert W. Jenson, *In One Body through the Cross* (Grand Rapids: Eerdmans, 2003).
23. On the geographical principle, see especially B. A. M. Luttikhuis, *Een grensgeval, Oorsprong en functie van het territoriale beginsel in het gereformeerde kerkrecht* (Gorichem: Narratio, 1992).
24. Brown, op. cit., 28.
25. Ibid.

Chapter 5

COMPREHENSIVE VISION: THE ECUMENICAL POTENTIAL OF A LOST IDEAL

Andrew Pierce

Introduction

This chapter revisits the notion of 'Anglican Comprehensiveness' and suggests that, since such comprehensiveness has often been considered a typically Anglican theological trait, it might appropriately be regarded as a candidate for Anglicans to offer in 'ecumenical gift exchange'. The first section reviews the extent to which comprehensiveness is evident in, or absent from, contemporary inter-Anglican contestings of identity, before the second section reviews briefly the emergence of a paradigmatic appeal to comprehensiveness in the Tudor and Stuart church reforms. A brief theological reflection on how comprehensiveness might be offered and received concludes the chapter.

Though written by an Anglican, this paper is not intended as an exercise in denominational navel-gazing. For those engaged in ecumenical dialogue, either with or as Anglicans, the present condition of Anglicanism and its fraught sense of self-understanding is all too evidently problematic. Yet, although Anglicanism's current state of internecine conflict is highly public, the issues under heated discussion are not unique to Anglicanism and resonate further afield. It is, for example, difficult not to catch theological echoes in recent Faith and Order attempts to articulate and commend an ecclesiology in which divided Christians may recognize the essential claims of their traditions.[1]

Setting the scene

Appeals to an 'Anglican comprehensiveness' appear to have fallen on hard times of late, at least in terms of the classical Catholic–Reformed dialectical tension. Traditionally, Anglican comprehensiveness was understood as a determination to ensure that the church's catholicity and its openness to be Reformed according to the truth of the gospel were not safely to be viewed as mutually opposed alternatives. Hence, comprehensiveness and its limits have been at the centre of intra-Anglican polemic over centuries, ensuring that comprehensiveness has gained the reputation of being a characteristic theological trait of Anglicanism. Once there is agreement on the fundamental articles of the faith, Catholic and Reformed expressions of Christian discipleship may enjoy full communion with one another. Yet, as present-day polemics make clear, it is at least questionable whether the currently competing articulations of Anglican identity replicate sufficiently the classical paradigm of Catholic and Reformed (even where, or even if, they appeal to one or the other tradition); it is doubtful if the partners in debate are willing to see that they and their opponents are, in fact, agreed on fundamental articles of the faith; and, more fundamentally, there may be – on the part of Anglican theology itself – a hesitancy in relation to the theme of comprehensiveness itself. There is a sense of foreboding in the index to Stephen Sykes' essays, *Unashamed Anglicanism*, where the reader is referred to 'comprehensiveness ... *see also* incoherence'.[2] Comprehensiveness, evidently, has earned a theological health warning, particularly courtesy of Sykes.[3]

As the ecumenical movement receives the language of 'gift exchange' to characterize the profound impact of ecumenical dialogue, it should not be surprising if some Anglicans might seek to offer their experience of comprehensiveness as their gift, and in the process, perhaps, to re-receive it themselves (nor is it surprising that some non-Anglican theologians have placed comprehensiveness high on their ecumenical wish-list).[4] But, if comprehensiveness appears synonymous with incoherence, a more robust case will have to be made for its positive ecclesial and ecclesiological value.

Introductory textbooks on Anglicanism are a reliable source of comforting noises about Anglican comprehensiveness, often making it appear as the happy outcome to bitter conflicts between (initially) English Christians. It thus bears the hallmark of a 'Good Thing', in the deliciously ironic terminology of W. C. Sellar and R. J. Yeatman. And not just a Good Thing for intra-Anglican polemic: as a traditional dimension of Anglican identity, comprehensive vision is also represented as sustaining widespread ecumenical engagement by Anglicans with other Christian churches and traditions that might find one pole of the Catholic–Reformed dialectic more congenial than the other. Yet such textbooks are also keen to make readers aware that this ecclesiological concept had – and has – its fair share of detractors. Is it not simply a fancy theological name for Elizabethan *realpolitik*, giving off more than a whiff of state-sponsored terror for those Roman Catholics, Puritans and others who did not conform within the limits of a Tudor or a Stuart national church? Was the concept coherent – or, if it possessed coherent expositors, did it not effectively amount to a protective charter for woolly-minded thinking? And, far from facilitating dialogue, surely appeals to comprehensiveness merely contributed to a muddying of the ecumenical waters: were Anglicans engaged in ARCIC dialogues *really* saying the same things to their Roman Catholic brothers and sisters as they were to those Scandinavian and Baltic Lutherans with whom they enjoyed full communion following the Porvoo agreement? Or were Anglicans merely – and conveniently – stressing one aspect of a more complicated and contested identity, which an appeal to 'comprehension' camouflaged, rather than named?

These are serious concerns, and they have undoubtedly contributed to a feature of some recent important works on Anglicanism – and on Anglican theology in particular – in which comprehensiveness shifts from being understood as an enduring characteristic, towards being seen primarily as an historic phase under the British monarchs Elizabeth I and Charles II.[5] The implication of this shift – that an adequate concept of comprehensiveness, once established, could be left to look after itself – errs rather on the euphoric side of optimism.

Whatever Anglicans may have said in the past about theological comprehensiveness, by their deeds they are increasingly becoming known for its absence. Indeed, the current strains on Anglican identity suggest that we are witnessing something that differs in interesting ways from the classic tension between Catholic and Reformed. The conflict that both preceded and followed the 1998 Lambeth Conference of Bishops concerning same-sex relationships among clergy – in particular among bishops – continues to impact on Anglican Christians. The 2008 Lambeth Conference was boycotted by a large number of bishops who consider that – globally – Anglicanism is colluding in a subversion of fundamental truths. Yet those who consider themselves marginalized are drawn from both extremes of Anglicanism's theological spectrum, Anglo-Catholic and Evangelical. Those interested in the potential of comprehensiveness are thus watching with interest as new patterns of oversight emerge: e.g., Anglo-Catholic parishes are moving under the pastoral care of evangelical bishops, or are seeking support from Roman Catholic dioceses. Only time will tell if hostility to openly gay clergy will be enough to sustain these *ad hoc* experiments in exclusive comprehensiveness.

Yet the Catholic–Reformed dialectic is still a part of Anglicanism's received account of its identity. And two points should be made – albeit briefly – concerning its nature, points that require substantiation at much greater length than this chapter allows. First, comprehensiveness is (or became) a *theological* concept to account for the (albeit limited) inclusive reality of Anglicanism, and in that regard, it might usefully be compared with the Chicago-Lambeth Quadrilateral which also accounted for Anglican identity in resolutely theological and historical terms. Second, both comprehensiveness and the Quadrilateral began to slip from prominence after Lambeth 1968. Ecumenists are used to seeing the 1960s invoked as the era in which global ecumenism, and especially the World Council of Churches, disengaged from the academy, and particularly from the discipline of theology. Is it too fanciful to see a similar theological disengagement by the Anglican bishops in the post-1968 period? The symbolism is striking: the Archbishop of Canterbury who presided at Lambeth in 1968 was the distinguished theologian Michael Ramsey, author of *The Gospel and the Catholic Church*, perhaps the most significant *apologia* for Anglican comprehensiveness written in the twentieth century.[6] It would be four decades before a professional theologian of similar stature, Rowan Williams, presided at a Lambeth Conference.[7] In the interim, Anglicans have debated, *inter alia*, the ordination of women as priests, the consecration of women bishops, new authorized forms of worship, and a range of issues raised by post-colonial ecclesiality.

It is, I think, significant that in these debates, there has been a tendency to deal with contentious issues, not by engaging with substantive theological reflection, but managerially. In *After Virtue*, Alisdair MacIntyre warned his readers that modernity offered us three important – and disquietingly prominent – characters: the manager, the aesthete and the therapist.[8] One does not have to affirm all aspects of MacIntyre's project to retrieve teleology in order to appreciate his wariness of instrumental managerialism. Anglicans are in conflict, but their conflict is not being conducted by way of theological debate: the current debate, in which is presupposed both the authority of scripture and personal ethics, has become a managed process of communion maintenance. The move from substantive theological debate on comprehensiveness and the quadrilateral to commissions, maintaining or policing *koinonia*, is part of the context in which the significance of comprehensiveness has been eclipsed. What kind of theology would assist in such a contesting is a moot question.

The next section of this paper looks at the emergence of comprehensive vision as a feature of Anglican identity in the Church of England in the traumatic aftermath of the Tudor and post-Commonwealth re-reforms.

The emergence of paradigmatic comprehensiveness

'Our Church stands on a different bottom from most of those in which the system-writers have been bred.' So wrote William Wake (1657–1737), Archbishop of Canterbury from 1716.[9] Wake's far-sighted capacity to engage productively with French Gallicans and English nonconformists goes to the heart of embodying comprehensive vision, but for now the point to note is Wake's celebration of the absence within Anglicanism of a foundational theological system.[10] A foundation there may be, but unlike the churches of the continental Reformations, Anglicans are not defined by their fidelity to the doctrinal system of a particular magisterial reformer (someone of the standing of Luther, Calvin, Bucer or Zwingli). Ramsey positively celebrates this lack:

> Amid the convulsions of religion in Europe in the sixteenth century the English church had a character and a story which are hard to fit into the conventional categories of continental Christianity. The Anglican was and is a bad Lutheran, a bad Calvinist, and certainly no Papist.[11]

Anglicanism's failure to observe conventional denominational lane-discipline has facilitated the recurrent allegation that it is purely an Erastian creation with little or no theological integrity. Aidan Nichols, for example, sees in Anglicanism a most un-Dominican rupture between nature and grace: 'Anglicanism testifies to the wisdom of Tudor government in the latter part of the sixteenth century. It does not testify to the "wisdom which is from above" of which the Bible speaks.'[12] Such views have often been expressed, both outside and within Anglicanism. Since the Reform of the Church of England under Tudors and Stuarts was state-led, rather than theologian-led, it is no surprise to find theological eyebrows raised at the ways in which Reform coincided suspiciously with the interests of contemporary rulers. Reform enabled Henry VIII to marry Anne Boleyn and Jane Seymour, and so on and so forth. But this Reform was kept on a tight leash: Protestants – especially Presbyterians – were dissatisfied with the pragmatic compromises of Elizabeth I and were unable to accept her attempts to create a national church. Such criticisms are, of course, well founded: Henry VIII requires considerable ideological reconstruction in order to appear as the Reformation ideal of a 'godly prince'. Martin Luther was not fooled by the Tudor, and neither was Thomas Cranmer, who managed to keep his zeal for more robust Reform safely under wraps during Henry's reign, and whose trust in the divine rights of the monarchy was sorely tried by the accession of Mary Tudor.

It is at this point that Wake's judgement may help to make sense of the various reforms of the English church in the sixteenth and seventeenth centuries. No single figure dominated either the Reform or Anti-Reform agenda. Competing voices and forces appear – sometimes to disappear, sometimes to reappear frequently. Thomas Cranmer (1489–1556) (Archbishop of Canterbury, 1533–53), for example, worked under Edward VI towards establishing England as the centre of European Reformed Protestantism. Had he succeeded, England's reformation would have been confessional, in the continental sense and would have aimed to become the lead partner in a pan-European Protestant communion. But only two-thirds of his agenda was accomplished at his death: the Books of Common Prayer (1549, 1552) and a (first) Book of Homilies (1547), to provide doctrinal teaching in the vernacular. The climax of Cranmer's Reform, a revision of canon law, which he attempted with the help of Peter Martyr, was left unfinished at his death. Because of the central role of the *Book of Common Prayer* in Anglican history, some have argued that Cranmer – via the Prayer Book – provided Anglicanism with its magisterial Reformer (a liturgist, not a maker of dogmatic systems). But this is difficult to accept, since the *Book of Common Prayer* that Cranmer left behind was amended under Elizabeth to permit a wider range of eucharistic theologies than the later Cranmer would have accepted. The eucharistic theology of the *Book of Common Prayer* that held Anglicans together until the early twentieth century would have sent its principal author spinning in his grave.

There was no single Reformer for the Church of England because the Church of England did not undergo a single Reformation. It underwent a series of contested reforming and counter-reforming strategies which were held in check to some extent because of the parameters set by the notion of a national church. And this notion was not a peculiarly English notion (though in England its role is prominent), but is simply a key characteristic of Europe's medieval ecclesial context following the abandonment of conciliarism, in which tension between heads of governments and the papacy was a regular feature.

The language of comprehensiveness is usually invoked with reference to two religious settlements reached by the English parliaments. First, the Religious Settlement of Elizabeth I, which began to be implemented from 1559 onwards, after she had been on the throne for one year. Second, over a century later, the Religious Settlement of Charles II in 1662. Elizabeth's settlement followed the rule of Mary Tudor (queen from 1553–58), who had reconciled the English Church with the papacy in 1555. Elizabeth's reformation was remarkably limited: she was declared Supreme Governor of the Church of England under the Act of Supremacy (unlike her father and half-brother, who had each been 'Supreme Head' of the English Church), and she also effectively combined Thomas Cranmer's two Books of Common Prayer (1549 and 1552) into the 1559 *Book of Common Prayer*.

The significance of this combination for Anglican comprehensiveness appears clearly in the eucharistic rite. Cranmer's first Prayer Book was a noticeably conservative revision of the mass in the vernacular. Communicants received the consecrated elements with words that satisfied the more conservative of English bishops, such as Stephen Gardiner, who found them compatible with the doctrine of transubstantiation:

> The Body of our Lord Jesus Christ, which was given for thee, preserve thy body and soul unto everlasting life.

> The Blood of our Lord Jesus Christ, which was shed for thee, preserve thy body and soul unto everlasting life.

By 1552, however, influences from Bucer and Zwingli were apparent on Cranmer's reformulation in his second Prayer Book, which provides the following wording:

> Take and eat this in remembrance that Christ died for thee, and feed on him in thy heart by faith with thanksgiving.

> Drink this in remembrance that Christ's blood was shed for thee, and be thankful.

By combining the two wordings, Elizabeth's Prayer Book of 1559 was able to satisfy the more conservative of her clergy about the identity of the 'this' that they were distributing:

> The Body of our Lord Jesus Christ, which was given for thee, preserve thy body and soul unto everlasting life. Take and eat this in remembrance that Christ died for thee, and feed on him in thy heart by faith with thanksgiving.

> The Blood of our Lord Jesus Christ, which was shed for thee, preserve thy body and soul unto everlasting life. Drink this in remembrance that Christ's blood was shed for thee, and be thankful.

Was this a pragmatic compromise or a principled theological decision? It is hard to know what a Tudor ruler would have made of this distinction. But one thing is clear, Elizabethan reforms did not follow the continental template suggested by the Peace of Augsburg in 1555, *cuius regio, eius religio*. The English people were not going to be either Lutheran or

Catholic, depending on their ruler's conviction. They were instead being required to conform to a national church that would satisfy neither Puritans nor Romanists, for whom respectively the Elizabethan reforms did not go far enough or went altogether too far.

Since the Elizabethan settlement, the 'settlement' of Anglican identity has had to be re-received on a regular basis, notably following the English Civil War, in which Episcopalian, Presbyterian and Independent theological identities were intimately connected with the issues under contention. The execution of Charles I and of Archbishop William Laud of Canterbury, together with the suppression of the episcopate and of the *Book of Common Prayer* under Lord Protector Oliver Cromwell, prepared the way for a reinvigorated Church of England with a far stronger theological attachment to episcopacy than before. In 1661, the newly returned King Charles II called together 12 bishops, 12 Presbyterian theologians and their advisors at the Savoy in London to consider a new Book of Common Prayer. Charles was more tolerant of dissent than either his parliament or his bishops, and his hopes for a revision of the Prayer Book that would enable his Presbyterian subjects to remain within the Church of England were frustrated. Within two years of Charles' return to England, more than 2,000 Protestant clergy were deprived of their living.

Historically, therefore, the experiment in ecclesial self-understanding undertaken by the Church of England has been far from tidy. Various 'system-writers' – to use William Wake's term – have *tried* to systematize the life and doctrine of the English Church, but with limited success. As reformations of various kinds continued to impact on the English Church, a number of writers have attempted to make theological sense of this peculiar branch of the Western church, and of its claim to be both Catholic and Reformed. It is important to acknowledge that these writers were – and are – by no means alone in articulating Anglican identity: there were (and there remain) contenders for one 'side' to dominate and possibly exclude the other. But the apologetics of those divines who tried to hold together Catholic and Reformed in one communion gave a shape and a theological integrity to the vision of comprehensiveness that continues to repay attention, especially in a context where the imperative to decide Anglican religious identity in terms of 'either/or' is gaining momentum. And it merits attention from non-Anglican ecumenical theologians too.

Is there, then, a classical vision of Anglicanism – what I have called a comprehensive vision – in which Catholic and Reformed are not regarded as mutually exclusive theological and ecclesiastical positions, and in which evangelicals and sacramentalists are equally at home? There is a short answer to this question, and it is 'No'.

'No', because Anglicanism exhibits itself, not in a finally binding settlement, but in an attempt – a continuously unsuccessful attempt – to reach a workable settlement for all God's people to live and worship together in a particular place. Those who are attracted to the ideal of comprehensiveness have to start with the acknowledgement of its historical failure, and with a realistic sense of its future potential for failure. Anglicanism's many settlements to date have been both premature and necessary.

The purpose of this hasty historical and theological sprint through key epochs in Anglican self-definition has been to underscore the continuous – and at times bloody – contestation in which the articulation of Anglican identity has been involved from its very beginnings until the present. Those who regard Anglican comprehensiveness as significant for Anglican unity as well as for trans-Anglican relationships may need to take more trouble to demonstrate its theological potential.

Theological reflection

In his 1995 encyclical, *Ut Unum Sint*, Pope John Paul II reflected at length on the Roman Catholic Church's commitment to ecumenism. Commenting in particular on dialogue he noted: 'Dialogue is not simply an exchange of ideas. In some ways it is always an exchange of gifts.'[13] Is comprehensive vision an idea, or a gift? Though it is often presented simply as an idea (e.g. 'holding together in one communion both Catholic and Reformed theological emphases and concerns'), the history of its emergence suggests that a vision of comprehensiveness is not just an abstract idea, but is an historically embedded and socially incarnated vision of how ecclesial life might develop, so as to nourish Christians away from positioning themselves among conventional oppositions (Catholic, Reformed; Word, Sacrament; etc.), and instead make an ecclesial home in the ambiguous tension between such conventional religious and ideological competitors.

The cost of comprehension is the knowledge that it might, in many ways, be easier to settle for something less apparently compromising. It is easier to be in communion with those who agree with us, and whose agendas look reassuringly similar to our own. This point was picked up twenty years ago, when Archbishop Robert Runcie gave the opening address at the 1988 Lambeth Conference. Then, the issue of the day concerned the consecration of women bishops:

> Let me put it in starkly simple terms: do we really want unity within the Anglican communion? Is our world-wide family of Christians worth bonding

together? Or is our paramount concern the preservation or promotion of that particular expression of Anglicanism which has developed within the culture of our own province? Would it not be easier and more realistic to work towards exclusively European, or North American, or African, or Pacific forms of Anglicanism? Yes, it might. Cultural adaptation would be easier. Mission would be easier. Local ecumenism would be easier. Do we actually need a world-wide communion?[14]

For Runcie, however, belief in one, holy, catholic and apostolic church precluded the vision of ecclesial clusters based on elective affinities. And yet, what is the alternative to a weakened communion where communion-dividing factors are contextual rather than doctrinal?

For inhabitants of a postmodern or high-modern age, the project of ecumenism (like all grand narratives and 'isms') sounds suspiciously like a hangover from modernity (or, in its restorationist expressions, quite possibly from pre-modernity). Critical ecumenism is acutely conscious of this suspicion: it has to engage not only with the history and theology of the churches, but has also to analyse and criticize the various contexts within which normative (or semi-normative) accounts of church were articulated, and within which they continue to be received. The project of an ecumenical ecclesiology, in particular, takes us into an intrinsically contested hermeneutical space. Or spaces.

Ecclesiology, like church history, is a post-Reformation discipline in the Western church, and has been shaped apologetically. Conflicting accounts of church – conflicting accounts of unity, holiness, catholicity and apostolicity – enter this arena already shaped by a variety of doctrinal (and non-doctrinal, yet still theological) perspectives and interests. Thinking about *the* Church, when such thinking is shaped in and by the Church*es*, calls for critical and self-critical theological reflection and for great ecumenical tact in its exercise.

This chapter has suggested that Anglicanism, if it wishes to be faithful to its own chequered history, should view its experience of seeking comprehension as a gift (at times a rather unlovely gift) that it ought to share with its sister churches and other communities within God's *oikoumene*. Such sharing obliges Anglicans to re-receive the experiences of Reformed Christianity that it once excluded and labelled as Puritan or dissenter, as well as to re-receive the Catholicism that it once rejected and labelled Popery. For what the principal articulators of comprehensive vision had in mind was not a synthesis of Catholic and Reformed theology, but a vision of a church militant here on earth in which the dialectical tension of catholicity and reform was not denied, repressed and projected, but rather expressed in and nourished by the church's liturgy. It is a vision for the

ecumenical long haul: if it were to remain solely an Anglican vision, it
would be corrupted beyond use.

Notes

1. For the text of *The Nature and Mission of the Church* (2005), together with a
   number of helpful interpretative essays, see Paul M. Collins and Michael A. Fahey
   (eds), *Receiving 'The Nature and Mission of the Church': Ecclesial Reality and
   Ecumenical Horizons for the Twenty-First Century*, Ecclesiological Investigations,
   vol. 1 (London and New York: T&T Clark, 2008).
2. Stephen Sykes, *Unashamed Anglicanism* (London: Darton, Longman and Todd,
   1995), 229.
3. See, especially, Stephen W. Sykes, *The Integrity of Anglicanism* (London and
   Oxford: Mowbrays, 1978), together with the debate sparked by Sykes' book, in M.
   Darrol Bryan (ed.), *The Future of Anglican Theology*, Toronto Studies in Theology,
   vol. 17 (New York and Toronto: The Edwin Mellen Press, 1984), particularly the
   papers by Donald Wiebe, 'Comprehensiveness: The Integrity of Anglican
   Theology', 42–57 and Stephen Sykes, 'Authority in Anglicanism, Again', 167–90.
4. The language of gift exchange, which echoes the language of Vatican II, has
   received renewed attention in the light of John Paul II's encyclical *Ut Unum Sint*
   (1995).
5. I consulted a number of justifiably well-received works, all of which focus on the
   current experience of Anglican adjustment to post-colonial realities together with a
   concern for re-examining some of the classical moments in Anglican tradition. In
   none of the following – which might reasonably be taken to represent a cross-
   section of key voices in the current debate on Anglican identity – do we find a
   separate index entry for 'comprehension' or 'comprehensiveness': Paul Avis,
   *Anglicanism and the Christian Church: Theological Resources in Historical
   Perspective*, revised and expanded edition (London and New York: T&T Clark,
   2002); Stephen Platten (ed.), *Anglicanism and the Western Christian Tradition:
   Continuity, Change and the Search for Communion*, Foreword by Archbishop
   Rowan Williams and Cardinal Walter Kasper (Norwich: Canterbury Press, 2003);
   Ephraim Radner and Philip Turner, *The Fate of Communion: The Agony of
   Anglicanism and the Future of a Global Church*, Foreword by Stanley Hauerwas
   (Grand Rapids, MI and Cambridge, UK: Eerdmans, 2006); William L. Sachs, *The
   Transformation of Anglicanism: From State Church to Global Communion*
   (Cambridge: Cambridge University Press, 1993); Kevin Ward, *A History of
   Global Anglicanism* (Cambridge: Cambridge University Press, 2006).
   Comprehensiveness is addressed briefly, but as an historical issue, in an
   introductory essay by Paul Avis in Alister E. McGrath (ed.), *The SPCK
   Handbook of Anglican Theologians* (London: SPCK, 1998), 3–28, at 10–11. It may
   be argued that the issue of comprehension/comprehensiveness is nevertheless
   present in these works (perhaps implicitly), but the point still stands that explicit
   treatment of this theme does not currently command a great deal of attention.
6. A. M. Ramsey, *The Gospel and the Catholic Church* (London, New York and
   Toronto: Longmans, Green and Co., 1936, 2nd edn 1956), see esp. 204–20.
7. Rowan Williams offers a reflection on what is, in effect, comprehensiveness, in his
   Anglican Identities (London: Darton, Longman and Todd, 2004).

8. Alisdair MacIntyre, *After Virtue: A Study in Moral Theory* (London: Duckworth, 1981).

9. For a discussion of Wake's ecumenical significance, see H. R. McAdoo, *The Unity of Anglicanism: Catholic and Reformed* (New York: Morehouse, 1983). McAdoo's discussion tends to emphasize Wake's significance for Anglican–Roman Catholic relations.

10. See Leonard Adams (ed.), *William Wake's Gallican Correspondence and Related Documents 1716–1731*, 4 vols, American University Studies Series VII: Theology and Religion, vols 26, 55 and 56 (New York, Bern, Frankfurt am Main and Paris: Peter Lang, 1988–90). Adams' introduction to Volume 1 (pp. 1–37) is especially helpful.

11. A. M. Ramsey, *The Gospel and the Catholic Church*, 204.

12. Aidan Nichols, OP, *The Panther and the Hind: A Theological History of Anglicanism*, Foreword by the Rt Revd Bishop Graham Leonard (Edinburgh: T&T Clark, 1993), xvii–xviii.

13. John Paul II, *Ut unum sint*, 28 (1995). The encyclical is referring to *Lumen Gentium* 13.

14. Robert Runcie, 'The Nature of the Unity We Seek', in R. Runcie and M. Pawley, *The Unity We Seek* (London: Darton, Longman and Todd, 1989), 3–21, at 10–11.

Chapter 6

INTEGRITY, ALTERNATIVE AGGRESSIONS, AND IMPAIRED COMMUNION

Wendy Dackson

A letter from Mrs Brenda Meakens in the *Church Times*, 12 October 2007, reads as follows: 'Sir – My grandchildren have a delightful wooden Noah's Ark. Both the lions have manes. Is there a message here for the Anglican Communion?' I think Mrs Meakens is on to something, especially if the other animals do not seem particularly bothered.

Since the summer of 2003, when the General Convention of the Episcopal Church (USA) confirmed the election of Gene Robinson as Bishop of New Hampshire, much has been said in Anglican circles about 'impaired communion', 'instruments of unity', and such things. Most of this talk has been at the level of primates' meetings and the Anglican Consultative Council, or has concerned who should and should not be invited to the 2008 Lambeth Conference, and which bishops would refuse the invitation if certain others were invited. *The Windsor Report* states that these three things (the Primates' Meeting, the Anglican Consultative Council, and the Lambeth Conference), along with the Archbishop of Canterbury, are the four 'instruments of unity' in the Anglican Communion. All of this presupposes that 'communion' exists in, and is determined by, the relationships between primates, bishops and other senior officials in the Anglican Communion. This raises the question concerning whether the primates, or even all the bishops, constitute the 'Communion', or if it actually includes the over 70 million Christians who claim membership in that worldwide association of churches. Do the primates and bishops actually represent the people in their provinces and dioceses? Are Anglican Christians at the 'grass roots' level experiencing 'impaired communion', and what would that look like if they were? Those are large questions, beyond the scope of this chapter, but ones that need addressing.

The first thing I wish to be clear about is that this essay is not about sexuality, but about questionable processes of theological reasoning which, together with dubious assumptions, have brought the Anglican Communion to a confused situation. I would like, therefore, to work with a few concepts. First, although the debate about same-sex unions, and actions taken by the US and Canadian churches, are cited as precipitating factors only, and despite the insistence from some quarters that the discussion is at heart about biblical interpretation and how to hold together as a communion, I think this is somewhat dishonest. There are serious violations of the concept of 'theological integrity' outlined by the current Archbishop of Canterbury. Second, the behaviours of some primates and bishops bear the marks of, and encourage participation in, 'alternative' aggressions: the attempt to control others by using words, relationships, exclusion, ridicule, constant unilateral shifting of the rules by which discourse is conducted, and escalation of demands by one group as the condition for continued relationship with others.

As already indicated, I wish to pay some attention to three things that have not been, to my mind, adequately addressed: first, the question of what constitutes the 'Anglican Communion', second, the lack of an agreed-upon working definition of 'impaired communion', third, the primary metaphor of 'illness', which dominates *The Windsor Report*, clearly privileges the claims and justifies the actions of conservative Anglicans. I think this is not only inappropriate, but counterproductive. As I will demonstrate, it prolongs illness, rather than promoting health.

Theological integrity and honesty

In a short essay written in 1993, Rowan Williams set out his vision of *theological integrity*, which can be summarized by the following four requirements:

1. It does not conceal its true agenda, but rather truly talks about what it *says* it is talking about.
2. It is open to genuine response from the concerned parties, rather than a prescribed or predetermined one.
3. It declines to take 'God's view' or claim to have a 'total perspective'.
4. It provides an 'imaginative resource for confronting the entire range of human complexity'.[1]

I can see several advantages to conducting ecclesiological discourse according to guidelines such as these. Not least, it requires humility on the part of all participants, and a real openness to each other's views and concerns. All parties to the conversation, as Andrew Shanks points out, have the possibility of being right – and equally, they may also be wrong.

Shanks expresses this rightness and wrongness as follows (although I am not sure about his use of only the liberal/orthodox terminology):

> Both are equally right to have suspicions of the other; both are wrong, in so far as those suspicions harden into conversation-inhibiting prejudices . . .
>
>   The 'liberals' are right, inasmuch as it is true that the saving element of true faith does not consist in any mere appropriation of propositional correctness as such, but much rather in the religious appropriation of *the most radical honesty*. And the 'orthodox' are right, inasmuch as the demands of deep honesty do indeed need to be accorded the most decisively absolute authority.[2]

The ability to acknowledge the truth in each other's positions would assist in reconciling conflicting views of what constitutes a 'tradition' – a major difficulty, as I see it, in the current debates in the Anglican Communion. Is it an unbroken deposit of faith based on a particular way of interpreting scripture, or is there more development and interaction with the culture, from which the church learns as well as which the church teaches? I believe that there is the possibility of both.

I question the degree to which *The Windsor Report* itself, and the chain of events that have resulted from it, follow Williams' criteria, or pursue the kind of theological honesty that Shanks envisions. The Report itself insists that it is 'not a judgement. It is part of a process. It is part of a pilgrimage towards healing and reconciliation.'[3] Furthermore, the Report claims that 'we have not been invited, and are not intending, to comment or make recommendations on the theological and ethical matters concerning the practice of same sex relations and the blessing or ordination or consecration of those who engage in them'.[4]

It is further claimed that the supreme authority for all church teaching and action is scripture, and that this is to be the primary bond of unity, and although the nature of its authority is debatable, it is not a 'static source of information or the giving of orders', but 'the dynamic inbreaking of God's kingdom'.[5] There is nothing particularly controversial in this, and when Peter Jensen, Archbishop of Sydney, says that 'the key issue is scriptural authority', there is no cause for disagreement.[6] However, it seems variably applicable, dependent on the issue at hand, and the highest degree of scrutiny is exercised for issues of sexuality.[7] Thus, it appears as though *The Windsor Report*, and the series of discussions following in its wake, have broken with Williams' first standard of theological integrity. *Windsor's* claim is that it is about reconciliation, and not a judgement on divergent theological understandings of same-sex relationships; the subsequent conversations have been precisely about using particular stances on this issue as a litmus test as to who is 'in communion' and to what degree.

Windsor fails on the second test of theological integrity as well – that of creating space for genuine response from all concerned parties, rather than moving towards predetermined conclusions. Paragraph 135 of *Windsor* requests

> A contribution from the Episcopal Church (USA) which explains, from within the sources of authority that we as Anglicans have received in scripture, the apostolic tradition and reasoned reflection, how a person living in a same gender union may be considered eligible to lead the flock of Christ. As we see it, such a reasoned response, following up the work of the House of Bishops of the Episcopal Church (USA), and taken with recent work undertaken by the Church of England and other provinces of the communion, will have an important contribution to make to the ongoing discussion.

However, this is not an invitation to a free response. It follows shortly after a foregone conclusion of wrongdoing on the part of the Episcopal Church, indicating that American Episcopalians disregarded the concerns of the wider Communion, and 'caused deep offence to many faithful Anglican Christians', but does say that those who consented to the election are not 'entirely or exclusively blameworthy' – merely ignorant of or insensitive to the opinions of other Anglicans.[8]

The American church provided the requested contribution, entitled *To Set Our Hope on Christ*, in 2005. In then-Presiding Bishop Griswold's Foreword, it is made clear that the question is not a recent one:

> The Episcopal Church has been seeking to answer this question for nearly 40 years and at the same time has been addressing a more fundamental question, namely: how can the holiness and faithfulness to which God calls us all be made manifest in human intimacy?
>
> Though we have not reached a common mind we have come to a place in our discussion such that the clergy and people of a diocese have been able, after prayer and much discernment, to call a man living in a same-sex relationship to be their bishop. As well, a majority of the representatives of the wider church – bishops, clergy and lay persons – have felt guided by the Holy Spirit, again in light of prayer and discernment, to consent to the election and consecration.

The Anglican Consultative Council and Anglican Communion Office found ECUSA's response to the concerns of *Windsor* to be adequate for that church to continue its participation in Primates' meetings, full representation on the Anglican Consultative Council, and at the Lambeth

Conference. However, various groups within the Communion, such as the Anglican Communion Institute,[9] and individual leaders such as Archbishop Peter Akinola of Nigeria, Bishop Robert Duncan of Pittsburgh (USA), and Archbishop Peter Jensen of Sydney (Australia) have indicated that the response of the American church has been inadequately penitential. The Institute, in particular, has acknowledged that the Anglican Consultative Council's declaration that ECUSA's response, although it has been a move in the right direction, has been 'far more generous than ours'.

It will become clearer in the next section how the last two indicators of theological integrity have been violated by *Windsor* and its aftermath. At the moment, however, it is important to flag the *humility* associated with theological integrity, which is tied to the refusal to take 'God's point of view'. The church, including its leaders, must remember that it identified with 'the unfaithful apostles at the table with Jesus ...'[10] One participant reminded the Primates' Meeting in Tanzania of this in saying, 'There is one thing that a bishop should say to another bishop. That I am a great sinner and that Christ is a great savior.'[11] To do otherwise, whether it be one person, or an entire province, to another, is an act of hubris.

Alternative aggressions

Psychologist Anne Campbell indicates that women use physical aggression as a means of expressing frustration, whereas men use it to control others. As her work focuses on actual violence, she does not explore the means by which women control others.[12] However, more recently, this has become an issue in public and mental health in the United States, most notably through Cheryl Dellasega at the University of Pennsylvania's medical school. A social phenomenon called relational, or *alternative*, aggression, involves the use of relationships to hurt peers, often through exclusion from the 'desirable' group;[13] the violence is verbal rather than physical. Those who are most likely to engage in relational aggression demonstrate a low level of empathy for others, are less goal directed, and less likely to articulate their values and act consistently with them.[14] As this form of behaviour is most commonly seen in female adolescents, a popular term for relational aggression is *girl bullying*. The inconsistencies between stated values and behaviours may be seen in the unilateral changing of agreed-upon rules so that they work to the disadvantage of the other party, ridicule, or build alliances with the intention of excluding others. As I mentioned earlier, although the Anglican Consultative Council agreed that the Episcopal Church had made as full a response to *Windsor* as is possible given its polity and constitutions, and thus this should be considered sufficient, some voices within the Communion have 'raised the bar' and made further demands.

Another technique of controlling others through verbal and relational means is what sociolinguist Deborah Tannen calls 'getting the lower hand' in a discourse.[15] This is done by the speaker's claiming a position of weakness in relation to his or her opponent, thus creating obligations to behave in ways that benefit the speaker. A comic example of this from popular literature is from the 'Just William' series of books, in which Violet Elizabeth Bott, the 'sweet little girl in white', coerces older, tougher boys into playing games with her. She 'exerted her sway over her immediate circle of friends solely' by the means of 'making her blue eyes swim with tears at will'.[16] When the game does not go her way, Violet Elizabeth makes her famous threat: 'I'll thcream and thcream and thcream till I'm thick. I can.'[17]

Windsor's governing metaphor for the aftermath of Gene Robinson's consecration is that of illness, setting up the idea that there are people who are somehow weakened by the action. I question, for three reasons, if this metaphor is the right one to use. The first is that of accuracy. While the Episcopal Church has expressed regret that some other Anglican churches have experienced pain as a result of their actions, 'illness' is not always the reason for pain. Sometimes, discomfort is a healthy sign – when a person begins a fitness programme, he or she is likely to feel much worse before feeling even the slightest bit better. Human gestation, long regarded in the Christian tradition as a self-evident good, also ends in a fair amount of discomfort. So, is it impossible to see this as a time of growth, strengthening, and new life, rather than merely interpreting it negatively as a period of 'illness'?

Second, there are very few responses that can be made to 'illness', except to remove its cause. Is this not a violation of Rowan Williams' criterion of integrity, which requires space for genuine response, rather than a predetermined outcome?

The third, and perhaps most important, reason that I question the 'illness' metaphor is that, when it is to a person or group's advantage to claim that they are ill or injured, there is little motivation to return to health or strength. The 'strong' people or groups are obligated to behave in ways that will cause as little discomfort as possible for as long a period of time as the 'weak' parties see fit.

A very recent instance of 'getting the lower hand' can be seen in Bishop Michael Nazir Ali's statement that he may choose to boycott the 2008 Lambeth Conference (*Church Times*, 12 October 2007). He said that it 'broke his heart', but hoped that the 'Conference would be summoned in such a way that it is easier for people like myself to be present at it'. That would require the exclusion of liberal bishops of the Episcopal Church – a clear use of taking a position of weakness to manipulate the behaviour of others.

Fourth, and most critically, in considering *Windsor*'s dominant metaphor of illness, is a fundamental lack of clarity concerning who is 'ill'. A reading of Susan Sontag's brilliant but disturbing 1978 essay, 'Illness as Metaphor',[18] sheds some light on this question. Sontag traces how literary uses of two serious illnesses – tuberculosis and cancer – pronounce judgement on the patient's moral character. As Sontag says, 'the romantic idea that the disease expresses character is invariably extended to assert that the character causes the disease – because it has not expressed itself'.[19] Thus, personal (and possibly, collective?) morality is symbolized by the illness from which one suffers and to which one may ultimately succumb. Sontag summarizes it as follows:

> For more than a century and a half, tuberculosis provided a metaphoric equivalent for delicacy, sensitivity, sadness, powerlessness; whatever seemed ruthless, implacable, predatory, could be analogized to cancer ... TB was an ambivalent metaphor, both a scourge and an emblem of refinement. Cancer was never viewed as anything but a scourge; it was, metaphorically, the barbarian within.[20]

The metaphor of virtue or innocence implied by an illness such as tuberculosis has something of a retrospective basis in medical science – TB is a monocausal disease, the result of a single, simple, pathogen. The sufferer *knows* the cause of the illness, and there is no discussion needed concerning diagnosis and treatment. In terms of the current state of the Anglican Communion, this is disturbing. The self-described 'Windsor-compliant bishops', who have called for a return to the simplicity of 'historic' Christian faith and a purification of authentic biblical practice (alongside pleas to respect those of 'weak' conscience or who actually have 'scruples' about the ordination of homosexual persons), wish to be seen, following Sontag's analysis, as innocent parties who have been unjustly damaged.

On the other hand, the metaphor of cancer – mysterious and multicausal, having the 'widest possibilities as metaphors for what is socially and morally wrong'[21] – seems applicable to those who attempt to make Christian faith intelligible and relevant in a post-Christian society, naming it a 'false accommodation to the world's ways of thinking'.[22] Although neither conservatives nor liberals are willing or perhaps able to be quite so crude as to apply one of these labels to themselves or others, there is the clear use of Sontag's notion of a metaphorical 'master illness'[23] which is used to 'propose new, critical standards of [individual] health, and to express a sense of dissatisfaction with society as such'.[24]

Following Sontag's analysis a bit further, it is interesting to note that although those who claim to hold a pure and simple form of traditional Christian faith are spread globally, they align themselves most strongly under the (now non-)geographical heading of the 'Global South'. Sontag notes that when a change of climate was prescribed for the refined and innocent TB sufferer, '[t]he most contradictory destinations were proposed. The south, the mountains, deserts, islands – their very diversity suggests what they have in common: the rejection of the city.'[25]

On the other hand, the modern city becomes both the metaphor and literal representation of 'the place of abnormal, unnatural growth'.[26] It is particularly the Anglican Communion Churches in Western industrialized democracies (primarily the Episcopal Church USA and the Anglican Church of Canada; to a lesser extent, the Church of England) that are seen as places of, and as suffering from, unwholesome development. Bishops in these northern hemisphere provinces who wish to flee the sick environment in which they are (geographically) located, seek the spiritual cure of oversight from primates in more salubrious places, such as Africa or South America. The irony is that in escaping from one form of 'sickness' in the developed world, they are banding together with those who 'suffer' from a different form of sickness – that which is associated with innocence and purity, in an enclave of new associates. Health does not seem to be the goal; rather it is safety in a sanatorium.

Conclusion

There is, on the surface, little question that there is damage to the Anglican Communion that will take time and careful work to repair. However, there are questions that need to be raised.

First, who or what *is* this thing called the Anglican Communion? The media coverage focuses on primates, bishops and official structures of governance. Leaders at that level appeal to the idea that the 'bonds of affection' between member churches have been strained, in some cases to breaking point. This may be true at the 'highest' level, but I doubt if it is equally true in the less formal, less authoritative structures and relationships between individuals, companion dioceses, institutions of learning and charitable organizations that link more than 70 million Anglicans in a network of positive relationships. Serious study is needed to discern whether any 'illness' or injury to the Communion is life threatening, or whether it is merely a surface wound that will heal with patience and care. But the language of illness, as it is being used currently, is not helpful.

It also raises the question of how 'impairment' is defined. *Windsor* insists that no province of the Communion should go forth with the ordination of someone whose ministry would not be accepted by all. This is problematic in two ways. First, women's ministries are not yet universally accepted (even in provinces where women are ordained). Second, there is little historic precedent for this requirement, and it has not been the practice of Anglican churches to have a full interchangeability of ordained ministers.[27] Most importantly, and the main thrust of all the foregoing, is a plea for taking Rowan Williams' concept of 'theological integrity' far more seriously than has been done in the process of producing *The Windsor Report*, and recognizing the posturing (rather than listening) which has characterized the ensuing discourse. The use of language needs reworking, and if a primary metaphor must be employed, it must be chosen more carefully than the one currently in use. It must not privilege one form of 'illness' above another, and encourage prolonging that disease. It must actually seek health.

In closing, it may be good to remember Archbishop Robert Runcie's thoughts on the tensions involved in exploring new ways of understanding scripture and being church. He cited the American Catholic bishop Fulton Sheen, 'not himself a notable moderate'. Runcie says he is 'comforted' by the story of Sheen at the Second Vatican Council, who, when questioned by journalists about the rift between conservatives and liberals, replied: 'These are political terms. In biblical terms there are two kinds of bishop: shepherds and fishermen. Shepherds care for the unity of the flock. Fishermen launch out adventurously into the deep. We need both!'[28]

Notes

1. Rowan Williams, *On Christian Theology* (Oxford: Blackwell, 2000), 2–6.
2. Andrew Shanks, *Faith in Honesty: The Essential Nature of Theology* (Aldershot: Ashgate, 2005), 1. Shanks says (p. 2) that 'to be radically honest is to love the prospect of the moral lessons to be learnt from your encounter with other people more even than you love the prospect of receiving their love and attention'.
3. The Lambeth Commission on Communion, *The Windsor Report 2004* (London: Anglican Communion Office), Foreword.
4. *Windsor*, 43. Italics in original.
5. *Windsor*, 53–5.
6. *Church Times*, 12 October 2007.
7. *A True Hearing*, produced by Anglican Mainstream UK and The Church of England Evangelical Council, for Anglican Mainstream International (Surrey, UK: September, 2005) is an example of a book-length response to *Windsor* that focuses

on almost nothing but the negative scriptural interpretation of same-sex relationships.

8. *Windsor*, 127–8.
9. Neither of these has any official status within the Anglican Communion.
10. Ibid., 10.
11. Elizabeth Kennedy, 'Anglican Leader Urges Humility over Rift', www.washingtonpost.com, 18 February 2007.
12. Anne Campbell, *Men, Women and Aggression: From Rage in Marriage to Violence in the Streets – How Gender Affects the Way We Act* (New York: Basic Books, 1993).
13. There can hardly be a worse exclusion than to imply that certain religious people are out of favour with God.
14. Adapted from Cheryl Dellasega and Charisse Nixon, *Girl Wars: 12 Strategies that Will End Female Bullying* (New York: Simon & Schuster, 2003), 9–11.
15. Deborah Tannen, *Gender and Discourse* (Oxford: Oxford University Press, 1994), 26–7.
16. Richmal Crompton, *Still William* (London: Macmillan, 1925), 129–30.
17. Ibid., 140.
18. Susan Sontag, *Illness as Metaphor and AIDS and Its Metaphors* (London: Penguin, 1991).
19. Ibid., 47.
20. Ibid., 63.
21. Ibid., 62.
22. *Windsor*, para. 32.
23. Ibid., 73.
24. Ibid., 74.
25. Ibid., 74.
26. Ibid., 74.
27. Colin Podmore, *Aspects of Anglican Identity* (London: Church House Publishing, 2005), 29–30.
28. Robert Runcie, *Authority in Crisis? An Anglican Response* (London: SCM, 1988), 38.

PART II

COMMUNION ECCLESIOLOGY AND OTHERNESS

Chapter 7

THE CHURCH AND THE 'OTHER': QUESTIONS OF ECCLESIAL AND
DIVINE COMMUNION

Paul M. Collins

Introduction

The question of the relationship of the church to the 'Other' emerges
against a background in current philosophical discourse concerning alterity,
diversity and difference which has arisen from concern for the marginalized
and the horrors of the 'civilized' West manifest in the Holocaust and other
parallel events in the twentieth century. Such theological discourse
concerning the 'Other' may relate to intra-Christian and extra-Christian
relations and dialogue. The 'Other' may be seen in terms of the different as
in a stranger/foreigner, whom 'we' might welcome or reject. So the
question emerges: how are such instances inscribed in language? One
answer might be 'in spaces of relation' such as ethnicity, city, state, nation.
Another might be in terms of the opposition of friend/foe (terrorist). This
in turn leads to the drawing of borders or boundaries and begs questions of
how the 'Other' is to be assimilated.

The question of the relationship of the church to the 'Other' also
impinges upon the theology of the church itself and by extension to recent
and current discourse on the connection(s) to be made between the church
and God as Trinity. Where are 'the spaces of relation' for the 'Other' in the
appeal to relationality and communion ecclesiology? So there are questions
to be asked at a number of levels and in a variety of areas concerning the
church and the 'Other'. I shall begin with an examination of the
relationship between ecclesial and divine communion.

What is the connection between church as communion and divine as communion?

In seeking to discern how space for the 'Other' is understood I will begin with an investigation of the identification of church and Trinity through an analysis of the construction of ecclesiology, mainly from the twentieth century. By this means I will set out a variety of understandings which illuminate each other and manifest their strengths and limitations, as a preliminary to a more searching interrogation of Trinity/church identity.

Leonardo Boff appeals to context and history as the basis for the identification of the church with the triune life *in se*.[1] He argues that the communion among Father, Son and Spirit constitutes the one God as a mystery of inclusion, and that '[t]he three divine Persons open to the outside and invite human beings and the entire universe to share in their community and their life'. Furthermore, '[t]he presence of trinitarian communion in history makes it possible for the barriers that turn difference into inequality and discrimination to be overcome ...'[2] For Boff the doctrine of the Trinity is the pattern for a programme of liberation and transformation for society and church. The identification of Trinity/church is something almost tangible and, certainly in his view, historical. He reiterates this claim as follows:

> We believe that in [the church] the substance of the incarnation is continued in history; through Christ and the Holy Spirit, God is definitively close to each of us and within human history. This mystery becomes embodied in history, because it is organized in groups and communities.[3]

The explicit appeal to human history in this passage leads me to reflect on how dependent Boff is on the philosophy of Hegel at this point. This is perhaps inevitable, as Hegel is *the* modern philosopher who highlighted and valued context. However, such an appeal is not without its problems, and I shall return to these below. It is interesting to note that, at least to some extent, there is an overlap here between Boff and Zizioulas in the thought that the divine communion can be seen/is manifest in the fabric of 'ordinary' society and communities.

Andrew Louth has worked on the ecclesiological understandings that are to be found in the writings of Maximus the Confessor.[4] In particular Louth discerns that Maximus suggests the church may be understood as an 'image and type of God' by imitating and representing God's activity (*energeia*). 'It is in this way that the holy Church of God will be shown to be active among us in the same way as God, as an image reflects its archetype.'[5] This identification of Trinity/church in terms of 'image' is a strong trajectory in modern Orthodox writings. However, it is far from clear what conceptuality or metaphysics is implied in this contemporary appeal to 'image'.

Zizioulas is one of those Orthodox writers who employ the language of 'image', in his construction of Trinity/church identity.[6] He also makes appeal to the conceptuality of event. Thus he argues that, 'True being comes only from the free person, from the person who loves freely – that is, who freely affirms his being, his identity, by means of an event of communion with other persons.'[7] Both ecclesiology and ontology are construed in terms of an 'event of communion'. This is qualified by his understanding that between the being of God and human being there is a gulf of 'creaturehood'. The being of each human person is 'given' to him/ her. The event of communion is possible between human persons, in the form of love or social or political life. However, this expression of freedom is relative; because human being is 'given'. This construction resonates with the conceptuality of 'Gift', to which I shall return below. Zizioulas argues that absolute freedom requires a 'new birth', a birth from above, which he identifies with baptism and the phrase 'ecclesial *hypostasis*'. He explains that, 'it is precisely the ecclesial being which "hypostasizes" the person according to God's way of being. That is what makes the Church the image of the Triune God.'[8] Zizioulas echoes Boff's view that the divine communion may be found and experienced in the 'ordinary' communities of everyday life; he also sees the limitations of these expressions and points to an 'absolute' expression; 'ecclesial being'. So Zizioulas may have seen the limitations of the Hegelian-based appeal to history, but his appeal to an absolute 'ecclesial being' or 'ecclesial *hypostasis*' is not without its problems: not least in terms of his articulation of this ecclesial reality in terms of the 'Other'.

An alternative construction of the identification of church and Trinity may be found in the works of Hans Küng on the church.[9] In *The Church*, he argues that the church as communion is to be understood in two senses: that of fellowship in Christ and with other Christians. He identifies Christ and the church in terms of the Body metaphor. This he roots in an understanding of the living and efficacious presence of Christ, especially in the worship of the congregation. However, he is keen to emphasize the reality of Christ beyond the church. He appeals, in particular, to the model of the body of Christ in which Christ is the Head of the body, to suggest that Christ relates to the world as well as the church. But most importantly he rejects any notion that the church is a 'divine-human' reality. He argues that there is no hypostatic union between Christ and the church. Rather the church is a fellowship of believers 'in Christ', and 'this relationship of faith is never altered'.[10] Küng's construction of Trinity/church identity is more restrained in the expression of its claims; which suggests a different kind of identity from that of the 'icon', or the Eucharist/body conceptuality.

Of the theologians discussed so far, Miroslav Volf is one who raises explicit questions about the conceptuality and expression of Trinity/Church identity.[11] He asks what correspondence there is between ecclesial and trinitarian communion, where such correspondences are to be found and what limits there are to such analogical thinking. In response, he seeks to sketch out the trinitarian foundation of a non-individualistic Protestant ecclesiology. He argues, as others have done before him, that the creature can never correspond to the Creator. Yet, in created reality he suggests that there must still be broken creaturely correspondence to the mystery of triunity. Such correspondence is to be rooted in an eschatological conceptuality that the world should be indwelt by the divine Trinity, i.e. the world will come to correspond to God. Having begun in reticence, he goes on to argue that, as the divine and ecclesial communion correspond to each other through baptism, so the churches are imprinted with the image of the triune God through baptism. Thus the churches share in a communion that is ontological because it is soteriological. Volf raises important questions; questions that are crucial for an understanding of the Trinity/Church identity, and, in particular, for an understanding of that identity in relation to the 'Other'. However, Volf's answers to the questions he raises are themselves infected with the problematic he criticizes.

By way of concluding this investigation of different approaches to the Trinity/church identity, I want to take up the argument set out by John Behr, concerning the problematic of divine/ecclesial communion.[12] Behr presents a review of the use of *koinonia* in the conceptualization of Trinity/Church identity, and concludes that, '[i]n this approach, the *koinonia* of the three Persons of the Holy Trinity, the very being of God, is taken as the paradigm of the *koinonia* that constitutes the being of the ecclesial body, the Church'.[13] Thus the Church as 'communion' is said to reflect God's being as communion, a communion that will be revealed fully (only) in the kingdom of God. He perceives that such understandings of ecclesiology fit with what is broadly understood as Eucharistic Ecclesiology, i.e. 'it is in the sacrament of eucharist, the event of communion *par excellence*, that the Church realizes her true being, manifesting already, here and now, the Kingdom which is yet to come'.[14] However, his response to this conceiving of Trinity/Church identity is insightful. He questions the way in which Trinity AND Church are juxtaposed. While what is said of the Church is based upon what is said of the Trinity, the effect of the AND is to separate church from Trinity as a distinct entity which now reflects the divine being. He argues that communion ecclesiology understands the Church to be parallel to the 'immanent Trinity'. That is to say, it is the three Persons in communion, the one God as a relational being, that the Church is said to 'reflect'. 'This results in a horizontal notion of communion, or perhaps better parallel "communions," without being clear about how the two intersect.'[15]

Behr goes on to argue that through his rejection of any sociological understanding of relationality, Zizioulas has jettisoned any possibility of starting with the human experience of relating to others, which in turn may be used to interpret the experience of God as Trinity. Rather, faith begins with the belief that God is 'very koinonia'. Behr identifies the problematic of the *a priori* characterization of the Trinity as a communion of three Persons, in that this approach does not adequately take into account 'economic' reality upon which trinitarian theology is based. While Zizioulas may stress that the Church is not any kind of Platonic 'image' of the Trinity, nonetheless he can assert that 'Church as communion reflects God's being as communion';[16] thus Behr argues that Trinity AND Church remain unconnected. Behr's questions are very important for the future of discourse in the conceptuality of Trinity/Church identity; and his focus on the AND which polarizes Trinity over against Church as separate entities is crucial. However, the possibility of collapsing the Church into the divine, prevalent in Behr's construction, is also surely to be avoided: Küng's warning that there is no hypostatic union between the divine and the Church needs to be heeded.

In the conceptualization of a connection between ecclesial and divine communion – where does the 'Other' stand ...?

In seeking to (re)construct divine and ecclesial communion in relation to the Other, it seems appropriate to discuss the deconstruction of the concept of community made by Derrida. Through an interpretation of a possible etymology of community, in which he suggests that part of the word relates to the origin of 'munitions', he argues that community as a defensive and enclosed concept is in need of deconstruction.[17] A reclamation of 'community' as a less defensive and more open concept might be made on the basis of an appeal to hospitality and alterity. Such an approach raises the issue of 'communion' *vis-à-vis* the 'other'. So the question emerges: in 'an event of communion' what place is there for the 'other'? Caputo suggests that the question of the place for the 'other' is unavoidable.[18] He reflects that:

Lévinas's idea is to rethink the religious in terms of our obligation to the other, not in terms of becoming happy, and to rethink God, not by way of a renewed experience of the truth of Being, but by getting beyond the anonymity of Being and experiencing the God whose withdrawal from the world leaves a divine trace on the face of the stranger.[19]

In the light of this it is important to examine the alterity of the 'other' in relation to the characteristics of *koinonia*. A 'hermeneutic of relationality' would need to be aware of how an approach to the 'other' might be included. Such a process raises issues concerning power. Derrida argues that in the usual reality of hospitality the host remains in control, and retains property. Thus in hospitality and hosting some hostility is always to be found.[20] However, Derrida does not suggest that this is a final outcome: rather hospitality is also 'the impossible', we must push against 'the limit'; thus hospitality is always to come.[21] The 'limit' suggests the dynamics of the economy of giving and receiving, including the debt of gratitude and the felt need to reciprocate. For Derrida, only the in-breaking of 'the impossible' can overcome such dynamics. For community to emerge that is unfettered by the dynamics of the economy of credit and the debt of hospitality, there needs to be 'an exposure to '*tout autre*' that escapes or resists community'.[22]

The language of *tout autre* has populated trinitarian thought in such writers as Karl Barth,[23] Jürgen Moltmann and Eberhard Jüngel. Barth, for instance, argues that God reveals himself, 'in the form of something He Himself is not'.[24] The reiteration or repetition of the divine (*Wiederholung Gottes*) in this conceptuality begs many questions, which I cannot pursue in this chapter. However, what is crucial for the understanding of *koinonia* is whether the divine self-revelation is simply that: the reiteration of the divine or absolute '*Ich*'. Is this an example of the influence of Hegel's use of *Aufhebung*? Hegel's own understanding of *Aufhebung* – annihilation, invalidation and also preservation – means that in annihilation there is also preservation: preservation of *Ich*. If such a conceptuality is extended to the church, this could mean that the ecclesial *koinonia* is no more than an 'absolute' '*Wir*'. In construing a 'space for the other' it is crucial therefore to have a clear concept of the place of 'the other'. Is alterity to be understood as within *Ich* or *Wir*? Or is it to be understood as in terms of externality?

Thesis of Zizioulas: communion and otherness

The relationship between 'Communion and Otherness', and thus by implication between the Trinity and the Other has been explored by John Zizioulas, in a collection of essays published under that name, as well as an article, also of the same name, originally published in 1994.[25] Thus Zizioulas has sought to engage in discourse concerning the 'Other', aware of the homogenizing and potentially hegemonic tendencies of an all-embracing communion ontology and ecclesiology. Indeed his ongoing concern for the relationship between 'the One and the Many' may be interpreted as a manifestation of this concern with the 'Other'. It is in the newly published essay, *On being Other: Towards an Ontology of Otherness*,[26] that Zizioulas provides the most extensive reflection on the 'Other'. Zizioulas begins by asking, '[w]hat can we learn about communion and otherness from study of the Trinity? First, *otherness is constitutive of unity*. God is not first One and then Three, but simultaneously One and Three'.[27] On the basis of his construction of trinitarian theology Zizioulas understands that otherness is not additional to the doctrine of the Trinity but inherent in it. 'Study of the Trinity reveals that otherness is *absolute*. The Father, the Son and the Holy Spirit are absolutely different (*diaphora*), none of them being subject to confusion with the other two.'[28] It is also expressed through the unbreakable *koinonia* (community) that exists between the three Persons, which means that otherness is not a threat to unity but 'the *sine qua non* of unity'.[29] The being of God as Trinity and communion is then held out as both a model and the ontological reality of otherness, and the space for the 'other'.

> There is no other model for the proper relation between communion and otherness either for the Church or for the human being than the trinitarian God. If the Church wants to be faithful to her true self, she must try to mirror the communion and otherness that exists in the Triune God. The same is true of the human being as the 'image of God'.[30]

Crucially, Zizioulas also argues that the construction of a space for the 'other', by the Holy Spirit, is within his conceptuality of 'an event of communion'.

> The Holy Spirit is associated, among other things, with *koinonia* (2 Cor 13, 14) and the entrance of the last days into history (Acts 2, 17–18), that is *eschatology*. When the Holy Spirit blows, he creates not good individual Christians, individual 'saints', but an event of communion which transforms everything the Spirit touches into a *relational* being. In this case the other becomes an ontological part of one's identity. The Holy Spirit de-individualizes and personalizes beings wherever he operates.

Where the Holy Spirit blows, there is community.[31] This passage perhaps tends to confirm the critics' view that an appeal to communion is likely to reduce the alterity of the other in a pervasive homogeneity. However,

Zizioulas is careful to argue for the distinctiveness of the 'individual other' at least in terms of ecclesial communion.

> The eschatological dimension, on the other hand, of the presence and activity of the Holy Spirit affects deeply the identity of the other: it is not on the basis of one's past or present that we should identify and accept him or her, but on the basis of one's future. And since the future lies only in the hands of God, our approach to the other must be free from passing judgment on him. In the Holy Spirit, every other is a potential saint, even if he appears be a sinner.[32]

Perhaps the main problem with these passages is the eliding of the discussion of divine and ecclesial communion, and thus a lack of a clear and necessary differentiation between the place of the 'other' within divine communion, and the alterity of individuals within the fellowship of the church, or human society at large.

While Zizioulas is explicit in his intentions to relate his argument concerning 'otherness' to the patristic period, his desire to read twentieth-century philosophy in the light of his interpretation of patristic sources is problematic in the sense that each source is, on the whole, treated as though it were a-contextual. In relation to late twentieth-century philosophy, what Zizioulas himself calls 'postmodernism', he demonstrates a careful reading of these writers. Finding in some of their ideas elements of a shared concern: e.g. in footnote 86 (p. 44) Zizioulas shares with Derrida the desire to liberate philosophy from the Greek domination of the Same to the One which is seen to be based on the assumption that ontology and comprehension are tied together. Indeed, Zizioulas declares that an aim of the essay is to question this assumption. However, Zizioulas does not engage with the underlying assumptions of those who have engaged with difference and *toute autre*, that is to say, issues of pluralism and cultural diversity. His essay remains primarily at a theoretical level, which removes the contemporary concerns for otherness from its purview. Also, while Zizioulas clearly perceives that postmodern philosophy is primarily a matter of method, he sidesteps any engagement with this philosophy on that basis.[33] However, I suggest that if theology is to engage with postmodern or deconstructive philosophy it needs to do so on the basis of this very matter of method. Indeed the method of 'reflexivity' raises many crucial facets for any understanding of the 'Other'/otherness.[34]

So what are the core preconceptions and values which Zizioulas espouses? First, he claims that the essay is an analysis of patristic interest in 'otherness'. This raises a number of difficulties. He acknowledges that concern for otherness impinges on intra-Christian dialogue as well as dialogue in society in general. He roots his discourse in an appeal to the notion of *creatio ex nihilo*, an appeal that resonates strongly with the understanding of Oliver Davies, to whom I shall return below. He clearly identifies the values of otherness and freedom with this doctrine, and in so doing sets his face against what he labels 'substantialism' or the appeal to substance as the origin of being.

Maximus is the one patristic source with whom Zizioulas engages in any detail. In particular, he highlights the distinction that Maximus draws between *logos* and *tropos* of (a) being, which he understands as allowing for communion.[35] 'Substance is relational not in itself but in and through and because of the "mode of being" it possesses.'[36] Thus (human) being is said to be 'tropical', i.e. personal and hypostatic. The 'tropical' element of the person allows for freedom – freedom for the other; and thus for

> ... an ontology of love: in which freedom and otherness can be conceived as indispensable and fundamental existential realities without the intervention of separateness, distance or even nothingness, or a rejection of ontology, as so much so-called postmodernity assumes to be necessary in dealing with the subject of otherness.[37]

Zizioulas makes appeal to Levinas quite simply because, in his view, Levinas comes closest to a patristic understanding of the 'other'; albeit that Levinas rejects any ontological interpretation. Zizioulas argues that for Levinas the 'other' is not constituted by the Self: nor by relationality as such, but by absolute alterity, which cannot be derived, engendered or constituted on the basis of anything other than itself. Levinas rejects communion; for him sameness and the general leads to the subjection of otherness to unity. This produces the inference that nothingness is the relationship between 'others', for Levinas insists on separation and distance as the alternative to that of relationship. This leads Zizioulas to make one of the most interesting and insightful claims in the whole essay: he argues that the crucial difference between patristic and postmodern conceptions of otherness lies in the way of 'filling the gap' between particulars. There is, he argues, a movement of constant departure from one to another in the name of the other. Patristic and postmodern writers share this understanding of constant new beginnings, he argues: 'but whereas for postmodernism alterity involves negation, rupture and "leaving behind", for patristic thought the "new" relates to the "old" in a *positive* way'.[38] Thus while postmodern suspicion of coincidence of otherness and communion as a totalizing reduction (and even violence) led Levinas and others to reject relational otherness, Zizioulas argues that communion does not produce sameness, because the relations between the particulars (persons) are not substantial but personal/tropical.

Zizioulas' appeal to the concept of creation *ex nihilo* is echoed by Oliver Davies in his examination of ontology and of the place for the other.[39] Davies sets four possibilities for an understanding of being. The first type of ontology, he describes, focuses on being itself, rather than on the self and the other, and stresses being as a unity or totality. Thus it tends to reduce the self and the many others to the same, which Davies attributes to the thought of Heidegger. A third type gives priority to the self. In this case, the other is set apart as separate, and yet risks being absorbed into the self in the process of thought, akin to the concepts of Descartes and Kant. The fourth type understands that ontology begins from the separate other. The other imposes itself on the self. It is to the second type of ontology that Davies appeals. This is rooted in

> ... the Judeo-Christian belief in creation *ex nihilo*[;] here being stands over against nothingness; thus being itself is a gift, originally a gift from God. Being, so understood, is inherently relational, and the relationship itself is personal in origin. Thus, in this way of thinking, the self and the other, which both receive the gift of being, are inextricably related to each other, in receiving, with their being, the capacity to give to others. The 'sameness' expressed in the (analogical) notion of being, does not obliterate the difference between the self and the other, nor the difference between the self and the other, and the transcendent other, God, who is the source of the gift of being.[40]

Davies' understanding of an ontology constructed in relation to *creatio ex nihilo* provides a bridge between Zizioulas' understanding of communion and the 'Other' and understanding of the 'Gift', in particular, of Milbank's construal of the divine Gift.[41] From this emerges a nexus of concepts which draw together a conceptuality of being, which is neither homogenizing nor hegemonic, with the conceptuality of 'Gift', which allows for difference between the self and the other.

Is it possible to conceive of a structure for *koinonia* that expresses the 'postmodern' understandings of hospitality and *tout autre*? The classic statement of the doctrine of the Trinity is constructed around notions of the monarchy of the Father, and of the begetting of the Son and the breathing out of the Spirit. Such classic concepts might be employed in a reconstruction of the concept of *perichoresis* in which the monarchy, begetting, and breathing out are each seen as examples of pushing against the 'limit', the limit of traditional monist ontology. In the perichoretic dance, monarchy, begetting, and breathing out might also be understood as signs of a transgressing of the economy of giving and receiving, through which hospitality and the 'impossible' characterize not only God *in se*, but also the encounter with mystery in the economy of revelation and salvation.

In his articulation of the issue of what lies between particular persons or 'others' Zizioulas offers an answer to the critique that the appeal to communion eliminates otherness through its homogenizing and hegemonic tendencies. Zizioulas' construction of the 'gap' between 'others' has created the space for the other within the structure of communion. In this sense Zizioulas' construction of an ontology of otherness does bear comparison with my suggestion for the reconceptualization of the classic ingredients of the doctrine of the Trinity in the metaphor of a perichoretic dance, which pushes against the 'limit' towards 'impossible' hospitality, allowing space for the other. Zizioulas' understanding of the 'gap' between persons, and my own exploration of a novel metaphorical understanding of *perichoresis*, may be seen as examples of the functionality of the doctrine of the Trinity in relation to alterity.

The Church and the 'Other'

As well as considering the identification of Trinity/Church *per se*, it is also important to consider the doctrines of the Trinity and the Church in light of the present-day context of pluralism in the West. Does the construction of the doctrines of the Trinity and of the church allow space for the other? And in the various structures of Trinity/Church identity is there space for the other? Among those who promoted an appeal to relationality Colin Gunton[42] argued that '[a] perichoretic unity is a unity of a plural rather than unitary kind'.[43] He develops an understanding of the different roles of the Son and the Spirit; attributing rationality to the Son, and freedom to the Spirit, which Dan Hardy and David Ford have called 'non-order'.[44] 'What becomes conceivable as a result of such a development is an understanding of particularity which guards against the pressure to homogeneity that is implied in modern relativism and pluralism.'[45] Thus Gunton sets out an understanding that 'Being is diversity within unity'.[46] He expounds this conceptuality further: 'God appears to be conceived neither as a collectivity nor as an individual, but as a communion, a unity of persons in relation.'[47] Within such a conceptuality he argues that there is space for the 'Other', i.e. a 'communion-in-otherness'.[48]

It is one thing to construct an understanding of relationality which has space for the 'Other', indeed, even an ontology of 'communion-in-otherness', but it is another thing to craft a structure which has place for those who may be considered 'radically Other' in regard to the communion of the church: i.e. the heretic, the excommunicate and those who do not confess Christ as Lord and Saviour. Küng argues that the church has to find space for the heretic, and no longer pursue the role of Inquisitor. He argues eloquently that as Christ's love is boundless, no one may be excluded, not even one's enemies.[49] Understandings of the Eucharist that include space for the 'Other' are to be found in the writings of Tissa Balasuriya, Timothy Gorringe, and Anne Primavesi and Jennifer Henderson.[50] However, there are, of course, alternative voices which argue that although the Eucharist is to be understood as making an eschatological community, this does not sanction intercommunion with the schismatic or heretic. The Eucharist is not a means of achieving unity. From a similar perspective there are those who argue that the reception of Holy Communion is related to an understanding of true or right belief. Andrew Louth argues that in the understanding of Maximus the Confessor, communion is only genuine communion if it is communion in the truth. It is difficult to see where space for the 'Other' is to be found in such understandings of the eucharistic community of the Church. Not only are 'other' Christians excluded but so also are the (Non-) Religious Other.

The place of the heretic, the schismatic, the excommunicate and the (Non-) Religious Other in relation to the Eucharist and/or the Church raises profound questions about exclusion and inclusion and the status of those 'outside', and thus about space for the other. How can the Church respond to demands for tolerance and/or hospitality? Can the Church facilitate participation and reciprocity in a universal cosmopolitan community? Serious questions are raised by the fractured reality of the Church and the ongoing exclusion of the heretic, the schismatic, the excommunicate and the (Non-) Religious Other. In seeking to respond to demands for tolerance and/or hospitality the construction of the Trinity/ Church identity in relation to the question of space for the other is thus not only a theoretical concern but is imperative for the churches' realization of their participation in the divine communion in and for the cosmos.

Notes

1. Leonardo Boff, *Holy Trinity, Perfect Community* (Maryknoll, NY: Orbis Books, 2000).
2. Ibid., 63.
3. Ibid., 65.
4. Andrew Louth, 'The Ecclesiology of Saint Maximus the Confessor', *International Journal for the Study of the Christian Church* 4, 2 (2004), 109–20.
5. Maximus the Confessor, *Mystagogia*, MPG 91, Chapter One; English trans. G. C. Berthold, *Maximus Confessor: Selected Writings* (London: SPCK, 1985).
6. John D. Zizioulas, *Being as Communion: Studies in Personhood and the Church* (London: Darton, Longman and Todd, 1985).
7. Ibid., 18.
8. Ibid., 19.

9. Hans Küng, *The Church* (London and Tunbridge Wells: Search Press, 1968).
10. Ibid., 237.
11. Miroslav Volf, *After Our Likeness: The Church as the Image of the Trinity* (Grand Rapids, MI and Cambridge, UK: Eerdmans, 1998).
12. John Behr, 'The Trinitarian Being of the Church', *St Vladimir's Theological Quarterly* 48, 1 (2004), 67–88.
13. Ibid., 67.
14. Ibid., 68.
15. Ibid., 68.
16. Zizioulas, *Being as Communion*, 8.
17. Jacques Derrida, *On the Name* (Stanford: Stanford University Press, 1993); Derrida, *The Politics of Friendship* (London and New York: Verso, 1994).
18. John Caputo (ed.), *The Religious* (Malden, MA and Oxford, UK: Blackwell, 2002).
19. Ibid., 5.
20. J. Caputo (ed.), *Deconstruction in a Nutshell: A Conversation with Jacques Derrida* (New York: Fordham University Press, 1996); see also J. Derrida, *Spectres of Marx* (New York and London: Routledge, 1993).
21. Ibid., 112.
22. Ibid., 124.
23. Karl Barth, *Church Dogmatics*, vol. 1.1 (Edinburgh: T&T Clark, 1975).
24. Ibid., 316.
25. J. Zizioulas, 'Communion and Otherness', *St Vladimir's Theological Quarterly* 38, 4 (1994), 349–50.
26. J. D. Zizioulas and P. McPartlan (eds), *Communion and Otherness: Further Studies in Personhood and the Church* (London: T&T Clark, 2006).
27. Ibid., 5.
28. Ibid.
29. Ibid.
30. Ibid., 4–5.
31. Ibid., 6.
32. Ibid., 6.
33. Ibid., 52.
34. Hilary Lawson, *Reflexivity: The Post-Modern Predicament* (La Salle, IL: Open Court, 1985).
35. Zizioulas, *Communion and Otherness*, 25.
36. Ibid., 25.
37. Ibid., 26.
38. Ibid., 54.
39. Oliver Davies, *A Theology of Compassion* (London: SCM, 2001).
40. Brian V. Johnstone, 'The Ethics of the Gift: According to Aquinas, Derrida and Marion', *Australian EJournal of Theology* 3 (August 2004): ISSN 1448–632; http://dlibrary.acu.edu.au/research/theology/ejournal/aejt_3/Johnstone.htm.
41. John Milbank, 'Can a Gift Be Given? Prolegomena to a Future Trinitarian Metaphysic', *Modern Theology* 11, 1 (1995), 119–61.
42. Colin E. Gunton, *The One, the Three and the Many: God, Creation and the Culture of Modernity* (Cambridge: Cambridge University Press, 1993).
43. Ibid., 212.
44. Ibid.

45. Ibid., 213.

46. Ibid.

47. Ibid., 215.

48. Ibid., 216.

49. H. Küng, *The Church*, 252.

50. Tissa Balasuriya, *The Eucharist and Human Liberation* (London: SCM, 1979). Timothy Gorringe, *Love's Sign: Reflection on the Eucharist* (Madurai: Tamilnadu Theological Seminary, 1986); Anne Primavesi and Jennifer Henderson, *Our God Has No Favourites: A Liberation Theology of the Eucharist* (Tunbridge Wells: Burns & Oates; San Jose, CA: Resource Publications, 1989).

Chapter 8

BEING CHURCH: A CRITIQUE OF ZIZIOULAS' COMMUNION ECCLESIOLOGY

Travis E. Ables

The ecumenical project of constructing a viable and truly catholic communion ecclesiology remains one of the lingering priorities of current theological discussion, a project to which this chapter hopes to contribute. To that end, my purpose here is to examine and test the attempt to ground communion ecclesiology in the doctrine of the Trinity. The question is not idle, for the consistently unthought moment in attempts to draw an analogy between the subsistents in communion of the Godhead, and the persons in communion in the church, is precisely what constitutes the analogy itself. Nonetheless, the invocation of the correlative structure of Trinity and church based upon an analogy of relationality has proven a fundamental and popular resource in ecclesiological constructions, most particularly in the seminal theology of Metropolitan John Zizioulas. It is his articulation of Cappadocian personalism that most directly and programmatically claims a basis for human relational personhood, realized exemplarily in the church, in the mode of perichoretic personhood of the hypostases in the Trinity. Realizing that Zizioulas' ecclesiology has been widely and enthusiastically appropriated, the purpose of this chapter is to raise the issue as to whether Zizioulas' proposal is theologically sustainable, and whether the conceptual structure of his thought is capable of underwriting a consistent and theologically generative vision of the nature of divine and human communion. I raise questions regarding his thought not to be captious or partisan, but rather out of a concern that, in the rush to appropriate a creative and rich theological vision that has spoken to deep needs in contemporary theology, critical tensions in Zizioulas' thought have been overlooked, tensions that bear upon the very heart of his theology.

In what follows, I presuppose the work of several recent critics of Zizioulas' interpretation of the Cappadocian Fathers, who argue for its dependence on the nineteenth-century synthesis of Théodore de Régnon with its trinitarian 'paradigm' opposing patristic-*cum*-Cappadocian personalism and scholastic-Augustinian essentialism.[1] This paradigm has been displaced and transformed through the mediation of Vladimir Lossky and Karl Rahner, and thus put to uses that de Régnon himself could hardly have imagined – not least a rigid dichotomy between Eastern and Western formulations of the Trinity, itself a lingering problem to be addressed in ecumenical discussions once current reflexes of Western self-abnegation are exhausted. But irrespective of Zizioulas' historical defensibility, I will focus instead on the cogency and plausibility of his systematic proposal as such.[2] In particular, I will be arguing here that the way he posits the relationship between the divine and human communion proves to be self-defeating.

Created and uncreated being: the ambiguity of analogy in Zizioulas' theology

In this first section, I will focus directly upon a theme which explicitly grounds Zizioulas' conception of communion ecclesiology, namely the dialectic of uncreated and created being. This theme, which takes various shapes in his thought, is the primary means by which Zizioulas articulates the relationship between divine and human communion at an ontological level. It will be my claim that in order to account for the nature of communion as an ontological category, Zizioulas is forced to proffer a pair of competing explanations for the primordial, ontological nature of communion, which turn out to be incompatible. I will proceed by revisiting the main argument of *Being as Communion*, before turning to examine Zizioulas' recent publication *Communion and Otherness*.

The project of *Being as Communion* is centred on the conceptual 'revolution' in ontology that Zizioulas attributes to the thought of the 'Cappadocians'.[3] By virtue of the doctrine of *creatio ex nihilo*, which ruptures the monism of Greek philosophical thought, being itself is made a product of freedom, the freedom of the being of God as graciously and freely choosing to create the world. But the being of God is inherently (although still freely) relational, as the second dimension of the Cappadocian revolution makes clear: as a result of the Arian disputes and the working out of the logic of the Nicene *homoousios* position, the Cappadocians made the divinity of God identical to the *monarchia* of the Father, a divinity which is nonetheless shared with the Son and the Spirit, the three of them being one God whose unity is not one of substance, but of communion. The conceptual apparatus that underwrites this communion is the dissociation of the category of *hypostasis* from that of *ousia*, and its linking to *prosōpon*. Being is thus identified with personhood via the notion of hypostasis: the person is the hypostasis of being, and being is thereby the product of freedom. Because God's mode of being, or *tropos huparxeōs*, the 'how' of God's existence, is identical to its constitution as a communion in the origination of Son and Spirit by the Father, Zizioulas argues that being itself is made relational.

> If God's being is by nature relational, and if it can be signified by the word 'substance,' can we not then conclude almost inevitably that, given the ultimate character of God's being for all ontology, substance, inasmuch as it signifies the ultimate character of being, can be conceived only as communion? ... *Communion belongs not to the level of will and action but to that of substance.*[4]

The logic here is simple: God (the Father) freely originates Son and Spirit and thus constitutes Godself, uncreated being, as communion; analogously, God freely creates the world, and because the 'substance' of God is itself relational, substance as such – being – is relational. Personhood, on the model of divine personhood, becomes the primordial ontological category, and the human *imago dei* is realized in human persons becoming hypostases, relational existents who exist ek-statically in freedom and love, having their being in the event of communion with the other. Hence, '*to be* and *to be in relation* becomes identical'.[5] An ontology of relation then can be deployed as the basis of an ecclesiology wherein persons (because they are persons like the divine hypostases are persons) are simultaneously particulars and in communion.

In turning to *Communion and Otherness*, Zizioulas expands the christological legitimation of this ontology via Maximus Confessor's thought.[6] For Zizioulas' ontology, as Aristotle Papanikolaou especially has been careful to point out, is premised upon a certain christological construal of the divine–human relation: the dialectic of the uncreated and the created, the relation of divine and human without confusion and without division. Christ, in short, just is the 'realism of the divine–human communion' in his person: divine and human exist in communion but as irreducibly other to one another – other precisely in their variegated union in a hypostasis.[7] Drawing upon Maximus,[8] Zizioulas makes a distinction between *diaphora* or 'difference', and *diairesis* or 'division' as a means of describing the relationship of particular existents in their individuation: creation is united in difference, in communion, in the Logos, a uniting not by nature but through a person, namely the Son; apart from the hypostasis of the person of the Logos, creation is subject to division and thus death, the reification of otherness into individualism and dissolution. The incarnation is itself the mode of God's being whereby God can unite

Godself to creation such that creation can be constituted in communion. The Logos of God constitutes the *logoi* of creation in their particularity and otherness. It is the hypostasis of the Son towards which creation and history are oriented, and towards which the logos of every existent is oriented for its fulfilment. For it is the relation of divine and human natures in communion, a communion that just is the person of Jesus Christ, that ultimately undergirds the relationship of the human hypostasis to its ultimate Other, the triune God.

Whatever the historical merits of Zizioulas' reading of Maximus' Christology, I wish only to point out the theoretical tensions resident here. There are two. First, the central thread of the earlier book focuses on the relationship of *analogy* between the relational 'substance' of God, and the relational substance of creation. The tenor of the later book, on the other hand, focuses upon a Chalcedonian Christology of divine–human communion. Zizioulas is at his strongest in his description of Maximus' Christology, but he is not careful to describe the relationship between this christological legitimation of communion, on the one hand, and that deployed more extensively in *Being as Communion*, where communion's ontological primordiality is grounded in the free creative agency of the Father.[9] If the nature of being itself is personal and relational insofar as the Father is the originator of being in freedom, communion is inscribed into the very nature of being as the free work of the Father. But then it is difficult to see just how the work of Christ adds anything to this ontological category of relationality: communion cannot simultaneously be an ontological category of being as such and the gratuitous work of Christ in deification, that is, unless *gratuity* is going to mean *superfluity*.

The natural reply for Zizioulas is that this criticism unfairly posits a disjunction between the two (he would no doubt charge that this is a typically Western mode of distinguishing creation and incarnation), and, in fact, his appropriation of Maximus' theology of the incarnation could demonstrate that the incarnation is a consummation and recapitulation of creation: the Logos becomes flesh, incarnating the divine–human communion of which he is already the ontological principle in the creation itself. This would, of course, require a strong theology of creation through the Son, as well as an affirmation of the incarnation as predetermined by God prior to creation and fall.[10] But, once this step is taken, the real issue emerges. Zizioulas is so strong on this point that he states that God *could not* relate to creation without the Logos.[11] Given the way Zizioulas conceives of the relationship of created and uncreated being, he is forced to inscribe the former within an almost total negative determination: created being, in fact, has no integrity or goodness of its own, and certainly no freedom. Recall his description of the human hypostasis as created: the biological hypostasis is a tragic figure, affirming itself without relation and thus an 'unsuccessful' hypostasis[12] – an existent that does not transcend its nature in freedom and communion but is rather agonistically bound to it. This basic argument recurs in *Communion and Otherness*, where he repeatedly stresses that human nature, in itself, has no power of survival and is oriented only to death.[13] Only by its uniting to uncreated nature – Christ – is the person hypostasized and made a free participant in communion. However, if the biological hypostasis is, in fact, completely bound to death and individualism *simply by virtue of being created*, this begins to look uncomfortably like a Manichean pessimism on the evil of created being as such – this *despite* the inherently relational nature of created 'substance' for which he argues on the basis of the Father's creatorhood.[14] This latter suspicion is exacerbated by Zizioulas' claim, noted above, that the Incarnation is required to overcome the (fatal and tragic) separation between God and creation – seemingly by the very nature of creation itself.

Zizioulas stresses the moribund nature of created being so strongly that the strict disjunction between freedom and necessity, or hypostasis and nature, that is at play here commits him to arguing strictly against any notion of a *potentia obedientialis* or capacity for grace:[15] it would seem that the biological human being is utterly incapable of becoming a hypostasis, which must mean that it is incapable of any degree of communion or relationality. But as we have already seen, Zizioulas also affirms that relationality is part of the very nature of being itself, such that it constitutes a 'capacity-in-incapacity'.[16] Faced with a contradiction here, in the (laudable) interests of making Christology the controlling factor in realizing the communion of the hypostasis, he tacks very close to making evil and fallenness analytic with created being: 'death ... belongs to the nature of what is created'.[17] One must confess a degree of perplexity on this point: Zizioulas' repeated assertion that created existents are by nature subject to change, death, and ultimately non-existence, and gain eternal existence only through participation in uncreated nature, bears more than a small trace of the Platonism he so despises. Regularly in *Communion and Otherness*, he avers that what is at stake in the incarnation and in deification is the eternal survival of the hypostasis, which by its own lights is condemned to fragmentation and perdition by virtue of it being merely a biological hypostasis. Because created being cannot survive eternally, it requires uniting with uncreated being; Christ's incarnation is merely the instrumentalization of addressing this necessity.[18] The relationship of uncreated and created being is not a dialectic at all; it is a rigid dichotomy, resurfacing between the biological and ecclesial hypostasis in what, in fact, looks like a strikingly modern, Western-style dualism[19] between nature and grace. Part of the problem here is that Zizioulas has no way to account for sin within his ontological schema:[20] by articulating the uncreated–created dialectic the way he does, he has no resources to describe how creation might be simultaneously good – as such and with its own integrity – and fallen.[21] The choice for non-being, which is sin, just is that which shows the ultimate contingency (which is not the same thing as reprobation or intrinsic moribundity) of created being; that Zizioulas cannot see this shows how the relationship of creation and redemption cannot line up in the terms with which he has set them forth. He is left with an insurmountable division between creation and redemption, despite positing a direct analogical relation between the two.[22]

The problem of ontology and transcendence

This chapter began by raising the question of the analogy that obtains between divine and human personhood: how are we to demonstrate that human persons are like divine persons? Zizioulas gives, as we have seen, two answers: first, that it is the nature of created being itself, by virtue of its being created – that is, in that it takes its origin from a personal cause, the Father. The Cappadocian logic of *creatio ex nihilo*, given expression through the concept of the Father as *aitia*, grounds the nature of all being as ek-static and tending towards communion – communion is grounded in the monarchy of the Father. Second, Zizioulas also argues that the mediatory character of the Logos is the principle of this analogical structure of communion, insofar as the uniting of natures in a person – a hypostasis – in Christ is the means by which all hypostases become personal and communal. I have argued that these two answers do not at all sit comfortably together, and, in fact, eventuate in an evacuation of the legitimacy of created being as such. The task is now to focus on why this irresolvable dilemma arises, and I will suggest in this section that the conflict is engendered by the very attempt to proffer an ontology of communion. This, in turn, raises serious problems for the project of communion ecclesiology, at least in Zizioulas' proposal.

I begin with the mediatory character of the Logos itself, as Zizioulas describes it. I noted above his strong position that God *could not* relate to the world without the Logos. This function of the Logos as bridging the 'ontological distance' between God and the world is then cast into sharp juxtaposition with the monarchical origin of substance qua communion as such, particularly inasmuch as this ontological distance is cast in a stark dualism of biological and ecclesial nature and grace. Thus when Zizioulas takes up the analogical question, cast in terms of the dialectic of created and uncreated being, he is unable to articulate the resulting complex of ideas –

incorporating the basic shape of the God–world relation, the christological mediation of redemption, and human nature as created and fallen – into a meaningful and consistent pattern. This is, I would submit, not simply a result of a failure to describe his conception of the connection of these doctrines – it is, in fact, a set of symptoms of a system-wide failure of his thought. The problem lies with the very heart of Zizioulas' proposal: a proffering of an *ontology* of communion, authorized by the analogy between the event of communion of persons that is the Trinity, and the event of communion in the church, where communion is an ontological category of the ekstasis of the hypostasis.

Simply put, there is no way to conceive of God as a being (even as uncreated being) and not cast God in a competitive relation with the world,[23] a relation which articulates itself in distance or duality, which, however, is a difference inscribed within a higher unity, namely that of being itself: God and objects in the world are specific individuations or modalities of being, which remains the ultimate neuter and indeterminate genus within which every other existent is posited. This is precisely what is at issue in the strong dualism emergent in Zizioulas' thought: given the competitive relation of divine and created being, in order for the priority of divine being to obtain, created being must be downgraded to the status of virtual *non*-being. Zizioulas must hold together the requirements of an ontological status for the capacity of communion, and for communion to be the prerogative of the Trinity, and consequently evacuates creation of its very status as the good creation of God. Furthermore, if God and world are posited within the general concept of being, even if they are two *orders* of being, God cannot truly communicate Godself to another being, for it is of the nature of beings to be incommunicable; it follows ineluctably that their distinction be cast as a distance between the two,[24] bridged only by a mediator, a hybrid, a *tertium quid* that manages to be two beings at the same time.

This is all a way, naturally, of talking about a standard objection to the crudest kind of articulation of the *analogia entis* which Zizioulas has, of course, not espoused; but this is because he has not even taken up the question to which the analogy of being thus conceived poses such an unsatisfactory answer! In fact, the analogical question is the consistently remaindered moment in contemporary trinitarian ontologies, of which Zizioulas' is perhaps the most exemplary, and its status as a kind of unthought surd is the disaster of every such ontology, even as an analogy is presupposed. But no matter what kind of analogical relationship is posited, whether it be via the quasi-univocal concept 'person'[25] by virtue of creation or via the mediatorial character of the Logos, if God and world are going to be placed under some overarching regulative concept 'being', then it is impossible to articulate how God and world are ultimately differentiated. The only recourse is to emphasize quantitative differences, such as a 'gulf' or distance, that separate them as furniture in their own particular storerooms of the universe. And some concept is going to have to be fixed to mediate between the two.

The Logos, we have seen, serves just this function for Zizioulas. But here is the true ruin of his trinitarian theology, which is again due to his desire to inscribe it within an ontology of communion. There are two insoluble dilemmas in deploying a Logos theology as he does (*viz.*, as a component, even the most important component, in an ontological system). First, configuring Christ the Son as a mediator in the particular manner Zizioulas does, as a functional concept designed to bridge an ontological chasm that combines two orders otherwise incommunicable, makes it impossible to actually account for the Chalcedonian logic Zizioulas makes so much of. Strictly speaking, God has no mediator: God is God's own mediator,[26] and despite the claims of many contemporary trinitarians regarding Irenaeus' 'two hands of God', supplementing the deity with a pair of mediators does nothing to ameliorate an otherwise cold and distant transcendence conceived spatially (it simply pushes it back one step further). God is either transcendent by virtue of 'being' altogether beyond being (and thus, impossible to subsume in any analogy of *being* as articulated above) and thereby is closer to every being than it is to itself as its source and end, such that God's transcendence is, in fact, precisely the condition of possibility of God's immanence; or God is a being altogether removed from the world while still not different in kind from the world, requiring mediation by a virtual demi-god whose necessity only exacerbates the remove at which God stands from all created being. Transcendence is not distance or remoteness; it is the surpassing intimacy of the creator who *im-mediately* sustains every creature in its existence.

But there is an even more basic problem internal to the type of mediatory-analogical Christology Zizioulas offers. In fact, this is an issue inherent to the very idea of an ontological system of relationality or communion. Ontology is, by definition, a philosophical level of description devoted to the study of essences or natures – beings. It is a discourse of the general. Any individual whatsoever is, in the ontological register, subsumed under a regulative concept or genus that flattens its concrete existence into the abstraction of an idea. This has, as Levinas in particular has shown, a lethal impact upon our ability to talk about particulars, once it is elevated to the level of the privileged descriptor of meaning.[27] Ontology once absolutized becomes a panoptic pretension to totality, thought's aspiration to inscribe all of being under the luminous vision of a masterful vision of cognition, and insofar as it reduces any particular to the white noise of being as such, the concreteness of the particular is irrevocably lost.[28] One cannot account for the particular apart from the very particular deifying relation of a person to Christ and thereby to the neighbour through the Spirit, for to abstract from that relation, which is finally only an encounter that escapes ontological categories, is to evacuate it of content. Put more schematically: to give a general account of the particular is precisely to reduce the many to one all over again. This is Levinas' point about the totalizing quality of all ontologies – a point, it must be said, that Zizioulas misunderstands entirely, for ironically, the movement from the particular to the general – from difference to unity – is a constant in Zizioulas, from his grounding of the trinitarian communion in the monarchy of the Father, to the centralizing of ecclesial communion in the unity of the bishop, to, finally, his dissolution of the particularity of the man Jesus Christ to one more exemplar – even if the highest exemplar – of a general structure of relationality and ekstasis. The incarnation for Zizioulas, even given its articulation via Maximus as discussed above, is consistently and immediately folded within a higher concept which it simply serves to instantiate: the Logos is a cosmic principle of the dialectic of uncreated and created being, the realization of an idea, an idea that fills a conceptual need for an analogical structure to hold between divine and created being such that reality in general can be characterized according to a regulative concept of the person.[29]

An ontology of communion is quite simply an excellent way of reifying an ontological distance between person and person, and between God and world: each an instance of a general structure of mediation required to bring two individuals together once they are locked into the self-referential solipsism of ontology. But we do not relate to concepts – and here is the utter failure of an ontology of communion. To relate to a person as a concept, or to conceptualize ontologically my relation to a particular person, is an erasure of that person – it is murder, in Levinas' language. We relate to persons, who are precisely particulars, who lay claim upon us and interpellate us and are the recipients of our love (and hate). And the incarnation of the Son of God is certainly not the concrete universal of a general concept of the hypostatic, an analogical principle bridging a gulf internal to being. The incarnation is nothing but the history of a Jewish man, Jesus Christ, who was identical to God's act in the giving of Godself, a man who by the giving of his Spirit calls forth a community of people who are characterized by their love, witness and worship. But this is not something that can be ontologized: my relationship to my neighbour is not the realization of an ontology of communion, or, in other words, a general concept of relationality, in anything more than a purely banal sense. The ontological may be the structure of the congening of two agents in a social correlation: but the *relationship* is the content of our fears, our hopes, our trusts, and our ventures in faith towards one another in service and in love. This is performative: a practice and an enactment of what it means to be deified insofar as the Spirit is the gift of God that is our love. It is indeed, as Zizioulas theorizes, freedom, but freedom as he conceives it would be an absolutizing of a *concept* of freedom, in which the meaning of my free relation with my neighbour serves simply to illustrate a universal principle. Thus the problem of transcendence that is inherent to the ontological conception of the God–world relation is a problem of ontology itself, showing up again in the incapacity of ontology to account for relations within the world: as long as communion or relation is inscribed within an order of being, there cannot be persons in relation, only concepts in instantiation.

We need to take a step back from the assumption that ecumenical and theological concerns are resolvable by recourse to a particular register of discourse – in this case, ontology. The ecclesial and thus ecumenical concern is one that is finally accounted for performatively, or not at all. Ontology is nothing but the discourse of conceptual mediation: to take recourse to ontology is to assume that, in order for the church to be church, it must fix a concept of itself in accordance with which it can establish its identity before entering into the question of its mission and discipleship. In fact, ontology functions as the evasion of the truly difficult task of being with the other, a way of talking about the difficult task of dialogue, respect and care, without actually enacting it. The striking thing about a relational ontology, thus, is just how superfluous it is: to enter into a relationship with my neighbour, whether that neighbour be a fellow Episcopalian, an Orthodox or Roman Catholic colleague, or a Southern Baptist friend, is simply a practice of charity that happens anew in the encounter with the ethical demand to attend, listen and serve. Ontology confuses the being of the church with simply *being church*: with every act of charity we are not encoding our being in the analogical folds of a totalizing ontology, but enacting the mystery of the love of God, the hope and venture of faith that is itself beyond being.

Notes

1. On the current debate, see Michel R. Barnes, 'Augustine in Contemporary Trinitarian Theology', *Theological Studies* 56, 2 (June 1995), 237–50; 'De Régnon Reconsidered', *Augustinian Studies* 26, 2 (1995), 51–79; Sarah Coakley, 'Re-Thinking Gregory of Nyssa: Introduction – Gender, Trinitarian Analogies, and the Pedagogy of *The Song*', *Modern Theology* 18, 4 (October 2002), 431–43, and 'Introduction: Disputed Questions in Patristic Trinitarianism', *Harvard*

Theological Review 100, 2 (April 2007), 125–38; Lewis Ayres, *Nicaea and Its Legacy: An Approach to Fourth-Century Trinitarian Theology* (New York: Oxford University Press, 2004); Bruce D. Marshall, 'Trinity', in *The Blackwell Companion to Modern Theology*, ed. Gareth Jones (Malden, MA: Blackwell, 2004), 183–203. Predating this was André de Halleux, in 'Personnalisme ou Essentialisme Trinitaire chez les Pères cappadociens?', in *Patrologie et Œcuménisme: Recueil D'études* (Leuven: Leuven University Press, 1990), 215–68. For a defence of Zizioulas against the Régnonian genealogy, see Alan Brown, 'On the Criticism of *Being as Communion* in Anglophone Orthodox Theology', in *The Theology of John Zizioulas*, ed. Douglas Knight (Burlington, VT: Ashgate Publishing, 2007), 35–78, which is hindered by his lumping together of a massively disparate variety of thinkers under the meretricious (and inaccurate) category of 'postliberal Anglican'; he primarily has Coakley in view with the term. Brown does not refute the Régnonian thesis.

2. For a similar strategy, see Edward Russell, 'Reconsidering Relational Anthropology: A Critical Assessment of John Zizioulas's Theological Anthropology', *International Journal of Systematic Theology* 5, 2 (July 2003), 168–86.

3. In the context of this chapter, I will forgo any attempt to examine to what extent Zizioulas' theological ontology is derived from modern sources. The standard critique here is Lucian Turcescu, '"Person" versus "Individual", and other Modern Misreadings of Gregory of Nyssa', *Modern Theology* 18, 4 (October 2002), 527–39. Cf. the riposte of Aristotle Papanikolaou, 'Is John Zizioulas an Existentialist in Disguise? A Response to Lucian Turcescu', *Modern Theology* 20, 4 (October 2004), 601–7, and of Zizioulas himself in *Communion and Otherness: Further Studies on Personhood and the Church*, ed. Paul McPartlan (New York: T&T Clark, 2006), 171–7.

4. *Being as Communion: Studies in Personhood and the Church* (Crestwood, NY: St Vladimir's Seminary Press, 1985), 84, 86, emphasis original.

5. Ibid., 88.

6. There is also a line of argument, especially in the opening essay 'On Being Other: Towards an Ontology of Otherness', that appears very much to proffer a general ontology of relationality that only deploys theological warrant *ex post facto*. Perhaps the most serious charge against a theological ontology of communion such as Zizioulas' is that, put flatly, one simply does not need trinitarian theology to argue that human beings are constitutively relational, as Zizioulas' engagements with Buber, Levinas or Macmurray show. However, in the interests of maximal interpretive charity, I will assume in the body of this essay that Zizioulas' motivations are, in fact, driven by the exigencies of trinitarian doctrine.

7. Aristotle Papanikolaou, *Being with God: Trinity, Apophaticism, and Divine–Human Communion* (Notre Dame: University of Notre Dame Press, 2006), *passim*.

8. See *Communion and Otherness*, 26ff.; 237ff. A similar though not identical argument is found in *Being as Communion*, 93ff.

9. These themes in fact sit side by side throughout both books; I am being somewhat schematic here for sake of clarity.

10. Zizioulas explicitly affirms this, *Communion and Otherness*, 237; cf. 116.

11. Specifically, 'without the Incarnation of the Logos, the ontological distance between God and the world cannot be overcome, since it is only through the

adjustment of a divine "mode of being", that is, a person, that communion and otherness can coincide'. Ibid., 28.

12. *Being as Communion*, 50ff.

13. *Communion and Otherness*, 257ff.

14. So also Douglas Farrow, 'Person and Nature: The Necessity–Freedom Dialectic in John Zizioulas', in *The Theology of John Zizioulas*, 122.

15. *Communion and Otherness*, 209; the entire essay, 'Human Capacity and Incapacity', is germane.

16. Ibid., 248, emphasis removed. Zizioulas' constant opposition of nature and freedom does not illuminate the matter, insofar as a capacity inhering in a nature is, by definition, constitutive of that nature, even if it is a purely negative capacity. Further, one of the cardinal assumptions of Zizioulas' thought, the equation of nature with necessity, is never defended in his work, but simply presumed; he seems to think it holds by definition, but there is no contradiction in conceiving a nature possessing an intrinsic capacity for freedom. If God simply is God's own nature, if God's act of existence, in other words, is identical to God's essence, as the West (or at least Aquinas) understands the matter, then nature and freedom are in fact identical in the divine. For one helpful exposition, see David Burrell, 'Distinguishing God from the World', in his *Faith and Freedom: An Interfaith Perspective* (Malden, MA: Blackwell Publishing, 2004), 3–19. The entire question of the freedom–necessity dialectic is fraught in Zizioulas; for an argument that Zizioulas, in fact, assumes freedom to be the capacity of a nature, see my 'On the Very Idea of an Ontology of Communion: Being, Relation, and Freedom in Zizioulas', forthcoming.

17. *Communion and Otherness*, 264, discussing Athanasius.

18. Ibid., 260.

19. To deploy an enormously overdetermined word that, nonetheless, seems required here.

20. Somewhat similar is Russell's concern that Zizioulas flirts with docetism in his Christology, insofar as both createdness as such, and, in particular, the significance of the cross, are undervalued, though I think the issue lies at a more fundamental level than the problem of emphasis Russell seems to diagnose here; see 'Reconsidering Relational Anthropology', 179. Russell argues that, had Zizioulas accepted the Lutheran *simul iustus et peccator*, he could have accounted for sinfulness as a continuing quality of the redeemed person, without drawing such a sharp disjunction between the biological and ecclesial hypostasis. This is right as far as it goes; but the implication of my argument here is that there is basic incoherency in conceiving creation and grace in Zizioulas, due to his totalizing of the ontological register, internal to this ambiguity *vis-à-vis* the notion of sin.

21. This is because, as the Augustinian conception of evil as privation makes clear, sin is by definition incomprehensible within an ontological register: it is the failure of a being in its being, a decision of a being for non-being, just as grace is the elevation of a being beyond being.

22. Or identity, for he claims that creation and grace coincide; ibid., 256. Zizioulas understands the West to have inscribed a dualism between the two that he wishes to refuse, but, in fact, it is a simple conceptual distinction, the necessity of which he has clearly overlooked.

23. The language of 'competitiveness' is, following Kathryn Tanner's work, superbly suited to express this issue; but Tanner's book *God and Creation in Christian*

Theology: Tyranny or Empowerment? (Minneapolis: Fortress, 1988) is simply an attempt to delineate the doctrinal grammar of a profoundly traditional theme, both in the East and the West.

24. Nicholas Lash uses the illuminating metaphor of the 'explorer' for the modern theist who conceives of God as a being with particular distinguishing attributes and whose transcendence is governed by the language of spatiality; see 'Considering the Trinity', *Modern Theology* 2, 3 (April 1986), 186–8. Cf. his discussion of the Thomist axiom *Deus non est in genere*, 191ff.

25. 'The notion of person, if properly understood, [is] perhaps the only notion that can be applied to God without the danger of anthropomorphism', *Communion and Otherness*, 224.

26. Rowan Williams makes a similar point in 'Word and Spirit', in *On Christian Theology* (Malden, MA: Blackwell Publishing, 2000), 107–27.

27. Most concisely, 'Is Ontology Fundamental?', in *Basic Philosophical Writings*, ed. Adriaan T. Peperzak *et al* (Bloomington: Indiana University Press, 1996), 1–10; cf. *Totality and Infinity: An Essay on Exteriority*, trans. Alphonso Lingis (Pittsburgh: Duquesne University Press, 1969).

28. This is explicitly to disagree with Papanikolaou's claim, in *Being with God*, 93, that Zizioulas is critiquing ' "onto-theology," or the inherent link between God, being, and thought'. On the contrary, Zizioulas epitomizes the onto-theological move. The logic of ontology and of apophaticism is by definition incompatible: one cannot give an ontological account of the *being* of that which is *beyond being*. The problem of erasure of the other applies to the human other and, *a fortiori*, the divine Other: the logic is the same.

29. Alternatively, Zizioulas' ecclesiology qua ontology represents the substitution of the particular relation to God in Christ that is redemption, and the content of the life of the church, for a *concept* of the church that mediates the formation of personhood: Douglas Farrow gives an excellent (if unwitting) illustration of this when he sympathetically states that, for Zizioulas 'When the Church is viewed . . . as the divine answer to the challenge to human personhood posed by necessity . . . it is immediately obvious that ecclesiology will rescue ontology' ('Person and Nature', 109). Put thusly, the church becomes yet another mediator of the ontologically remote deity: a virtual concatenation, then, of mediatorial structures begins to come into view – exacerbated still further by the fact that, for Zizioulas, the church does not exist without the mediation of the bishop. Farrow's desideratum for supplementary Latin resources for an 'ecclesial ontology of personhood' (123), does not, in my judgement, resolve this problem in the least.

Chapter 9

RETRIEVING EUCHARISTIC ECCLESIOLOGY

Radu Bordeianu

The eucharistic ecclesiology of Nicholas Afanassieff represents a milestone in the development of Orthodox theology, with its emphasis on the eucharistic nature of the church as it is fully manifested in the local ecclesial community. Orthodox theologians such as John Zizioulas and Dumitru Staniloae found Afanassieff's proposition unsatisfactory. Consequently, in contemporary Orthodox consciousness, communion ecclesiology has replaced eucharistic ecclesiology.

In this chapter, after an analysis of Afanassieff's position, I compare the communion ecclesiologies of Zizioulas and Staniloae, as they both respond to Afanassieff. Next, I identify the strengths of these three Orthodox theologians, introducing two models of ecclesial unity based on their emphasis on either the local or universal church and on the Eucharist as either means or sign of unity. Finally, I submit a constructive proposal aimed at advancing the dialogue between the Orthodox and Catholic Churches.

Afanassieff's eucharistic ecclesiology

Afanassieff first proposed a eucharistic ecclesiology in 1932–33.[1] He claimed that the early church had a 'eucharistic ecclesiology' in which the eucharistic assembly of the local church contained the fullness of the church universal. Local churches were autonomous and independent, but at the same time related to other local churches through the communion of their bishops, through the acceptance of other local churches' ecclesial life, and, most importantly, through mutual identity, as they each represent the fullness of Christ's presence in the local eucharistic assembly. It was Cyprian of Carthage, Afanassieff argued, who later replaced eucharistic ecclesiology (which affirms the fullness and independence of the local church) with universal ecclesiology, where only the universal church possesses fullness and is made up of parts, i.e. local churches that do not possess fullness.[2] All these parts are united into the universal church through the 'multiplicity united by peace' of their bishops.[3] Consequently, the limits of the church are drawn by the episcopate, and outside of these limits there is no church. According to Cyprian's formula: 'The bishop is in the Church and the Church in the bishop, and if anyone is not with the bishop, he is not in the Church' (Epist. LXVI, VIII, 3).[4]

In Afanassieff's estimation, even though Cyprian's understanding of universal ecclesiology has never been accepted in its entirety, the basic principles of his doctrine still perpetuate the schism between the Orthodox and Catholic Churches.[5] To end this schism, Afanassieff proposed the application of eucharistic ecclesiology to twentieth-century Orthodox–Catholic relations, in order to manifest the (forgotten) unity that still exists between these two distinct but full manifestations of the same eucharistic presence of Christ in the church. Several aspects of Afanassieff's eucharistic ecclesiology are relevant today.

First, because Christ is fully present in the Eucharist, the eucharistic assembly of the local church fully manifests the *Una Sancta*, which is the body of Christ. Consequently, Afanassieff submitted the fundamental thesis of eucharistic ecclesiology:

> ... the Church is where the eucharistic assembly is. It is also possible to formulate this in another way. Where the Eucharist is, there is the Church of God, and where the Church of God is, there is the Eucharist. It follows that the eucharistic assembly is the distinctive, empirical sign of the Church ... The actual limits of the Church are determined by the limits of the eucharistic assembly. In affirming that the eucharistic assembly is the principle of the unity of the Church, the thesis that the bishop is the distinctive empirical sign of the local church is not excluded, because the bishop is included in the very concept of the Eucharist. According to its very nature, the eucharistic assembly could not exist without its president or, according to the terminology established by usage, without the bishop. The foundation of the ministry of the bishop is the eucharistic assembly.[6]

Thus, if Cyprian's universal ecclesiology regarded the bishop as the principle of unity of the church and the point of reference for the limits of the church, Afanassieff attributed these roles to the eucharistic assembly that includes the bishop as its president. Hence, eucharistic ecclesiology does not stand in tension with the hierarchical aspect of the church, but includes it.

Second, Afanassieff affirmed the autonomy and independence of the local church based on the fullness of the local eucharistic assembly. He wrote that in the apostolic age, and throughout the second and third centuries, every local church was autonomous and independent; autonomous, for it contained in itself everything necessary to its life; and independent, because it did not depend on any other local church or any bishop whatever outside itself.[7]

Shortly after this affirmation, however, as if knowing how prone to criticism this affirmation would be, Afanassieff added yet another clarification: 'the local church is autonomous and independent, because the Church of God in Christ indwells it in perfect fullness. It is independent, because any power, of any kind, exercised over it would be exercised over Christ and His Body.'[8]

Third, and complementary to the previous contention that nothing can stand above the local eucharistic assembly, Afanassieff affirmed that the *Una Sancta* is not subordinate to the local church, thus attempting to affirm a proper balance between the universal and local aspects of the church (Afanassieff ended up giving priority to the local church). He emphasized a unity by 'mutual identity'[9] among diverse local manifestations of the same reality:

> Each local church would unite in herself [all] the local churches, for she possessed all the fullness of the Church of God and all the local churches together were united because the same Church of God dwelt in them all … [T]his is not an association of parts of the Church or of diverse churches, but the union of different manifestations of the Church of God in actual human existence. It is the union of the Church of God with herself, through diverse representations.[10]

This kind of unity preserves the universal character of the church since, as Afanassieff continued, 'what was celebrated in one church was also celebrated in the others, because everything was celebrated in the Church of God in Christ. Because of this universal nature, the local churches were neither locked in themselves, nor "provincial".'[11]

Fourth, Afanassieff contended that both Catholic and Orthodox Churches celebrate the same Eucharist, which unites all those who receive it, whether they be Catholic or Orthodox, in spite of their canonical and dogmatic divergences. He consequently criticized Cyprian's affirmation that separated Churches place themselves outside of the church (*Una Sancta*), thus rendering their sacraments invalid.[12] Paradoxically, however, both Catholic and Orthodox Churches have adopted Cyprian's position, each of them considering itself to be the true Church. They have altered Cyprian's position and affirmed that the other Church contains a 'diminished existence of the Church, or certain "vestiges" of the Church, which allow the separated parts of the Church to continue their ecclesiastical life and for the sacraments to be administered'.[13] Afanassieff considered that such a position cannot be defended theologically, since 'the nature of the Church presupposes that either she exists in her fullness or she does not exist at all, but there can be no partial existence nor can there be vestiges existing here and there'.[14] Interestingly, Afanassieff did not accept differing degrees of belonging to the church, forcing him implicitly to uphold Cyprian's position, in the sense that there is no church outside the community celebrating a valid Eucharist.

Fifth, based on the affirmation of the Nicene-Constantinopolitan Creed that the church is 'one, holy, catholic, and apostolic', Afanassieff reinforced his contention that the church is one, even in the present context of dogmatic disunity. Consequently,

> if one recognized the quality of Church in [either] part of the divided Church, one would be minimizing the importance of dogmatic differences, leaving them integral as they are. If one or the other parts are both the Church, then this means the sacraments are celebrated and salvation is possible in both, for this is the purpose of the Church.[15]

Afanassieff was subtle here; applied to the present Orthodox–Catholic situation, this statement means that the two Churches recognize each other's sacraments and character of church (each being a local church of the same *Una Sancta*).[16] Hence, in practice, these Churches actually de-emphasize the importance of the dogmatic differences between them, even though they might be reluctant to admit it officially. I return to this aspect shortly.

Sixth, Afanassieff considered the possibility of ecclesial unity without episcopal communion. He criticized universal ecclesiology for considering that the principle of church unity is not the fullest manifestation of the church in the Eucharist, but only one of its elements, namely the episcopate, which, 'though being most essential for the Church, does not manifest her entirely . . . Therefore, in universal ecclesiology, the episcopate does not find itself within the eucharistic assembly, but above it'.[17] According to eucharistic ecclesiology, however, 'the unity of the Church . . . finds concrete expression in the eucharistic assembly'.[18] This is an essential argument, since it implicitly poses the question: does disunion in episcopacy preclude union in the Eucharist? The answer to this question will determine whether the Orthodox and Catholic Churches are still united or not.

Seventh, Afanassieff contended that the lack of eucharistic communion between the Orthodox and Catholic Churches has never affected the essence of their unity because it is based merely on canonical grounds (which is quite surprising coming from a professor of Canon Law). He wrote:

> Our separation, even if provoked by dogmatic differences, nevertheless has a canonical character. This separation always remains but on the surface of ecclesial life and never extends to its depths. Our canonical division (provoked by dogmatic differences), a division that in turn has given rise to even more profound dogmatic differences, has despite all of this never entirely broken our eucharistic unity. Nevertheless, this unity does not find its concrete expression – for canonical reasons – because we cannot transform in reality our ecclesiological *koinonia*.[19]

For Afanassieff, exclusion from the Eucharist is the expected result of any schism, and it certainly does not imply the impoverishment or even cessation of ecclesial status:

> [S]uch a church did not cease to remain in itself the Church of God despite its isolated situation. If we think that such a local church is no longer the Church, we reject the only distinctive sign by which we can judge the existence of a Church: where there is the eucharistic assembly, there is Church, and there is the Church of God in Christ. This sign applies not only to churches that are part of the multitude-of-churches-linked-by-Love-and-peace but also to those that are separated.[20]

Afanassieff seems inconsistent here, by allowing a church to exist in isolation from other local churches, an assertion he has previously denied. Moreover, I disagree with Afanassieff that lack of love is not a church-dividing issue, since two local communities cannot share in the same eucharistic celebration without love.

The previous points illustrate Afanassieff's theology according to which the church scattered throughout the world is at the same time one, and fully manifested in each local eucharistic assembly. Moreover, the unity of the church depends primarily on the same Eucharist being celebrated in different local churches, and not on interdependence of local communities, dogmatic union, episcopal communion, or bond of love. The implicit argument that Afanassieff is making is that no universalist element (bishop or council) stands above the local church, demanding submission (doctrinal or jurisdictional) as a condition for union, but union happens by mutual identity in the Eucharist. However, Orthodox and Catholic Churches have forgotten these eucharistic ecclesiological principles and have concentrated on their canonical disunity.

As a solution, Afanassieff called for a return to the eucharistic ecclesiology of the early church, meaning that, today, those who receive the Eucharist 'are united with all those who at that moment also participate in eucharistic assemblies – not only those of the Orthodox Church but also those of the Catholic Church – for everywhere there is only the one and the same Eucharist being celebrated'.[21] Because of this unity manifested in the Eucharist, 'the links between the Catholic Church and the Orthodox Church were never entirely broken and continue to exist until the present. The essential link between us is the Eucharist'.[22] Thus, Afanassieff arrived at the heart of eucharistic ecclesiology: since both Orthodox and Catholic Churches celebrate the same Eucharist, they are united through their mutual identity in the Eucharist.

As a practical consequence of his theology, Afanassieff recommended that the Orthodox and Catholic Churches should work towards manifesting their already-existing unity by renewing their communion and postponing the solution of dogmatic divergences for the time when they would be able to address them in the spirit of love:

> By an effort of Love, the Orthodox Church *could* reestablish communion with the Catholic Church, the dogmatic divergences notwithstanding and without demanding that the Catholic Church renounce the doctrines that distinguish her from the Orthodox Church … [The Catholic Church] *could* consent not to demand that the Orthodox Church accept these new dogmas. Within herself she would have remained what she is today, preserving the content and the doctrines that she actually possessed. Certainly, to attain this, the effort in Love is necessary, a great sacrifice, an element of self-renunciation.[23]

Afanassieff's main argument here is that if the Orthodox and Catholic Churches acted based on love, they could renew their communion despite their dogmatic divergences. As if knowing that his daring affirmation would be met with strong criticism, Afanassieff defended his proposal by contending that, even though ideally different local churches should enjoy absolute dogmatic harmony, this has never been the case in history, and is certainly unattainable in the present state of animosity. Afanassieff claimed that he did not minimize the importance of dogmatic formulations and he did not advocate doctrinal relativism or indifferentism, but hoped that differences could be solved in the spirit of love.

What does renewing the communion between the Orthodox and Catholic Churches mean? Ware contends that Afanassieff regarded intercommunion (i.e. sharing in the Eucharist among separate churches) as a practical consequence of his theology. He believed that Christians need to share in communion, so that they discover the unity that already exists in Christ and in the Eucharist. This union would be built from the inside, rather than from the outside.[24]

The reception of Afanassieff's theology varied from enthusiastic embrace (Paul Evdokimov)[25] to vehement rejection (Ware,[26] Zizioulas and Staniloae). In the next section, I concentrate on Zizioulas' and Staniloae's criticisms of eucharistic ecclesiology.

Zizioulas and Staniloae: communion ecclesiology

Zizioulas' main criticism of Afanassieff is that churches cannot have eucharistic communion without sharing in the same teaching and without communion among bishops. Alternatively, Zizioulas proposes communion ecclesiology which emphasizes episcopal communion.

Zizioulas first challenges Afanassieff's historical analysis of the contrast between the eucharistic ecclesiology of Ignatius and the universal ecclesiology of Cyprian.[27] Second, Zizioulas contends that unity of faith and the Eucharist are interdependent, while eucharistic ecclesiology minimizes the importance of dogmatic differences. Third, he criticizes the term 'intercommunion' as being inept, arguing that eucharistic communion can only take place in a fully united Church.[28] Zizioulas' fourth criticism coincides with the heart of his early communion ecclesiology. Because he identifies the bishop with the entire local church, the necessary condition for Christian unity is episcopal communion.[29] Fifth, Zizioulas contends that, for a local church fully to exist, it must exist in communion with other local churches, the Eucharist pointing to the simultaneity of both local and universal.[30] This principle stems from his understanding of the person as 'being in communion', where a person (applied to God, humanity, and the church) exists fully only in communion with other persons.[31] Over time, Zizioulas' communion ecclesiology became more and more centred on his theology of personhood and less on an historical analysis of the role of the bishop in the early church. In his recent book, *Communion and Otherness*, he reformulates some of these previous criticisms.

Zizioulas continues to reject the possibility of intercommunion and emphasizes the necessity of excluding the non-Orthodox from the Eucharist, even though his major premise is that communion embraces and presupposes otherness. He writes:

> In the Eucharist the Other is inconceivable as autonomous or independent 'individual.' The Eucharist is *communion*, and this means that otherness is experienced as *relational*. The eucharistic ethos, therefore, precludes any exclusiveness in otherness. The only exclusion that is permissible – even imperative – is of exclusiveness itself ... [U]ntil the causes of [disunity] are removed, communion with the 'other' suffers.[32]

Zizioulas thus disagrees with Afanassieff's contention that schism does not affect essentially the church unity still manifested in the Eucharist.

Moreover, Zizioulas attempts again to balance 'one' and 'many', 'nature' and 'person', 'universal' and 'local' aspects of ecclesiology.[33] But despite his announced intention, he repeatedly gives priority to 'many', 'person' and 'local'.[34] This brings Zizioulas closer to Afanassieff than he would probably want, since Afanassieff also gave priority to the local church despite his claim to maintain the universality of the church.

Thus, Zizioulas proposes communion ecclesiology as a response to Afanassieff, emphasizing the interdependence between the Eucharist and the bishop, and rejecting intercommunion. However, Zizioulas' departure from Afanassieff is not entirely satisfactory concerning the relationship between the local and the universal church.

Staniloae likewise criticized several aspects of eucharistic ecclesiology, but not the relationship between the Eucharist and the bishop – so prominent in Zizioulas – because Staniloae believed that Afanassieff did actually emphasize this relationship.[35]

First, Staniloae considered that eucharistic ecclesiology is relativistic because it does not adequately stress the importance of the right faith as a condition for the Eucharist, thus creating a compromise that brings a disservice to the ecumenical cause.[36] Consequently, he rejected inter-communion, affirming that eucharistic communion is based on unity of faith; the role of the non-ordained to profess a common faith; the love among members of different communities; the unity between the priest and the bishop who appoints him to preside over the eucharistic assembly; and the communion between the bishop and the rest of the church. All these elements are interrelated.[37] Second, Staniloae disagreed with Afanassieff's assertion that the division between the Orthodox and Catholic Churches has affected only the surface of their ecclesiastical lives and has merely a canonical character.[38] Third, Staniloae considered that this theory includes Orthodoxy in a universal church under papal primacy instead of proposing a future united church in which the pope would be *primus inter pares*.[39] Fourth, Staniloae accepted the idea of a local church's plenitude, but only qualified by the existence of the local church within the framework of the universal church. Offering a more balanced position than Afanassieff and Zizioulas, he considered that local churches are united by sharing in the same Spirit, faith, Eucharist,[40] and episcopal communion. Sometimes, Afanassieff and Staniloae agreed on these principles of union, yet at other times Afanassieff was inconsistent in his theology of the independence and self-sufficiency of the local church.[41]

Staniloae ended his analysis on a more reconciliatory tone, recognizing the validity of the Eucharist and the preservation of apostolic teaching in the Catholic Church, even if it has also added the dogmas of papal primacy, papal infallibility, the *Filioque*, and purgatory. Among these, only the dogmas of papal primacy and infallibility are church dividing.[42] Orthodox and Catholic Churches, although both having a valid Eucharist, cannot share the same Cup because they do not profess the same faith concerning the papacy. Thus Staniloae's main contribution is that doctrinal communion is necessary for unity and that the local and universal aspects of ecclesiology are interdependent.

I suggest that sometimes Zizioulas and Staniloae have dismissed Afanassieff unfairly, taking the consequences of his theology to an extreme. For example, Afanassieff tried (though sometimes unsuccessfully) to balance the independence of the local church with the affirmations that 'no church could separate from the others'[43] and that

> All the multitude of local churches forms one union founded on concord and love. ... [E]very local church accepts and makes its own anything that happens in other churches, and all the churches accept everything that happens in each fellow-church. This acceptance (its regular designation is the word *reception* or *receptio*) is the witness of a local church indwelt by the Church of God, witnessing the work being done in other churches also indwelt by the Church of God – the Spirit bearing witness of the Spirit.[44]

The process of reception mentioned here refers to the entire church life of a local community, and one can safely assume that this includes teachings; so Afanassieff did not deny the importance of dogmatic unity as a necessary ingredient for Christian unity. Understood intrinsically, he was consistent with this principle, since he did not see the differences between the Orthodox and Catholic Churches as church dividing, even though he was inconsistent about whether papal primacy is a canonical or doctrinal issue. Thus he did not minimize the teaching role of the bishop or the importance of the unity of faith as transmitted and received by the whole Church. But he did question the status of 'church-dividing' issues that separate Orthodoxy and Catholicism.

Retrieving eucharistic ecclesiology

After Zizioulas and Staniloae, eucharistic ecclesiology was regarded with suspicion and replaced by communion ecclesiology. It is now time to retrieve the aspects of eucharistic ecclesiology that have been unjustly dismissed and to outline a communion ecclesiology that incorporates the strengths of Afanassieff, Zizioulas and Staniloae. Thus, Afanassieff's ecclesiology, quite influential on Vatican II,[45] would regain its ecumenical significance.

There are two models for Christian unity, based on their emphasis on either the local or universal church and on the Eucharist as either a means or sign of unity. According to the first model, the representative of which is Afanassieff, the local church has priority over the universal, so unity is accomplished through the mutual identity of different local churches celebrating the same Eucharist. The merit of this model is that it explores the ecclesiological consequences of the mutual eucharistic recognition in the Orthodox and Catholic Churches. Moreover, it calls for a re-evaluation of the issues that were historically considered church-dividing.[46] Unfortunately, it presents the Eucharist exclusively as a means towards unity, hoping that doctrinal and episcopal differences will eventually be overcome through intercommunion.

According to the second model for Christian unity, the representatives of which are Zizioulas and Staniloae, union is accomplished through sharing in the same faith and through visible communion among bishops, thus providing a richer unity than the first model. There is, however, the risk to regard the Eucharist exclusively as a sign of unity (or lack thereof), and to transform canonical issues into church-dividing elements. Moreover, if Zizioulas tends to overemphasize the hierarchical character of church unity, Afanassieff and Staniloae present a more balanced ecclesiology, where the non-ordained play a crucial ecumenical role, especially through reception and strengthening the bond of love among local churches.

These two models show that there is a need to create a balance between them, by emphasizing their strengths. First, Christianity needs to seek doctrinal unity. Even though there are several points of divergence that can be regarded as diversity within unity, it appears that the only church-dividing issues between Orthodoxy and Catholicism are papal primacy and infallibility. Afanassieff's proposal that these issues would temporarily remain dogmas in the Catholic Church, though unaccepted by the Orthodox, is not acceptable for either Church at the present time. However, it suggests the way towards future doctrinal unity, hoping that the Catholic Church understands primacy to refer only to the West and views infallibility from the perspective of conciliarity and reception. The East regards the Bishop of Rome as *primus inter pares*. If in the past the emphasis fell on *inter pares*, now Orthodoxy must state positively what *primus* means and propose concrete forms of exercising papal ministry in a united Christendom, with a unified council of bishops. While Zizioulas and Staniloae do not advance this issue considerably, Afanassieff proposed that 'the bishop possessing primacy acts with the agreement of the whole body of bishops: this agreement is made manifest in the council in which the primate bishop participates as its president'.[47] Thus, the second element of unity is episcopal communion.

The third aspect of unity is love. Disagreeing with Afanassieff, I consider (with Staniloae) that eucharistic communion cannot be justified where there is only a fragile bond of love between the members of the Orthodox and Catholic Churches. Such a contention might appear inadequate to a Western audience where there is relative harmony between the two churches. However, in other places such as ex-Yugoslavia or Russia, there are considerable tensions resulting in mutual accusations and even violence. This affirmation is not intended to create an unfairly hostile picture of the Orthodox–Catholic relations in general, especially given the positive aspects of this relationship, such as the successful bilateral dialogues, the exchange of students and professors, common charitable projects, and so forth. However, the Orthodox and Catholics need to strengthen the bond of love between them, and only then will they be able to solve their theological differences and re-establish eucharistic communion.

Fourth, the unity between the Orthodox and Catholic Churches will be a full reality only when they re-establish their eucharistic communion. At that point, the Eucharist would be both a sign and a means towards greater unity: a sign, because there would be doctrinal and episcopal communion, as well as a strong bond of love between them. The Eucharist would also be a means towards greater unity, because important differences would still require a solution, but their resolution can only emerge within the context of harmony and love of a united church, where the members approach the same Cup, continually strengthening their communion.

Thus church unity encompasses four elements: doctrinal unity (while maintaining diversity), episcopal communion (where the pope would be *primus inter pares* within a unified synod of bishops), love (sharing in the Eucharist cannot be justified where there is only a fragile bond of love between churches), and eucharistic communion where the Eucharist is both a sign and means towards unity.

In conclusion, I suggest that Afanassieff's eucharistic ecclesiology can be retrieved and improved in light of Zizioulas and Staniloae to provide a valuable tool for the long journey towards communion ecclesiology and, ultimately, towards Christian unity.

Notes

This chapter, which has been revised and updated, first appeared in a more extensive form in *Journal of Ecumenical Studies* 44, 2 (2009), and is reproduced with permission.

1. Marianne Afanassieff, 'The Genesis of "The Church of the Holy Spirit"', in *L'Église du Saint-Esprit*, Nicholas Afanassieff, trans. Marianne Drobot, *Cogitato Fidei 83* (Paris: Cerf, 1975), 17. Unless otherwise stated, all translations from French and Romanian are mine.

2. According to Cyprian, 'just as we can distinguish members in the Church, the Body of Christ, so the one and only Church, physically speaking, is made up of different local churches, which are her limbs or members: *ecclesia per totum mundum in multa membra divisa*' (Epist. LV, XXIV, 2; cf. Epist. XXXVI, IV, 1). Nicholas Afanassieff, 'The Church Which Presides in Love', in *The Primacy of Peter: Essays in Ecclesiology and the Early Church*, ed. John Meyendorff (Crestwood, NY: St Vladimir's Seminary Press, 1992), 95.

3. Cyprian, *De unitate ecclesiae*, V.

4. Nicholas Afanassieff, 'Una Sancta', in *Tradition Alive: On the Church and the Christian Life in Our Time: Readings from the Eastern Church*, ed. Michael Plekon (Lanham, MD: Rowan & Littlefield, 2003), 12–13. French original: Nicholas Afanassieff, 'Una Sancta', *Irénikon* 36, 4 (1963), 449–51. Henceforth I provide the page numbers corresponding in English and French under the following format: English/French.

5. Afanassieff, 'Una Sancta', 440 (French). This phrase is missing from the English translation.

6. Afanassieff, 'Una Sancta', 14/452–3.

7. Afanassieff, 'The Church Which Presides in Love', 107.

8. Ibid., 109.

9. Timothy (Kallistos) Ware, *Communion and Intercommunion* (Minneapolis, MN: Light and Life Publishing Co., 1980), 11.

10. Afanassieff, 'Una Sancta', 15/454–5. Most contemporary Orthodox and Catholic theologians would agree with Afanassieff's affirmation based on the principle of catholicity, according to which the whole is present in the part and the part is in the whole ('catholicity' derives from *cath'olon*). This principle is valid both for the Eucharist, where every communicant receives the entire Body and Blood of Christ, and for the church, as a description of the relationship between the local and universal aspects of the church. A further reason for Orthodox theologians to agree with this statement is that here Afanassieff seems to come close to the model of autocephalous Orthodox Churches, where they are administratively autonomous and independent, but united in faith and Eucharist. This comparison with contemporary autocephalous Orthodox Churches, however, needs even further qualification. Afanassieff criticized this model because it ascribes autonomy only to the autocephalous church, and not to the dioceses (as eucharistic centres) that make it up.

11. Afanassieff, *L'Église du Saint-Esprit*, 29.

12. Afanassieff, 'Una Sancta', 442 (French).

13. Ibid., 443–4 (French). Translation mine.

14. Afanassieff, 'Una Sancta', 8/444.

15. Ibid., 5–6/439–40.

16. Afanassieff wrote:

> For eucharistic ecclesiology, the Orthodox Church and the Catholic Church are both Churches, or to be more exact, each local church of both groups remains a Church – as it was before so it is after the 'separation.' I put 'separation' in quotation marks for it did not take place and there is no

separation. The Church of God is forever and remains one and unique. The break in communion was not able to produce the division of the Church which, by her very nature, cannot be divided into parts.' Ibid., 22/465.

17. Ibid., 15/454.

18. Ibid., 14/453–4.

19. Nicholas Afanassieff, 'The Eucharist: Principal Link between the Catholics and the Orthodox', in *Tradition Alive: On the Church and the Christian Life in Our Time – Readings from the Eastern Church*, ed. Michael Plekon (Lanham, MD: Rowan & Littlefield, 2003), 49. Original French: Nicholas Afanassieff, 'L'Eucharistie, principal lien entre les Catholiques et les Orthodoxes', *Irénikon* 38, 3 (1965), 339. (The last phrase is author's translation.) History supports Afanassieff's affirmation, since the events that led to the schism in 1054 were not so much doctrinal differences as canonical (although not completely separate from dogma), and the schism was sealed only in 1204 with the fourth crusade. Even in the earlier Photian schism (867–70), unity was restored after agreement was reached on canonical issues, without solving the theological issue of the *Filioque*.

20. Afanassieff, 'Una Sancta', 18/458–9.

21. Ibid., 24/468.

22. Afanassieff, 'The Eucharist: Principal Link', 48–9/337, 339.

23. Afanassieff, 'Una Sancta', 25–6/470.

24. Summarized in Ware, *Communion and Intercommunion*, 18–21. Although Afanassieff called for the re-establishment of communion (see previous quote) – to warrant Ware's summary – Afanassieff has also affirmed that, for canonical reasons, 'we cannot transform in reality our ecclesiological *koinonia*' (Afanassieff, 'L'Eucharistie, Principal Lien', 339). He seems inconsistent on this matter.

25. In his book, *L'Orthodoxie*, Evdokimov dedicated an entire chapter to eucharistic ecclesiology and expressed his unreserved agreement with Afanassieff. Paul Evdokimov, *L'Orthodoxie* (Paris: Desclée de Brouwer, 1979), 128–31, 156.

26. Ware affirms that the Eucharist alone does not create the church, but that two other ingredients are necessary: communion in faith and unity in the local bishop. Moreover, Ware disagrees with Afanassieff's view on intercommunion. Ware, *Communion and Intercommunion*, 7–13.

27. John D. Zizioulas, *Eucharist, Bishop, Church: The Unity of the Church in the Divine Eucharist and the Bishop During the First Three Centuries*, trans. Elizabeth Theokritoff (Brookline, MA: Holy Cross Orthodox Press, 2001), 126. See also Ware's similar criticism in Ware, *Communion and Intercommunion*, 38, note 20.

28. Zizioulas, *Eucharist, Bishop, Church*, 257–8.

29. Ibid., 116.

30. John D. Zizioulas, *Being as Communion: Studies in Personhood and the Church*, Contemporary Greek Theologians, No. 4 (Crestwood, NY: St Vladimir's Seminary Press, 1985), 133.

31. Zizioulas accuses Afanassieff of regarding Christ first as an individual who *then* becomes corporate personality, which would determine Afanassieff to affirm that the faithful are *identically* Christ rather than *differentiatedly* Christ and that local churches are united through their mutual identity. Instead, Zizioulas (in McPartlan's summary) suggests that the unity of the local churches 'derives not from their sameness but from their existence in this differentiated configuration'; see Paul McPartlan, *The Eucharist Makes the Church: Henri De Lubac and John Zizioulas in Dialogue* (Edinburgh: T&T Clark, 1993), 229, 233–5. In my

estimation, Afanassieff did not work within the framework of Christ as individual/ corporate personality, or the local churches united identically/differentiatedly, but Zizioulas 'forces' Afanassieff to fit into this scheme.

32. John D. Zizioulas, *Communion and Otherness: Further Studies in Personhood and the Church*, ed. Paul McPartlan (New York: T&T Clark/Continuum, 2006), 7–8, 91–2.

33. Ibid., 38.

34. E.g., ibid., 142.

35. Dumitru Staniloae, 'Biserica universala si uoborniceasca [The Universal and Catholic Church]', *Ortodoxia* 18, 2 (1966), 168–9.

36. Dumitru Staniloae, *Spiritualitate si comuniune in Liturghia Ortodoxa* [Spirituality and Communion in the Orthodox Liturgy] (Craiova: Editura Mitropoliei Olteniei, 1986), 397. See also Staniloae, 'The Universal and Catholic Church', 169–72.

37. Dumitru Staniloae, 'Teologia Euharistiei [The Theology of the Eucharist]', *Ortodoxia* 21, 3 (1969), 357, 361.

38. Staniloae, 'The Universal and Catholic Church', 195; Staniloae, *Spirituality and Communion*, 397–8.

39. In 1966, before these considerations from *Spirituality and Communion* (p. 398), Staniloae considered that Afanassieff's theory intended to challenge the kind of Catholic ecclesiology that affirms the interdependence between the church and the pope. But, Staniloae continued, Afanassieff did not contradict only the idea of a universal church centred on the pope, but also the idea of the universal church in general, which runs against the teaching of the first Christian centuries and of the second ecumenical council that affirmed the church to be universal, or catholic. Staniloae, 'The Universal and Catholic Church', 173.

40. See, for example, Staniloae, *Spirituality and Communion*, 81–8.

41. Staniloae, 'The Universal and Catholic Church', 170–7.

42. Staniloae, *Spirituality and Communion*, 401–2.

43. Afanassieff, *L'Église Du Saint-Esprit*, 29.

44. Afanassieff, 'The Church Which Presides in Love', 112. Similarly, Afanassieff wrote that

> ... the isolation and introversion of a particular local church was excluded ... Each local church would accept all that took place in another church and all the churches accepted that which occurred in another ... This acceptance, or to employ a term used more regularly with a slightly juridical nuance, this reception was not at all juridical nor social in general. (Afanassieff, 'Una Sancta', 15/454–5)

45. Olivier Rousseau mentions that Afanassieff was quoted at Vatican II where the participating bishops were asked to read his works. His influence can be seen especially in the sections on the local church and on the laity of *Lumen Gentium* ('Preface' by Olivier Rousseau, in *L'Église Du Saint-Esprit*, 8–9). Moreover, Bruno Forte refers to the 'eucharistic ecclesiology of Vatican II', influenced by Afanassieff's contention about the fullness of the local church as expressed in the eucharistic assembly headed by the local bishop; see Bruno Forte, *The Church: Icon of the Trinity – A Brief Study*, trans. Robert Paolucci (Boston: St Paul Books & Media, 1991), 71–4, 78. However, I consider that *Lumen Gentium* articulated a more balanced relationship between the local and universal aspects of the church, properly stressing the communion among local churches and their bishops –

elements that most Orthodox theologians would have hoped to see more prominently in Afanassieff. At the same time, the Orthodox might say, Vatican II placed too much emphasis on the role of the bishop of Rome in creating unity. Thus, there is room for growth in a common Orthodox–Catholic understanding of church unity. I would also add that Afanassieff's book, *The Church of the Holy Spirit* (defended as a dissertation in 1950), approaches first the mystery of the church, then the people of God and the common priesthood, and then ordained priesthood, a scheme that preceded *Lumen Gentium* by 15 years. In my estimation, it is probable that Afanassieff's work has influenced this document, given Rousseau and Forte's remarks, Afanassieff's presence at Vatican II as an official Orthodox observer, and Afanassieff's personal contacts with influential participants, such as Yves Congar.

46. For example, in 2003, the North American Orthodox–Catholic Theological Consultation concluded 'that our traditions' different ways of understanding the procession of the Holy Spirit need no longer divide us'.

47. Afanassieff, 'The Church Which Presides in Love', 102–3.

Chapter 10

COMMUNION ECCLESIOLOGY AND ECUMENICAL EXPERIENCE: RESOURCES FOR INNER-DENOMINATIONAL OTHERNESS

Brian P. Flanagan

Introduction

In the last forty years, as real progress has been made on some of the church-dividing issues of the fifth, eleventh, and sixteenth centuries, new issues, especially in areas of church practice, sexual morality, and other ethical questions, have threatened the visible communion of Christians. Numerous commentators have noted that the lines of division between Christians no longer fall neatly along denominational boundaries (if such a vision was ever entirely accurate), but also divide Christians internally in denominations or communions that were presumed to be relatively cohesive. The serious crisis in the Anglican Communion sparked by differences regarding same-sex sexual relations and the supposed polariza-tion of Roman Catholics between 'traditionalists' and 'progressives' are two oft-mentioned symptoms of this phenomenon. Even in less fraught circumstances, increasing awareness of internal 'otherness' between global South and global North, between urban, suburban and rural Christians, and between different ethnic, immigrant and national groups in a globalizing world, have all made denominational or inner-ecclesial cohesion more difficult to discern.

At the same time, as the experience of the Anglican Communion suggests, the need for structured maintenance of communion within local churches, denominations and worldwide communional bodies may never have been greater. While the great gift of postmodern consciousness to the Christian churches may be what Jonathan Sacks calls 'the dignity of difference',[1] those differences no longer impair full, visible communion only *between* churches and denominations, but also are threatening full, visible communion *within* churches and denominations. If the challenge of twentieth-century ecclesiology was to develop theories of inter-denomin-ational communion flexible enough to embrace the otherness of Christian faith in different denominations, the challenge of twenty-first-century ecclesiology may be to appropriate a theory of communion flexible enough to embrace the otherness of Christians who, officially and juridically, are already in communion.

This essay outlines an ecclesiological thesis and suggests the practical utility of that thesis for the negotiation of inner-denominational[2] otherness that I expect will be a hallmark of ecclesiology in a postmodern situation. The thesis is this: while there are some significant dissimilarities between the differences that have historically divided the Christian churches into multiple churches and denominations, and differences at the foundations of contemporary inner-ecclesial conflict and divisions, the problems of negotiating ecclesial otherness are more similar in both situations than different. In both cases the reconciliation of Christians with Christians who are 'other', individually and communally, is an important, even essential, aspect of ecclesial existence. The first part of this chapter emphasizes the importance of this 'unified theory of communion', arguing that there ought not to be separate theories of Christian communion for extra-denominational and intra-denominational ecclesial relationships. Differences between Christian relations across denominational boundaries and those existing within denominations are specific, and not generic. This theory is rooted in the life and work of Jean-Marie Tillard, both in his theoretical understanding of communion, as well as in the progression of his thought on communion from a theory utilized to address ecumenical otherness to its utility within his own Roman Catholic Church.

The second part of the chapter then asks how, in practical response to the situation of inner-ecclesial pluralism and strained, if not broken, communion within churches, the churches might follow this same progression in appropriating some of the skills, structures and values developed within the ecumenical movement to negotiate their own, inner-denominational otherness. As a Roman Catholic from the United States, I will primarily address some of the possibilities that I see in such an appropriation for life within the Christian communion with which I am most familiar, with the hope that my explorations might not only be helpful to my own community, but may also provide some starting points for similar appropriations within other Christian communities and within other Roman Catholic contexts.

A unified theory of communion

A. *The life and thought of Jean-Marie Tillard, OP*

The contributions of the priest, ecumenist and theologian Jean-Marie Tillard to the church and the ecumenical movement were evident during his lifetime, and have continued to bear fruit since his untimely death in the year 2000. Tillard is most well known today as a leading contributor to the language and theology of communion in contemporary theology. Reviewing Tillard's first major volume on communion in ecclesiology, *Église d'Églises*,[3] Francis A. Sullivan commented:

> Tillard is not the first Catholic theologian to have developed an ecclesiology based on the concept of communion ... However, no one, to my knowledge, has done so with the thoroughness, the depth of insight, the mastery of the biblical and patristic sources, and especially with the ecumenical sensitivity, which Tillard has displayed in this work.[4]

In two subsequent substantive works on communion in ecclesiology, *Chair de l'Église, chair du Christ*,[5] and *L'Église locale*,[6] Tillard deepened the vision of communion outlined in *Église d'Églises*, clarifying its patristic sources and showing more explicitly the relationship of communion to ecclesial catholicity and apostolicity.

But in addition to Tillard's *theory* of communion, Tillard's intellectual *biography*, the theological journey by which he came to address questions of ecclesial communion, provides an important supporting explanation for his ecclesiological position.[7] Tillard's earliest theological work was not focused upon questions in ecclesiology proper, but on sacramental theology, particularly eucharistic theology, and on the theology of religious life. Tillard attended the Second Vatican Council, but worked primarily upon the document on the renewal of religious life, not on any of the major ecclesiologial or ecumenical texts. At the Council he became acquainted with some of the ecumenical observers and soon after became directly involved in the ecumenical movement. He went on to have a distinguished ecumenical career that involved further dialogue with the Anglican Communion, the Orthodox Churches, and the Disciples of Christ; a major role in the drafting and redaction of the Faith and Order consensus statement *Baptism, Eucharist, and Ministry*; and a long period of service to the World Council of Churches and to that body's Faith and Order Commission.

From his earlier studies of the Eucharist and religious life, Tillard's research in this period increasingly focuses upon ecclesiological issues, in two senses. First, the particular questions Tillard asks in his published works from the late 1960s to the 1990s are almost always related to questions raised in the multilateral and bilateral dialogues in which he took part. This is particularly true of the dialogues with Anglican and Orthodox Christians, which often returned to core ecclesiological questions of authority, papal primacy, locality/universality, and episcopacy. In this sense the ecumenical community became one of the determining contexts of Tillard's theology. The second and broader sense in which Tillard's work increasingly focuses upon ecclesiology in this period relates to the development of new and more flexible language for Christian unity within ecumenical dialogue. The language of 'communion' became prominent, especially in the documents of the Anglican–Roman Catholic International Commission, as a way of speaking about the insight that Christian unity involved nuances and degrees of 'fullness' or 'partiality' beyond a binary conception of unity as being *extra-* or *intra-ecclesia*.[8] In connection with his earlier work on the Eucharist, Tillard helped recover theological language adequate to the reality of churches that could recognize the same shared faith in and through their differences of practice, ritual, and theological/ doctrinal expression.

One of Tillard's most important insights was the need to carry the concerns and theological achievements hammered out in the ecumenical dialogues back to the theology and practice of his own Roman Catholic Church. One good example of this pattern is Tillard's 1982 work *L'Évêque de Rome*.[9] The book is the product not simply of individual research, but of investigations carried out with Anglican and Orthodox ecumenists on the nature of papal primacy. Tillard's insight was to draw upon the ecumenical dialogue's results in addressing a text about the dangers of 'papolatry' to a primarily internal, Roman Catholic audience. This movement also holds true for Tillard's research into the overarching question of the nature of Christian ecclesial unity.

B. Communion, salvation and difference

The dialogues with which Tillard was involved used the concept of communion to talk about the value of Christian difference across denominational and ecclesial boundaries. In the three major works of his 'ecclesiology of communion', however, Tillard develops this idea of communion to talk about Christian unity as a unity-in-difference in all Christian conceptions of unity, not only those responding to the divisions of the church. This 'unified theory of communion', Tillard's theory of Christian unity as unity-in-difference, was not only a stopgap concept needed for ecumenical progress, but is a constant of Christian life – including, Tillard argues, within his own Roman Catholic Church. His theory of communion provides a theological foundation for drawing upon ecumenical experience in addressing questions of inner-ecclesial otherness.

Given the wide diversity of uses of communion language in contemporary ecclesiology,[10] and the critiques that have arisen in response to the seemingly infinite flexibility of the term,[11] determining the origins and context of Tillard's idea of communion is essential. In his case, the most important thing to note is that, unlike theories of communion rooted primarily in comparisons to the relations of the trinitarian persons,[12] or theories focused upon the concept of 'hierarchical communion',[13] communion is a *soteriological* concept for Tillard before it is an ecclesiological concept.[14] The nature of communion in the church can only be understood by first understanding communion not only as the *result* of salvation, but as the *substance*, the concrete working out, of that salvation:

> If the concrete content of the Salvation announced in the Gospel of God, both individual and collective, had to be summarized in a single word, we would use, following many of the Fathers, 'communion,' the word that brings together the summaries of Acts [2.42–47; 4.32–35; 5.12–16]. For biblical thought, as the first centuries understood it, Salvation's proper name is 'communion'.[15]

Communion is the salvation of human sociality, not simply a matter of ecclesiastical functionality or ethics. 'The Church of God', Tillard writes, 'appears as the realization of the mystery, that is, the accomplishment in Christ of the eternal plan which forms the drama of Revelation and which has as its object the reconnection of humanity, the reunification of the universe'.[16] The failure of the church to live this communion, as in divided Christianity, or as is threatened by internal division and conflict, is not simply a matter of practical difficulty, but is a countersign to the accomplishment of the plan of salvation.[17]

Tillard is particularly concerned about affirming this unity as a unity-in-difference, a unity in which the many differences that characterize human existence in time and space are valued as goods of creation, rather than hardened into divisions. 'Salvation', he notes, 'has the effect of abolishing the barriers enclosing each human being in her individuality, each human group in its specificity, each human category in its "difference".'[18] Rooted broadly in a Thomistic appreciation of the value of created nature, Tillard argues that salvation-as-communion is the reversal of Babel through the reconciliation of Jew and Greek in Christ through the power of the Spirit.

Those who were far apart – 'in the strong sense in which the link with hatred gives this term [*loin*: far apart]' – have become close in Christ,[19] not by eliminating their differences, but by removing that which turned otherness into enmity, difference into division.

> Within the logic of the rule of incarnation, the *communion* of each local church – and that of the local churches among themselves – thus corresponds to the variety of creation and the connections of history. It is not a vague reality, ignoring the riches of the natural solidarities that constitute one of the joys of humanity. These are part of the realities that grace assumes, conserves, and promotes by making them into the good of catholicity. The Church is catholic in joining together within the *communion* of Christ Jesus the diversities rooted in creation ... The ecclesiological status of 'difference,' therefore, is positive. It is – in all of its forms – one of the riches in which catholicity is embodied.[20]

Tillard's valuation of the difference between incarnations of Christianity across time and space, and a theory of communion that gives those differences salvific significance, are crucial foundations for his theology of the local church, the relations between the local churches, and for collegial, conciliar and primatial structures. In his major ecclesiological works, Tillard is not speaking only about the differences of theology and practice that separate the Christian churches, but about diversity throughout Christian ecclesial experience. Tillard, writing about 'the church' and 'the local church', attempts to speak not only about difference within the Roman Catholic Church, nor only about difference across ecumenical divisions, but about the relation of unity and difference in the church in both of these situations. I highlight the importance of this judgement by naming it a 'unified theory of communion', emphasizing its formal similarities to a theoretical breakthrough in early modern mechanics. Newton's universal law of gravitation demonstrated that the laws of gravitation were the same for terrestrial and celestial objects; the different interactions observed in the heavens and on the earth were not explained by two different sets of principles, but by one unified theory that analysed both kinds of motion.

Similarly, Tillard's soteriological and ecclesiological theory of communion suggests that there are not two separate kinds of Christian unity, one appropriate for internal relations among those canonically in communion, and another appropriate for external relations among separated Christian churches. The differences between inner-denominational and extra-denominational Christian communion are specific, and not generic. It makes more sense to talk about the universal negotiation of Christian otherness as occurring in (at least) two ways: between 'officially', institutionally separated Christians, and in internal dialogue between Christians who are officially 'already in communion'. Questions about diverse inculturations of Christianity within a worldwide denomination or communion, and about the diverse traditions of Christianity in a divided church, are therefore properly understood as two aspects of the same issue.

This understanding of the connection between inner- and extra-denominational communion is not something unique to the work of Jean-Marie Tillard, nor to contemporary ecclesiology. But what does seem possibly new in Tillard, and newly relevant in the postmodern moment, is the explicit linkage of these two major aspects of Christian communion. Conscious appropriation of the continuing reality of Christian unity as a unity-in-difference makes these areas of negotiation and dialogue both easier, and more difficult. Easier, in that resources, best practices and theoretical frameworks used in one context might be more easily utilized in addressing questions in another area or context. It might make some approaches to understanding the Christian church more difficult, however. Full recognition of diversity within Christian denominations may be profoundly threatening to the cohesiveness of Christian denominations. Recognition that the active negotiation of unity-in-difference, of apostolic fidelity and catholic appropriation of human cultures and histories, is a constant of ecclesial existence and even, following Tillard, the material working out of human salvation, calls into question theories of church which make claims for a context-less Christianity only subsequently incarnated in various forms.

Ecumenical experience and inner-denominational realities

A. Ecumenical experience as a source of practical wisdom

Within this vision of Christian communion as a unity-in-difference that is always already negotiating otherness, there are a number of resources in Christian history and experience to assist the churches in the negotiation of their own otherness. The ecumenical movement is not the only, or necessarily the best, source of practical wisdom for addressing inner-denominational otherness. But there are reasons for taking the experiences of ecumenical dialogue and the movement for Christian unity as a privileged source for inner-denominational dialogue and communion-maintenance. First, both of these kinds of dialogue are explicitly Christian; they are not only about issues of membership, acceptable diversity, and authority in the abstract, but about how to address these issues within explicitly Christian attempts to live out the gospel. Ecumenical experience is uniquely valuable as a source for discussing how to read scripture, interpret the tradition, and share experience within a particular world denomination aware of its diversity. Second, ecumenical dialogue in a variety of forms has become a common experience for many Christians. Individuals with practical experience in dialogue and negotiation between distinct incarnations of Christian faith and life therefore are potential guides that could aid the churches practically and theoretically. Finally, the theological rationale outlined above suggests that, despite their particularities, dialogue between separated Christians and dialogue between diverse, officially united Christians, is not only similar, but more similar than different.

There are some potential difficulties with institutionalizing practices of intra-denominational dialogue by analogy to the ecumenical movement. One, in particular, should be addressed and weighed carefully. Ecumenical dialogue proceeds from a situation of explicit, institutionalized division between Christian churches. Membership in a denomination, church, or world communion provides both dialogue partners with their identity in the ecumenical conversation. Giving a strong identity to disagreeing groups within a Christian communion might further solidify and institutionalize those differences. This danger will vary from case to case and from church to church. The situation in the Anglican Communion is sadly approaching a situation more obviously analogous to the situation of separated churches, but what about the situation in my own denomination, the Roman Catholic Church? There is an obvious danger in setting up dialogue groups between 'traditional' Catholics and 'progressive' Catholics, if by doing so one calls into existence rival and polarized blocs of Catholics at the expense of a vibrant, moderate middle.[21]

B. The need for dialogical structures

One lesson that the ecumenical experience of the past century might give to those seeking to address inner-denominational polarization is the need to emphasize the dialogical nature of such structures. It may be helpful to draw upon the 'working definition' of dialogue with which Bradford Hinze begins his study of dialogue within the Roman Catholic Church. Hinze identifies 'the distinctive dynamic feature of dialogue' as 'the back-and-forth movement in communication between individuals in which people are acting both as speakers and as listeners and there is an exchange of messages that provide the condition for possible common understandings, judgments, decisions, and actions'.[22] He expands the term beyond this model of propositional communication and of one-on-one interaction in defining various modes of practice 'as dialogical because they are premised on an exchange between speakers and listeners striving for mutual understandings, judgments, decisions, and actions'.[23] One can further address the existential dimension of dialogue as an encounter not only of ideas, but of persons, as John Paul II does in the encyclical *Ut Unum Sint*: 'Although the concept of "dialogue" might appear to give priority to the cognitive dimension (*dia-logos*), all dialogue implies a global, existential dimension. It involves the human subject in his or her entirety; dialogue between communities involves in a particular way the subjectivity of each.'[24] These definitions, and others, highlight the existential, 'back-and-forth' encounter between two or more individuals or communities who recognize each other as relative equals, as speakers worthy of listening to and as subjects of action worthy of recognition as such.

In the history of ecumenism, the move to conceive the relations between the churches as a dialogue was a major achievement. It remains a controversial and fragile achievement, both with regard to the historic pillars of the ecumenical movement and with regard to those churches and communities that cannot yet conceive of their relations with other Christians as dialogical. Before this breakthrough, the overwhelming model of interchurch relations was an 'ecumenism of return', in which other Christians were expected to come to their senses and recognize their own church as the true Christian church. While the Roman Catholic and Orthodox churches' positions were most clearly described in terms of the 'return' of their 'wayward daughters', many Protestant churches similarly expected an eventual conversion to what they thought was the obvious destination of Protestantism. It was only when the churches began to recognize each other, despite their differences, as communities to whom one might speak *and* listen, that the ecumenical thaw of the twentieth century began.

The Catholic Common Ground Initiative, launched in 1996 under the initiative of Joseph Cardinal Bernardin of Chicago, is perhaps one of the more important dialogical structures within the Roman Catholic Church in the United States.[25] The methods and 'working principles' enumerated in its founding document, *Called to be Catholic: Church in a Time of Peril*, are strongly consonant with, if not explicitly drawn from, the experiences and 'best practices' of ecumenical dialogue.[26] Its principles attempt to draw members of a church community perceived as polarized into an explicitly dialogical relationship of shared speaking and listening, without falling into a facile relativism. And, like the ecumenical movement, this dialogue was initiated not simply for the sake of cordial discussion, but with a purpose: to strengthen the mission of their church in the United States.[27] In its practice, the Initiative's yearly conventions look strikingly like formal bilateral and multilateral ecumenical dialogues: a core group of approximately twenty-five members, and roughly the same number of invited speakers and guests, meets over a weekend to discuss a topic in formal sessions within a context of shared meals, prayer, and life.[28] In its call for polarized Roman Catholics to abandon their 'Catholicisms of return', in the recognition that such a dialogue was necessary for the continued mission of the church, and in its practice of formal and informal dialogue, the Common Ground Initiative provides one excellent example of a particular denomination appropriating some of the experience and theory first hammered out ecumenically.

The approach of the Catholic Common Ground Initiative to inner-ecclesial otherness has had its critics. The more substantial critiques of the Common Ground Initiative came from conservative members of the Roman Catholic Church in the United States who argued that any entry into dialogue, particularly in matters of faith, opened up the church to relativism. The most trenchant critique came from David L. Schindler in an editorial in the journal *Communio* in 1996.[29] Schindler critiqued the document *Called to be Catholic* not for a particular doctrinal or theological position, but 'rather in [the document's] *ordering and integration* of these christological-ecclesiological principles [called for by Schindler]: it is precisely the lack of this proper ordering and integration', he wrote, 'that distorts already at the beginning the model of dialogue appealed to by the document'.[30] Despite the Initiative's attempts to make 'Jesus Christ, present in Scripture and sacrament ... central to all that we do',[31] Schindler argued that the model of dialogue proposed by *Called to Be Catholic* assumes an ecclesiology eviscerated of its sacramental/hierarchical principles before the conversation even begins.

It is important to take the critiques of Schindler and other critics seriously.[32] Schindler's critique reminds those who would enter into denominational dialogue of the danger of prejudging difficult questions for dialogue, and, as in the case of the ecumenical movement, of the need for regular 'dialogue on the dialogue'.[33] The danger of what is often caricatured as a 'least common denominator' solution to difficult questions is real, both ecumenically and inner-ecclesially.

But while there may be a need to be careful, it seems inadmissible in a Christian ecclesial context to refuse dialogue *tout court*. Even if some of the dialogue partners maintain that the dialogue is more analogous to that between Christians in separated communities than to one between those in full communion, one could not withhold oneself from such dialogue without calling into question the understanding of many Christian churches, the Roman Catholic Church included, that prayer and practice on behalf of greater Christian unity is of the *esse* and not only the *bene esse* of the Christian life. 'To believe in Christ means to desire unity.'[34] The suspicion of polarized conservatives or liberals, who can sometimes appear as dogmatic in their *a priori* refusal to consider the legitimacy of their counterparts' otherness, should provide a careful counterweight to an easy, insubstantial inner-denominational dialogue.

C. Shared conversion

A second lesson that the ecumenical movement provides for inner-denominational dialogue is an awareness that unity is not a project for completion, but a grace to be received, and therefore not simply a matter of theological discussion, institutional negotiation and diplomatic skill.[35] The ecumenical movement teaches that receiving the gift of ecclesial unity is a matter of shared conversion to Christ. The structures developed to promote ecumenical dialogue are inadequate on their own in promoting ecclesial unity. Position papers, dialogue statements and theological proposals are crucial to the sort of dialogue envisioned above, but without a context of shared life and shared prayer leading to mutual conversion, these tools become lifeless, if not hazardous to the pursuit of Christian unity.

Real ecclesial dialogue requires a shift from a 'face to face' encounter of the other to a 'side by side' exploration of a new way of being church together. This is the language developed by the Catholic–Protestant dialogue of the Groupe des Dombes.[36] The group has been active in various forms since the 1930s, and has been a leader in ecumenical dialogue and methodology. It has remained, since its beginnings, an explicitly private initiative, in two senses. First, unlike official ecumenical dialogues, the Groupe des Dombes has always operated with the approval of the competent ecclesial authorities, but not at their initiative or behest. Its choice of topics for conversation, and the ordering of its affairs, has always been its own prerogative. Second, the group focused first upon its own conversations, and on the shared prayer and dialogue of its members, rather than attempting to influence ecumenical discussions in a more public way. The focus of the Groupe des Dombes on starting small, and starting with prayer, provides some useful points for reflection for intra-denominational dialogue.

Catherine Clifford analyses the progression of the Groupe des Dombes as a movement from an initial, critical realist encounter, to a period of dialectic and dialogue, to a period of shared conversion and agreed foundations. She discusses the way in which the group's members began in the initial encounters by meeting one another 'face to face' and then, building upon their mutual trust, turned to work on difficult questions 'side by side'. Clifford emphasizes the importance of the concept of conversion from the initial inspiration of Abbé Couturier, but the history she presents shows the ways in which the mutual conversion to Christ occurred only through a slow and patient process of shared life and sustained conversation.

The history and the success of the Groupe des Dombes can be an important example for inner-ecclesial dialogues. It is a commonplace to note the need for mutual trust in any disputed dialogue between parties, but this example suggests that the growth of trust over time allowed for new possibilities in shared dialogue and discernment not available before entering into the difficult work of long-standing dialogue. The continual focus upon making the group a place not only of shared discussion, but of shared prayer and life, seems to have been crucial in forming and maintaining that trust. The ability of the Groupe des Dombes not only to negotiate statements of consensus, but to turn together, 'side by side' in a call for continued, mutual conversion to Christ, was the result not only of negotiation, but of a sustained conversation between brothers and sisters in Christ.

Within denominational or church bodies, the language of mutual conversion to the will of Christ through a shared reading of the tradition has great potential. It identifies the already shared identity of dialogue partners as those seeking to follow Christ according to the norms and practices of a shared ecclesial tradition. But the example of the Groupe des Dombes suggests that there are better and worse ways to read the Christian tradition together. Within my own Roman Catholic tradition, one can easily see how simultaneous reading of the documents of the Second Vatican Council has not led to shared reading of those texts. The '*relecture convertie*' for which Clifford and the Groupe des Dombes call requires a shared reading rooted not in an attempt to find prooftexts for one's own positions, and that shared reading does not seem to occur without the conscious intentionality, the relative continuity of members, and the intimate prayer life fostered by structures like that of Dombes.

This example and others suggest that a crucial element of inner-ecclesial dialogue must be a certain stability, a relative continuity of shared life outside the formal dialogue. In my own context, one might dare to hope for a dialogue between, say, the editors of *First Things* and the editors of the *National Catholic Reporter*, but ecumenical experience suggests that a single meeting would be worse than no meeting at all, resembling the debates of the sixteenth century far more than the dialogues of the twentieth. Learning to debate without rancour and to trust the goodwill of one's partners requires a sustained, prayer-filled commitment. Without such a context, inner-denominational dialogue seems bound to fail, or at least to remain only at the level of face-to-face negotiation rather than the side-by-side conversion necessary for communion.

D. Multilevel ecclesial dialogue

A third lesson that contemporary intra-ecclesial dialogue might draw from the history of ecumenism is a warning about what Michael Kinnamon has termed the 'professionalization' of the ecumenical movement.[37] In tracing the serious challenges facing contemporary ecumenism, Kinnamon notes that what began as a grassroots protest movement against the scandal of Christian division was domesticated over time in an increasingly professionalized and often clericalized institution. While praising the faithfulness and hard work of those who have made ecumenism their life's work, he writes:

> Ecumenism cannot be left for denominational specialists and theological experts to do on our behalf. It cannot be something that the laity leave for the clergy to worry about. Unless the movement becomes less clericalized, less dominated by 'professional ecumenists', ecumenism will seem increasingly remote and irrelevant to persons in our congregations.[38]

In the case of instances of strained communion within the Christian churches, the difficulties that the ecumenical movement has faced in creating dialogue at numerous levels in the church, and in helping Christians appropriate the consensus statements and other documents produced through formal dialogue, provide an important warning about the need to make inner-denominational dialogue relevant at a number of levels of the churches' life. To take an example from my own context, the Catholic Common Ground Initiative seems to be replicating some of the most successful and least successful strategies of the ecumenical movement. The yearly conventions are by all accounts quite successful in providing a forum for leaders in the United States – lay and ordained, academic and pastoral – to come together in a spirit of dialogue. Like ecumenical bilateral and multilateral dialogues, the participants retain a lasting impression of their real communion with those whom they thought to be irrevocably other. And, like the ecumenical movement, the Initiative has also produced a number of high-quality resources sharing the results of these dialogues and encouraging non-elites to carry on that dialogue at the local level. But how are these resources being used at the local level? Not for lack of effort on the part of the Initiative, the process has not yet been widely engaged beyond its immediate members. The ecumenical experience provides a warning of how easily the professionalization of communion can be its undoing.

One of the more notable and successful attempts to involve Christians at a variety of levels in the churches in ecumenical dialogue was the 'living room dialogues' that occurred in the United States after Vatican II. The dialogues were based on a programme pioneered by Paulist Father William B. Greenspun and the Revd William A. Norgren, the Episcopal Director of the National Council of Churches Faith and Order. The publication of a book suggesting topics for conversation in 1965 brought the model of monthly small group discussions, involving twelve to fifteen lay Christians, to national attention.[39] Within two years, over five thousand groups met in the United States and Canada.[40] By addressing such topics as the nature of dialogue, Christian worship, common heritage, common witness, and eucharistic sharing, these dialogues, by all accounts, greatly energized lay Christians in the work of ecumenism by allowing laypeople at a number of levels to take part in the conversations that drew upon the 'official' conversations of ecumenists and theologians. They not only achieved their primary goal of allowing divided Christian neighbours to encounter each other authentically in a dialogical setting; they also helped to enlist these laypeople in the multilayered project of ecumenism.

In inner-denominational dialogue, there is a need for similar, and more creative, attempts to cultivate dialogues at a variety of levels within a church or denomination. Otherwise, agreements or understandings reached at the level of ecclesial elites will have little or no effect upon large segments of the church. In a United States Catholic context, for instance, where congregations are increasingly determined by their ideological positions rather than their geographic limits, something as creative as the 'living room dialogues' in bringing people together in response to strains in communion will be needed for the long-term maintenance of communion.

E. The challenges of dialogue with the other

Finally, the last lesson that the history of the ecumenical movement teaches those promoting inner-denominational dialogue is the logic of the cross. As the responses to the Common Ground Initiative show, attempts within the Roman Catholic Church to bridge internal divisions have not always been welcome. Those attempting to maintain the unity of the Anglican Communion can testify to the difficulty of remaining in a centre between two coalescing institutional poles. This difficulty ranges from the simple awkwardness of being misunderstood by one's colleagues, peers, and sisters and brothers in Christ, to the institutional and financial risks of refusing to be drawn into one of two antagonistic camps.

A look at the history of the ecumenical movement should be sobering to those who would attempt inner-denominational dialogue. One could point to the crucified years of one of the Roman Catholic Church's greatest ecumenists and theologians, Yves Congar, OP. Congar's struggles demonstrate the personal, material and spiritual danger of pursuing dialogue with one's brothers and sisters.[41] While it would be pathological to enter into dialogue to provoke suffering, it would be irresponsible not to recognize that discipleship in the pursuit of communion carries the same costs as all true discipleship. Whether through marginalization, material insecurity, misunderstanding, or the suspicion of one's friends and peers, those expressing their love of Christ and of his church through the pursuit of dialogue will be uncomfortable, at best, in their position between the quasi-Donatist certainties of others in their communities.

Conclusion

Despite the need for authentic 'Christian pessimism' in these endeavours, the theology of communion with which I began, the history of the Christian church, and the particular history of the ecumenical movement, all suggest that some way of negotiating difference within Christianity is not optional. Communion between those who are 'others' is a mark of the church, not a mere concession to a situation of imperfection. Given the increasing recognition of pluralism within our churches, it is no longer possible or advisable, if it ever was, to assume the coincidence of structural or juridical communion and the graced communion of Christian believers. The experience of Christian difference in the ecumenical movement provides some signposts for attempts to respond to internal ecclesial division. It is my hope that members of other Christian denominations may find my attempts to explore some of the practical implications of ecumenical theology and practice of communion in my context helpful in theirs. The reality of the reconciliation as sisters and brothers of those who were once enemies is the proclamation of Good News for our globalized, pluralist times. Allowing the church to be a sign of that reality, and bearing the burden of being active and creative in mending and tending communion within and without our churches, will be a crucial task for this generation.

Notes

1. Jonathan Sacks, *The Dignity of Difference* (New York: Continuum, 2002).
2. One indication of the complexity of these issues is the lack of good vocabulary to talk about otherness between and within those churches. In this chapter I will be using the terms 'intra-denominational' and 'inner-denominational' interchangeably to discuss relations within Christian churches and communions, despite the awkwardness of those terms as well as the objection some communities raise, including the Roman Catholic and Orthodox Churches, at being identified as a 'denomination' in parallel to other denominations.
3. Jean-Marie-Roger Tillard, OP, *Église d'Églises: L'Ecclésiologie de Communion* (Paris: Cerf, 1987).
4. Francis A. Sullivan, 'Recent Ecclesiology', *Modern Theology* 9 (1993), 419.
5. Jean-Marie-Roger Tillard, OP, *Chair de l'Église, Chair du Christ: Aux Sources de l'Ecclésiologie de communion* (Paris: Cerf, 1992).
6. Jean-Marie-Roger Tillard, OP, *L'Église Locale: Ecclésiologie de Communion et Catholicité* (Paris: Cerf, 1996).
7. See Brian P. Flanagan, 'Communion, Diversity, and Salvation: The Contribution of Jean-Marie Tillard, OP, to Systematic Ecclesiology' (PhD Diss., Boston College, 2007), 84–9.
8. The Lutheran theologian Michael Root has addressed the need for 'scalar categories' ecclesiology that avoid the 'all-or-nothing' conceptions of unity, validity, membership, etc. See Michael Root, 'Bishops, Ministry, and the Unity of the Church in Ecumenical Dialogue: Deadlock, Breakthrough, or Both?', *CTSA Proceedings* 62 (2007), 32–4.
9. Jean-Marie-Roger Tillard, OP, *L'Évêque de Rome* (Paris: Cerf, 1982).
10. See Dennis Doyle, *Communion Ecclesiology: Vision and Versions* (Maryknoll, NY: Orbis, 2000).
11. Prominently, that of Nicholas M. Healy. See 'Ecclesiology and Communion', *Perspectives in Religious Studies* 31 (2004), 273–90; and *Church, World and the Christian Life: Practical-Prophetic Ecclesiology*, Cambridge Studies in Christian Doctrine 7 (Cambridge: Cambridge University Press, 2000), esp. 44–6. See also Thomas P. Looney, '*Koinonia* Ecclesiology: How Solid a Foundation?', *One in Christ* 36 (2000), 145–66.
12. As, for instance, that of John Zizioulas, *Being as Communion: Studies in Personhood and the Church* (Crestwood, NY: St Vladimir's Press, 1985); and, *Communion and Otherness* (London: T&T Clark, 2006); and that of Miroslav Volf, *After Our Likeness: The Church as the Image of the Trinity* (Grand Rapids: Eerdmans, 1998).
13. As that of Joseph Ratzinger, summarized most thoroughly in *Pilgrim Fellowship of Faith: The Church as Communion*, ed. Stephan Otto Horn and Vinzenz Pfnür, trans. Henry Taylor (San Francisco: Ignatius, 2005). Ratzinger's thought exemplifies what Gerard Mannion, following the analysis of Philip Murnion, refers to as the 'official communion ecclesiology'. See G. Mannion, *Ecclesiology and Postmodernity* (Collegeville, MN: Liturgical Press, 2007), 55–71.
14. For a more extensive treatment, see Flanagan, 139–49.
15. *Église d'Églises*, 33. See also ibid., 33–6; *L'Église Locale*, 135–41. Translations are my own, unless otherwise noted.
16. *Église d'Églises*, 68. See also *L'Église Locale*, 83–8.
17. Cf. *Église d'Églises*, 186–215; *L'Église Locale*, 89–104.

18. 'L'Universel et le Local', *Irénikon* 61 (1988), 28–9.
19. *Église d'Églises*, 69–70.
20. *Chair de l'Église*, 23.
21. See Mark S. Massa, SJ, 'Beyond "Liberal" and "Conservative"', in *Inculturation and the Church in North America*, ed. T. Frank Kennedy (New York: Crossroad, 2006), 127–44.
22. Bradford E. Hinze, *Practices of Dialogue in the Roman Catholic Church* (New York: Continuum, 2006), 8.
23. Ibid., 9.
24. John Paul II, *Ut Unum Sint*, §28. Also cited in Konrad Reiser, 'The Nature and Purpose of Ecumenical Dialogue', *Ecumenical Review* 52 (2000), 288–9.
25. For background and analysis, see Hinze, 112–29. See also Joseph Bernardin and Oscar H. Lipscomb, *Catholic Common Ground Initiative: Foundational Documents* (Eugene, Oregon: Wipf and Stock, 1997).
26. Bernardin and Lipscomb, ibid., 42–3.
27. Ibid., 44.
28. See Hinze, *Practices of Dialogue in the Roman Catholic Church*, 119–23.
29. David L. Schindler, 'On the Catholic Common Ground Project: The Christological Foundations of Dialogue', *Communio* 23 (1996), 823–51. See also Robert P. Imbelli, 'The Unknown Beyond the Word: The Pneumatological Foundations of Dialogue', *Communio* 24 (1997), 326–35; Terry Tekippe, 'With Whom Do We Dialogue?', *Communio* 24 (1997), 336–8; Gary Culpepper, 'Dialogue within the Church', *Communio* 24 (1997), 339–46; and Schindler, 'The Pneumatological Foundations of Dialogue: Response to Imbelli, Tekippe, and Culpepper', *Communio* 25 (1998), 366–76.
30. Schindler, 'On the Catholic Common Ground Project', 826.
31. Bernardin and Lipscomb, *Catholic Common Ground Initiative: Foundational Documents*, 40.
32. I am grateful to Prof. Dennis Doyle for encouraging me to attend to this critique.
33. Indeed, the critiques of Schindler and others provided the impetus for a fuller clarification of the method and goals of the Initiative. See Oscar H. Lipscomb, 'Dialogue: A Labor in Love', in Bernardin and Lipscomb, *Catholic Common Ground Initiative: Foundational Documents*, 79–96.
34. *Ut Unum Sint*, §9.
35. See Michael Kinnamon, *The Vision of the Ecumenical Movement and How It Has Been Impoverished by Its Friends* (St Louis: Chalice Press, 2003).
36. In this section I am drawing on the excellent work of Catherine E. Clifford, who, in her 2005 study, outlined the history of the Groupe and detailed how it grew from the founding vision of Abbé Couturier to make major contributions to Catholic–Protestant dialogue in France and beyond. Catherine E. Clifford, *The Groupe des Dombes: A Dialogue of Conversion* (New York: Peter Lang, 2005).
37. Kinnamon, *The Vision of the Ecumenical Movement*, 75–86.
38. Ibid., 84.
39. William B. Greenspun, CSP, and William A. Norgren, *Living Room Dialogues* (Glen Rock, NJ: National Council of Churches of Christ in the USA and Paulist Press, 1965).
40. William B. Greenspun, CSP, and Cynthia C. Wedel, *Second Living Room Dialogues* (Glen Rock, NJ: National Council of Churches of Christ in the USA and Paulist Press, 1967), ix.

41. See Congar's journal of his period of exile, *Journal d'un Théologien (1946–56)*, ed. É. Fouilloux (Paris: Cerf, 2000); and Alberto Melloni, 'The System and the Truth in the Diaries of Yves Congar', in *Yves Congar: Theologian of the Church*, ed. Gabriel Flynn (Louvain: Peeters, 2005), 277–302.

Chapter 11

EVANGELICAL ECCLESIOLOGY AS AN ANSWER TO ETHNIC IMPAIRED CHRISTIAN COMMUNITY? AN INQUIRY INTO THE THEOLOGY OF MIROSLAV VOLF

Eddy Van der Borght

Introduction

Being Christian means being a member of the church. At the same time, Christians belong by nature to other communities, such as families, tribes, ethnic groups, nations, and so forth. At various periods in history and at specific places, the relationship between those identities has become problematic. Ethnicity has been a challenge for the identity of the church throughout the history of the church. In fact, the first major crisis in the church during the New Testament period was related to an issue in which ethnicity played a central role. Could Gentiles become Christians without conforming to Jewish identity markers such as circumcision and food laws? Recent developments have highlighted the need for a new and more thorough investigation of the issue. The reshaping of Europe as well as the globalization that causes the resurgence of many diaspora churches and migrant churches challenge Christian theologians to rethink ethnicity as a factor in church identity. Is the traditional Protestant relaxed attitude to national and ethnic churches justified? Or should more gain be expected from the Petrine ministry of the bishops of Rome to counter a too close relationship between national and/or ethnic communities and the church? How can the unity, the catholicity, and the apostolicity of the church be confessed if churches are ethnically co-defined?

This chapter offers an analysis of ethnic factors that impair Christian communities and focuses on the question whether the evangelical ecclesiology of Miroslav Volf is able to overcome the church-dividing potential of ethnic differences. My point of departure is the claim of Zizioulas that the ethnic factor is a non-legitimate form of otherness within the Christian community.

Zizioulas' remark as a recent example

In the introduction of his 2006 volume *Communion and Otherness*, John Zizioulas described an embarrassing example of a Christian community dividing otherness from within his own Orthodox tradition.[1] After indicating the unifying potential of the office of the bishop, protecting diversity within the Christian community, and after reminding us of the rule of canon 8 of Nicaea – there can be only one bishop in a church – he continues with the following remark:

> The present-day situation of the Orthodox diaspora is such an unfortunate, dangerous and totally unacceptable phenomenon. It allows ethnic and cultural differences to become grounds of ecclesial communion centred on different bishops. A bishop who does not in himself transcend ethnic and cultural differences becomes a minister of division and not of unity. This is something that the Orthodox should consider very seriously indeed, if distortion of the very nature of the Church is to be avoided.[2]

He expresses fear of ecclesial chaos in diaspora situations, in which one church in one region is no longer led by one bishop. In this case the multitude of bishops in one area is not legitimated with theological differences but with ethnic and/or cultural variation. Ethnic differences have the potential to become church divisive. Community on the basis of ethnic identity runs the risk of building communion by excluding otherness.

At the same time, Zizioulas' remark about the danger of ethnicity as a basis for ecclesial communion has a limited scope. It is only a side-remark, which is not repeated in the rest of the articles in the volume. The approach through episcopal authority tends to reduce the issue to a canonical one. Additionally, it is limited to the Christian diaspora context. This approach suggests that division within the Christian community on the basis of ethnicity is a real but at the same time minor problem.

There is reason to doubt this implication. The ethnic threat to church unity is also present in the homeland. Greece and the Greek Orthodox Church, both 'home' for Zizioulas, illustrate this. In Greece, the Orthodox Church is the centre of the defence of Greek national identity. And the church considers itself as the soul of the nation. This example can be broadened to most of the Eastern and Oriental Orthodox Churches, which tend to define their identity as local churches not only in terms of region, but also in terms of a link with a people, nation, language, and a specific interpretation of history. The development of autocephalous churches within the Orthodox tradition has been a canonical instrument that allows for even closer links between church and ethnicity.

This Greek example can also be brought into the context of the relationship between church and nations in the whole of Eastern and Central Europe. A close link between the various peoples and nations and different religions, in most cases Christian confessions, marks the whole region. In many other countries, a strong link between the Roman Catholic Church and the nation developed. Poland, Ireland, Italy, Croatia and Spain are well-known European examples. These examples show that linkage of church and nation is not only an issue in central and eastern Europe.

However, within Western Christianity the strongest examples of defining the church by ethnic elements are to be found in the Protestant traditions, which often have weaker forms of episcopal ministry to protect the unity of the church and in which differences often lead to divisions. Otherness in relation to confessional or ethnic difference too often has given way to separate denominations that are in many cases not even on speaking terms with one another – thus not recognizing each other's baptism, not extending eucharistic hospitality to those outside their denomination, and not recognizing each other's ministries. This situation has led to Protestant state churches, established churches and national churches.

The conclusion of this overview can only be that it is not a coincidence that migrant churches often have problems integrating in the local churches that stem from the same confessional tradition. The fact that churches are often co-determined by ethnic features makes the integration of individual believers in congregations with different ethnic roots a serious problem. It is not only a challenge for the newcomers, but also for the congregations and churches with a long history in the region. Does the cultural and ethnic determination of the church leave enough space for a Christian who does not have the same cultural roots? How much room is there for cultural and ethnic diversity in the parishes and churches? How local can a church be without losing its global calling? What holds the Christian community together, the common faith or the common culture?

The inability to cross cultural and ethnic boundaries within the church is a major obstacle on the way to communion with God in Christ and with one another. Paul's powerful claim that once one is baptized in Christ 'there is neither Jew nor Greek' challenges an attitude that is tempted to accept the primacy of cultural and ethnic identity markers. The ethnic and cultural determination of churches places the fundamental confession of the catholicity and unity of the church under great pressure. The issue is not limited to some specific regions, nor is it limited to some confessional families. It is a global issue that is a challenge for all Christian denominations. Moreover, in our globalizing world the pressure to deal with it has become more urgent.

A past ecclesial issue theologically neglected

We should be aware that the challenge is not new. The twentieth century has witnessed massive violence on a scale never seen before. Genocides were committed and ethnically legitimized for the higher cause of the future of the nation. European churches, in particular, had to deal with a gulf of nationalism that has swept over the continent since the second half of the nineteenth century.

In recent years I have analysed some of the ecumenical documents that have dealt with ethnicity reacting to violent and exclusive forms of nationalism in the twentieth century. One of the most well-known examples is the Life and Work Conference (1937) on *Church, Community and State* that was an answer to the nationalistic governments of Italy and Germany, in particular, which used ever more threatening and violent language.[3] Renewed outbreaks of nationalist conflicts in central and south-eastern Europe in the 1990s stimulated the Reformation churches gathered at the Leuenberg Church Fellowship to study the issue once again. The Fellowship accepted a study document *Church – People – State – Nation* at their fifth General Assembly in Belfast in 2001.[4] The third document I used in my research was *The Charta Oecumenica*, which was also accepted in 2001.[5]

These are my conclusions:[6]

The limitation of a pastoral approach

In the past, the ecumenical movement only reacted when a major nationalistic or ethnic upsurge occurred. In these cases, major international crises demanded a careful, diplomatic, and – in the case of the churches – pastoral reaction. Although the pre-Second-World-War conferences of the ecumenical movement condemned an extreme nationalistic or racist approach of humanity, they always were very careful not to state positions that could unnecessarily hurt the churches and individual Christians who where suffering under nationalist violence (especially in Nazi Germany.) When the crisis was over, the ecumenical movement returned to its own agenda of which nationalism was not considered to be a key issue. So the discussion on the value of nation and country for the global society and the church was not executed in depth. The ecumenical movement of the twentieth century has left us with a heritage of mainly pastoral reactions to nationalism in situations of crisis.

The absence of Faith and Order

Conferences of Life and Work (Stockholm 1925 and Oxford 1937) and of the International Missionary Council (Edinburgh 1910 and Tambaram 1938) reacted to the threat posed by nationalism. Accordingly, the response had a practical and mission-strategic nature. Life and Work and the International Missionary Council should not be blamed for this. On the contrary, they did what was expected of them and delivered good work. The problem is that the third pillar of the twentieth-century ecumenical movement, Faith and Order, was absent in the debates. The theological department let the opportunity pass by. We can only observe that the second World Conference of Faith and Order, held in Edinburgh (August 1937) one month after the Oxford conference of Life and Work, did not discuss the theme of the identity of the church in relation to the nation. The national church is only mentioned under the heading of obstacles to church unity, in part, theological or ecclesiological, and, in equal part, sociological or political: 'Such obstacles are met in the case of a national Church which hallows the common life of a given people, but is at the same time exposed to the perils of an exclusive provincialism or of domination by a secular state.' After giving examples of obstacles due to historical factors, we read about churches that have different cultural origins agreeing on doctrinal matters. 'These Churches are not conscious of any obstacles to such union because of mutually exclusive doctrines. They are, however, kept apart by barriers of nationality, race, class, general culture, and, more particularly, by slothful self-content and self-sufficiency.'[7] It is remarkable that, in these two quotes, descriptive language is mixed with normative language. The heading 'Non-theological obstacles for church unity' suggests the issue relates to cultural elements that do not influence the theological identity of the church.

The weaknesses of the theological argumentation

The line of reasoning always travels from a universality that is based on creation theology and soteriological elements towards a supranational world order with a need for international solidarity. Striking is the lack of ecclesiological argumentation. Therefore, the line of theological argumentation tends to address the world and its structure. The world – not the church – has to learn its theological lesson.

Rereading the harvest of theological argumentations, a second weakness becomes obvious. The conferences of Paris (1934) and Oxford (1937) focused more on the threat posed by the state than by the nation. Both state and nation are elements of the new type of nationalism that emerged – together with the appearance of the new phenomenon of the nation-states – during the nineteenth century. The Paris Conference has the relationship between church and state as its theme. The Oxford Conference chose the title, *Church, Community and State.* However, the main challenge was to give an answer to the claims of totalitarian states, such as the fascist state in Germany and the communist state in the Soviet Union. Oldham, the organizer of the Oxford Conference, was well aware of the particular challenge posed by the nation as an identification marker for people, but aggressive types of states formed the main frame of his perception. It is not by chance that the ecumenical movement reacted more strongly to the state than to the nation challenge. In the first half of the twentieth century, the ecumenical movement was almost uniquely a Protestant cause. And Protestants were better equipped to deal with the issue of state than that of nation. Since their origin, the Protestant churches discussed their authority *vis-à-vis* the state after the decline of the religious monopoly position of the Roman Church in western and central Europe from the end of the Middle Ages. But how to relate to a country, nation or people was a far less certain issue for most Protestant churches.

Miroslav Volf

In recent years when I discussed the issue with students, they often referred to Miroslav Volf, the current director of the Center for Faith and Culture and professor of systematic theology at Yale University. He wrote an ecumenical ecclesiology from a Free Church perspective,[8] and, in the same period, finished a theological exploration of identity, otherness and reconciliation.[9] The stimulus for the latter work stemmed from the ethnic violence that led to the dissolution of the former Yugoslavia. Born in Croatia as the son of a Pentecostal preacher, he grew up in Novi Sad in Serbia during Tito's Yugoslavian regime. In his 2006-published volume, *The End of Memory: Remembering Rightly in a Violent World,* he tells how during his military service in 1984 in the then communist Yugoslavia, he had been a victim of interrogations by a security officer who accused him of being a spy for the West and threatened to lock him in jail for eight years.[10] His revelation of the haunting memories of abuse indicates the existential and personal nature of the issue. In the last part of this contribution, I want to investigate whether Volf – as an ecclesiologist and theologian dealing with the issue of identity and otherness – has been able to deal with the issue of ethnicity in relation to the identity of the church. I will begin with an analysis of the volume on the theme 'identity', followed by a close reading of his major work on ecclesiology as far as it is relevant for our theme. The conclusion will answer the question whether his contribution is relevant to the issue of church and ethnicity.

Exclusion and embrace

In the introduction to *Exclusion and Embrace*, Volf begins his analysis with the observation that ethnic and cultural conflicts are part of the larger problem of identity and otherness, which form the heart of our social realities.[11] Leaving the suggestion of social arrangements to social scientists, the theologian Volf focuses on 'fostering the kind of social agents capable of envisioning and creating just, truthful, and peaceful societies, and on shaping a cultural climate in which such agents will thrive'.[12]

In the next chapter, he indicates how the church has missed the opportunity to be a social agent of reconciliation. 'The overriding commitment to their culture serves churches worst in situations of conflict. Churches, the presumed agents of reconciliation, are at best impotent and at worst accomplices in the strife.'[13] Identification with the claims of ethnic and cultural communities leads, among parishioners and clergy, to legitimization and even sacralization of ethnic conflict. As a consequence, a distancing of particular cultures is needed that asks for a departure for which Abraham is the model. 'At the very core of Christian identity lies an all-encompassing change of loyalty, from a given culture with its gods to the God of all cultures.'[14]

At the same time, 'the grounding of unity and universality in the scandalous particularity of the suffering body of God's Messiah is what makes Paul's thought structurally so profoundly different from the kinds of beliefs in the all-importance of the undifferentiated universal spirit . . .'.[15] Unity is not the result of 'sacred violence' which obliterates the particularities of the 'bodies', but a fruit of Christ's self-sacrifice that breaks down the enmity between them (Eph. 2.14). As a consequence, baptism into Christ should not be understood as a wiping out of bodily inscribed differences, but as being brought into a differentiated body of Christ.[16] The conclusion of the first leg of his argument – religion must be de-ethnicized so that ethnicity can be de-sacralized – is now complemented with a second leg: each culture can retain its own cultural specificity. Christians are distant, and yet they belong. Their difference is internal to the culture.[17]

He then argues why Christians should distance themselves from their own cultures. It is the consequence of the work of the Spirit who recreates people in 'catholic personalities', enriched by otherness.[18] A catholic personality requires a catholic community. For Volf, catholicity has a specific meaning. In contrast to the Roman Catholic understanding that links catholicity, in the first place, with the universal church and understands the local church as catholic insofar as it is linked to the universal church, Volf prefers to understand catholicity in a Free Church tradition: every local church is a catholic community insofar as it does not isolate itself from other churches in other cultures, and insofar as it does not declare itself sufficient to itself and its own culture. In this way every local church is a catholic community because all other churches are part of that church, and all of them shape its identity. All churches together form a worldwide communion that Volf qualifies as 'ecumenical', reserving the qualification 'catholic' for these local churches that are open to other churches in other cultures.[19]

In conclusion, four observations can be made. First, by introducing the concepts of 'distance' and 'belonging', Volf has tried to bridge the cultural gap between particularity and universality and between the one and the many in a Christian perspective. It is an alternative for the traditional understanding of Christian existence as 'in' but not 'of' the world. Second, although he refers to the Christian church, he is not so much interested in the identity of the Christian churches as he is in the consequence for the Christian understanding of the unity of the diverse cultures in society. Third, he abruptly introduces the concept 'catholicity', in the first place, to qualify individuals, and only in the second place to define a specific Christian community. Fourth, catholicity of the church is a label for the local church and not for the universal church.

After our likeness

In the introduction to the American edition, he explains that the purpose of the book is to counter individualism in Protestant ecclesiology by giving proper due to both person and community through an inquiry into the relevance of the doctrine of the Trinity for the relation between person and community.[20] After analysing Ratzinger's and Zizioulas' actual examples from the Western and Eastern traditions to relate personhood and community in the church through an interpretation of the doctrine of the Trinity in Part I, Part II is dedicated to building a Free Church variant. The church is, in the first place, a community of people (*Wir sind die Kirche!*), an assembled community of faithful people coming together in the name of the Lord Jesus in order to worship Christ and to bear witness to him. But the intra-trinitarian relationships should shape the ecclesial relationships as well. Only when individual believers participate in the Spirit of God who indwells the community can this community correspond to the Trinity. Next, the *perichoresis* of the divine persons has also inter-ecclesial relevance. Like the divine persons, different churches have different identifying characteristics, by means of which they should enrich one another.[21] In the same way as the identity of the Son is determined by his relations with the Father and the Spirit, the identity of the local churches is co-determined by their relations with other churches. In order to develop this further, in this volume he also introduces the concept of catholicity – the topic of the last chapter of the book.

He defines the catholicity of the entire people of God as 'the ecclesial dimension of the eschatological fullness of salvation for the entirety of created reality'.[22] Because of this eschatological approach to the catholicity of the church, the local church as the church *in via* can only live its catholicity in an anticipatory way, only partially realizing its catholicity. Volf identifies openness to other churches and loyalty to the apostolic tradition as the two marks of catholicity for the local church. With Congar, Volf recognizes the catholicity of creation as a second source for the catholicity of the church. He does not see this creational dimension of catholicity expressed in a territorial principle of one church in one specific locality, but in universal openness for all human beings who confess faith in Christ without distinction. 'Any church that excludes certain people on the basis of race or social class, or that is willing to tolerate such exclusion with indifference, is denying its own catholicity.'[23] Finally, he describes the subjective dimension of catholicity in relation to personhood, which consists not only in the internalization of what is common to all, but also in the adaptation of what is specific to each.[24]

Conclusion

To conclude this section, I will try to answer three questions. First, is Volf giving a topical answer to the challenge of church and ethnicity, as some of my students suggested? Not really. In *Exclusion and Embrace*, the challenge is cultural, not ecclesial – how to combine identity and otherness in society – and the answer is found in theological anthropology. In *In Our Likeness*, the challenge is not ethnicity, but individualism within Free Churches. The answer is found in the community of the local church. Second, do these books contribute to solving the problem of ethnicity within the churches? Not really. In fact, for Volf it is not truly a problem since the church in the

Free Church perspective is an assembly of individual faithful. Their new relationship with Christ simultaneously links them to other believers. Their cultural identities are not erased, but they do not influence the identity of the church. Third, is the Free Church model the answer to the question of ethnicity in the church? In some way it is, especially for the magisterial Protestant and for the Orthodox Churches, which identify local churches with states, nations, language and regions. But at the same time, the basic model of the Free Church is very vulnerable, especially because the local church is, in reality – though often not officially – a very locally culturally determined church. With its exclusive definition of catholicity as local church without ministerial catholicity, the local congregations are always under great pressure to identify their culture with the gospel.

Notes

1. John D. Zizioulas, *Communion and Otherness: Further Studies in Personhood and the Church* (London and New York: T&T Clark, 2006), 1–3.
2. Ibid., 8–9.
3. In the series, *Church, Community and State*, eight volumes appeared in the years 1937 and 1938: vol. 1: *The Church and its Function in Society*, vol. 2: *The Christian Understanding of Man*, vol. 3: *The Kingdom of God and History*, vol. 4: *The Christian Faith and the Common Life*, vol. 5: *Church and Community*, vol. 6: *Church, Community, and State in Relation to Education*, vol. 7: *The Universal Church and the World of Nations*, vol. 8: *The Churches Survey Their Task: The Report of the Conference at Oxford, July 1937, on Church, Community and State* (London: George Allen & Unwin, 1937). For a detailed analysis see E. A. J. G. Van der Borght, 'Oxford Revisited: A Re-reading of the Report on Church and Volk at the Life and Work Conference in Oxford 1937', *Exchange* 33, 4 (2004), 372–400.
4. *Kirche, Volk, Staat, Nation: ein Beitrag zu einem schwierigen Verhältnis: Beratungsergebnis der Regionalgruppe der Leuenberger Kirchengemeinschaft Süd- und Südosteuropa* (Frankfurt am Main: Lembeck, 2002). See for a detailed analysis, E. A. J. G. Van der Borght, 'The Leuenberg Document *Church – People – State – Nation*: A Critical Assessment', *Exchange* 3, 3 (2002), 278–98.
5. It was accepted by the Conference of European Churches, which includes almost all Orthodox, Protestant, Anglican, Old Catholic and independent churches in Europe, and by the Council of European Bishops Conferences, which represents all Roman Catholic Bishops Conferences in Europe. Viorel Ionita and Sarah Numico (eds), *Charta Oecumenica: A Text, a Process and a Dream of the Churches in Europe* (Geneva: WWC, 2003). See for my analysis, Eddy Van der Borght, 'Uniting Europe as a Challenge to the Future of National Churches', in *Charting Churches in a Changing Europe: Charta Oecumenica and the Process of Ecumenical Encounter*, ed. Tim and Ivana Noble, Martien E. Brinkman, Jochen Hilberath (Amsterdam and New York: Editions Rodopi, 2006), 105–25, especially the part 'The Charta Oecumenica on Divisions', 118–23.

6. See, Van der Borght, 'Uniting Europe as a Challenge to the Future of National Churches', 123–5.
7. L. Hodgson (ed.), *The Second World Conference on Faith and Order held at Edinburgh, August 3–18, 1937* (London: SCM, 1938), 258–9.
8. His Habilitationsschrift under supervision of Jürgen Moltmann at the Evangelical Theological Faculty of the University of Tübingen, entitled *Wir sind die Kirche!* (1993), was originally published in German: *Trinität und Gemeinschaft: eine ökumenische Ekklesiologie* (Neukirchen-Vluyn: Neukirchener Verlag, 1996), and later in English: *After Our Likeness: The Church as the Image of the Trinity* (Grand Rapids, MI and Cambridge, UK: Eerdmans, 1998).
9. M. Volf, *Exclusion and Embrace: A Theological Exploration of Identity, Otherness, and Reconciliation* (Nashville: Abingdon Press, 1996).
10. M. Volf, *The End of Memory: Remembering Rightly in a Violent World* (Grand Rapids, MI and Cambridge, UK: Eerdmans, 2006).
11. Volf, *Exclusion and Embrace*, 13–20.
12. Ibid., 23.
13. Ibid., 36.
14. Ibid., 40.
15. Ibid., 47.
16. Ibid., 48.
17. Ibid., 49.
18. Ibid., 51.
19. Ibid., 51.
20. Volf, *After Our Likeness: The Church as the Image of the Trinity*, 2.
21. Ibid., 213.
22. Ibid., 267.
23. Ibid., 278.
24. Ibid., 281.

PART III

ECCLESIOLOGY IN GLOBAL CONTEXTS

Chapter 12

ON BEING A EUROPEAN CATHOLIC:
THE POLITICS OF INCLUSION ENCOUNTERS AN ECCLESIOLOGY
OF EXCLUSION

Julie Clague

The politics of inclusion: from The Hague to Lisbon

Sixty years ago, Europe was trying to piece itself together and understand itself anew following the destruction, carnage and genocide of its catastrophic conflict that had escalated into the deadliest war in history. There was no stomach for ideologies; ideologies had done enough damage. A strong dose of pragmatism was needed. Under the auspices of the newly formed United Nations, and despite historical antagonisms based on national, political, economic, religious and cultural differences, nation-states that could normally do no more than agree to differ signed up to the 1948 *Universal Declaration of Human Rights* (UDHR). As Catholic philosopher Jacques Maritain, one of the drafters of the document, observed, political opponents could agree on the list of human rights, but not on reasons why.[1] No matter. This camel-like product of a committee has become the cornerstone of customary international law and remains a landmark statement of humanity's shared values.

That same year, delegates from across Europe convened The Hague Congress, which set out plans for greater European political and economic unity and cooperation. Ten nations concretized these proposals by forming the Council of Europe. Reflecting this growing momentum in favour of peaceful coexistence and mutual assistance, French foreign minister Robert Schuman put forward a plan to overcome Franco-German enmity through the pooling of resources. A peaceful, united Europe cannot be created overnight, Schuman argued, it will be built step-wise 'through concrete achievements which first create a *de facto* solidarity'.[2] Recognizing the strategic and economic importance of coal and steel as the ingredients necessary to fuel economies and fight wars, Schuman saw that such a pact would offer much-needed employment and urban regeneration to industrial areas previously devoted to the production of armaments. Furthermore, by taking coal and steel production out of the hands of any one nation, war would become 'not merely unthinkable, but materially impossible'. Seeing the potential benefits of overcoming mistrust, France and West Germany were joined in the venture by Italy and the Benelux nations, thus giving birth to the European Coal and Steel Community (ECSC), from which grew the European Economic Community (EEC). Schuman announced his practical plan for postwar reconciliation and cooperation on 9 May 1950, the date now associated with the birth of the European Union (EU).

Since these founding events there have been further episodes in the story of the unification of Europe expressed primarily through enlargement of the European Union, greater cooperation between Member States, relaxation of border restrictions, the emergence of the eurozone, and many other initiatives. On paper, the latest stage in the process of clarifying the aims and objectives of the European Union is the text of the Treaty of Lisbon, which was signed by the Heads of the 27 EU Member States on 13 December 2007.[3] The Treaty of Lisbon combines the sort of practical aims espoused by the ECSC and the visionary sentiments of the UDHR. It contains within it both an expression of the mission and values of the EU and an outline of the nuts and bolts operations that allow the EU to function. The aims of the Treaty were to make the EU economically stronger and its mechanisms more efficient, democratic and transparent. It arose out of an awareness that the behemoth-like structures of governance at the EU were making its citizens feel estranged from, irrelevant to and disillusioned with its democratic and participatory mechanisms. The Treaty attempted to strike that difficult balance between investing sufficient power in the structures of governance to allow the effective running of the EU, thereby preventing self-interested Member States derailing its objectives, and at the same time ensuring Member States retain legitimate autonomy, that decision-making is as far as possible devolved, and the EU avoids disempowering the very citizens it represents.

Lisbon grew out of the EU Constitution of 2004, which was in large part brokered during Ireland's Presidency of the EU by the then prime minister, Taoiseach Bertie Ahern. In the absence of the wisdom of Solomon to negotiate between the competing interests and concerns of Member States, Ahern had to resort to shuttle diplomacy, draw on a career of coalition politics and employ the same shrewd pragmatism that had helped secure the Good Friday Agreement of 1998 – no doubt convinced in the light of that experience that, against the odds, political will can overcome ideological differences and historical hurt. Ahern's achievement confirms his place in the EU's history books but, ironically, Ireland's voters flexed their democratic muscles in a referendum on 13 June 2008, rejecting the Treaty which had been due to come into force on 1 January 2009, thereby stalling the process of ratification and interrupting the European Project once again.

As we will see, the political achievements and setbacks of the EU in its efforts to build an inclusive, peaceful and prosperous Europe are not unrelated to the sort of ups and downs faced by Churches charged with instituting humane structures, teachings and practices that express and embody their mission and values. Here attention will be focused on the Roman Catholic Church and what we can learn about its ecclesiological identity from its dealings in Europe. We will find that the political vision of the EU provides an interesting context for exploring Roman Catholic ecclesiology and what it means to be a European Catholic today.

The political vision of the European Union

The stated goals of the European Union are to promote peace, security and solidarity within Europe and beyond. The values that inspire and shape these objectives are described in the Preamble of the Treaty on European Union as Europe's cultural, religious and humanist patrimony, and are outlined in Article 2 of the same text:

> The Union is founded on the values of respect for human dignity, freedom, democracy, equality, the rule of law and respect for human rights, including the rights of persons belonging to minorities. These values are common to the Member States in a society in which pluralism, non-discrimination, tolerance, justice and equality between women and men prevail.[4]

Thus the Treaty sets out the moral trajectory and political mission statement of a European Union that comprises 450 million citizens, and establishes the next phase of the collaborative effort that is the European Project. Not since the *Universal Declaration of Human Rights* has there been such an ambitious political effort to characterize and realize the marks of a moral civilization. The Treaty's lofty ideals capture the aspirational goal to do away, once and for all, with the conflicts, grievances, prejudices, nationalisms and racisms that have afflicted the continent, through the building of a united Europe and the creation of a hospitable and socially inclusive political space that accommodates any lifestyle that can coexist alongside others peaceably. Europe's strong social conscience is also in evidence. The Treaty pledges to help eradicate poverty, to assist developing countries and those hit by natural or man-made disasters, and to work with other nations to manage natural resources sustainably and protect the environment.

What has Lisbon to do with Rome?

Approximately a quarter of the world's 1.3 billion Roman Catholics live in Europe, and Catholics are to be found in each of the 27 Member States of the EU. What should Catholics make of the European Project, and how compatible are Catholicism's and the EU's vision of social life? Pope John Paul II viewed the European community's growing unity as a sign of hope, because it was occurring peacefully and with respect for human rights and democratic processes.[5] He reminded Catholics that they are called to make an 'indispensable contribution to the building in Europe of a civilization ever more worthy of man',[6] and he indicated the applicability of the church's social teaching in this regard:

> In building a city worthy of man, *a guiding role should be played by the Church's social teaching*. Through this teaching the Church challenges the continent of Europe about the moral quality of its civilization ... By the body of principles which it sets forth, the Church's social doctrine helps lay solid foundations for a humane coexistence in justice, peace, freedom and solidarity. Because it is aimed at defending and promoting the dignity of the human person, which is the basis not only of economic and political life, but also of social justice and peace, this doctrine proves capable of upholding the supporting structures of Europe's future.[7]

European Catholics who delve into the dense texts of the two Treaties covered by Lisbon may be reassured to see a notable correspondence between their Church's vision of moral and political life and the vision statement of the EU. There is substantial overlap on issues such as human dignity, the duty to establish a just social and political order, the obligation to care for the needy, and humankind's responsibility for the environment. In many respects, therefore, it is possible to see in the statements of these major representatives of humanity, the EU and the Roman Catholic Church, overlapping values and shared concerns.

Yet despite the apparent compatibility of the moral language, John Paul and his successor Benedict XVI have both repeatedly expressed grave misgivings about the aims of the European Project, and the values that shape it. A central concern is the fact that even the most avid of readers will find no explicit mention of God or Christianity in the texts of the various EU Treaties. Why should this be of such concern? Should one not rest content to see the evident correlation between the non-negotiable dimensions of European and Christian moral values? Is not the EU's reluctance to invoke religious terminology a straightforward recognition of the existence of varied religious and non-religious worldviews held by Europeans, and an appreciation of the many valuable and enriching contributions made by non-Christians to Europe's moral and cultural fabric? While some may accept or prefer the EU's form of words, representatives of the Church in Rome have seen these omissions as indicative of a more sinister secularist agenda gripping the continent of Europe. The most serious of these omissions, to judge by the extensive column inches devoted to the topic by Popes John Paul II and Benedict XVI, is the absence not of God from the pages of the EU's key texts, but of explicit reference to Europe's Christian roots. What is going on?

Recovering Europe's Christian identity?

The publication of John Paul's Apostolic Exhortation *Ecclesia in Europa* coincided with public debate over the wording of the EU Constitution and he used the opportunity to appeal for the inclusion of 'a reference to the religious and in particular the Christian heritage of Europe'.[8] This was a request not for a roll-call of religious influences on the shape of Europe, in which Christianity takes its place alongside other faiths, but for the singling out of Christianity as chief influence:

> The history of the European continent has been distinctively marked by the life-giving influence of the Gospel ... There can be no doubt that the Christian faith belongs, in a radical and decisive way, to the foundations of European culture. Christianity in fact has shaped Europe, impressing upon it certain basic values. Modern Europe itself, which has given the democratic ideal and human rights to the world, draws its values from its Christian heritage.[9]

Around the same time, Cardinal Ratzinger published personal writings that echo and extend John Paul's analysis of Europe.[10] Europe was once 'the Christian continent', Ratzinger writes. There Christianity received 'its most effective cultural and intellectual imprint and remains, therefore, identified in a special way with Europe' and yet, he notes with regret, there is no room for Christianity in the wording of the Constitution. He dismisses the suggestion that to do so would offend those of other faiths, on the basis that reference to Europe's Christian history would be a simple statement of fact. Rather, an aggressive anti-religious secularism is the true reason for 'the banishment of Christian roots'.

Catholicism's problem with Europe

For John Paul and Benedict, that the EU has effectively airbrushed Christianity out of European history is symptomatic of Europe's secular condition and reflects a corresponding evacuation of the religious underpinnings that give authentic meaning and specificity to Europe's moral values. According to the logic of these two papacies, it is no coincidence that the moral malaise affecting the modern world is writ large in the continent that gave birth to that most influential yet ambivalent of cultural revolutions, the Enlightenment. In its emphasis on the value of freedom, Enlightenment culture has distorted European social life and created an opposition between itself and Christianity.[11] As a consequence, argues John Paul: '[European] culture is marked by a widespread and growing religious agnosticism, connected to a more profound moral and legal relativism rooted in confusion regarding the truth about man as the basis of the inalienable rights of all human beings.'[12] Europeans are suffering from a crisis of how to apply their hard-won, precious values not because the situations in which they find themselves raise morally complex quandaries, but because freedom to act has been prioritized over obedience to the truth. Such an outcome is inevitable once God is made superfluous to human reasons for acting, and is ejected from humanity's political horizon.

Nostalgia ain't what it used to be

The sad consequence is a culture in moral decline, and the emotional response is to look back to an era when Europe's Christian (and therefore moral) identity was much more secure than today.[13] The theological outlook expressed both by John Paul and Benedict is not unique. The nostalgic desire for a return to Christian Europe is found in the writing of Catholic apologist Hilaire Belloc (d. 1953) who, in dramatic overstatement, in the closing lines of *Europe and the Faith*, implausibly identified all that is great about European culture and its sustainability with Roman Catholicism: '[T]his our European structure, built upon the noble foundations of classical antiquity, was formed through, exists by, is consonant to, and will stand only in the mold of, the Catholic Church. Europe will return to the faith or she will perish. The Faith is Europe. And Europe is the Faith.'[14] Belloc's rhetoric has the effect of making most other Christian apologists appear muted in comparison. Yet the distress at the rise of the secular is also apparent in the yearning expressed in the opening of John Milbank's defining work, *Theology and Social Theory*: 'Once there was no "secular" ... Instead there was the single community of Christendom ... The secular as a domain had to be instituted or *imagined*, both in theory and in practice.'[15] With the inconvenient presence of Christianity evacuated from European history, a free-floating secular political space can open, in which historical irritants such as the destructive force of age-old religious resentments are neutralized – so it might be argued. For John Paul and Benedict, however, the advent of the secular is not the moral triumph that is often claimed for it. Secularity is too flimsy and insubstantial to paper over the deep-rooted imprints of a culture's religious identity that are indelibly written on the pages of history.

Christian Europe encounters the Islamic other

The debates concerning the wording of the Constitution took place in the immediate aftermath of the 9/11 atrocities, as the so-called war on terror began in earnest. Islam was on the political agenda as never before, and new questions were being asked about Turkey's long-standing application for membership of the EU. It is against this backdrop that John Paul spoke of 'the notable gap between European culture, with its profound Christian roots, and Muslim thought'.[16] Shortly afterwards, Cardinal Ratzinger gave an interview to French weekly *Le Figaro* which took up the question of Turkey's bid for EU membership. Confining himself to the expression of personal views, rather than speaking in an official Vatican capacity, he opined that admission of Turkey to the EU would be an error that would put Europe's common identity based on Christian roots at risk:

> Europe is a cultural continent, not a geographical one. It is its culture that gives it a common identity. The roots that have formed it, that have permitted the formation of this continent, are those of Christianity ... In this sense, throughout history Turkey has always represented another continent, in permanent contrast with Europe ... That is why I think it would be an error to equate the two continents ... Turkey, which is considered a secular country but is founded upon Islam, could instead attempt to bring to life a cultural continent together with some neighbouring Arab countries, and thus become the protagonist of a culture that would possess its own identity but would also share the great humanistic values that we should all acknowledge.[17]

Try as it might, a secularized Europe cannot erase its Christian past. And by the same token, argue John Paul and Benedict, a secularized Turkey cannot ignore its Muslim identity.

Despite the controversy these opinions provoked, the Cardinal, undeterred, revisited the matter in his Subiaco lecture. The EU's omission of explicit mention of Christianity in its constitutional documentation is part of its secularizing strategy, involving the creation of a new inclusive identity: '[T]he dead roots cannot enter into the definition of the foundations of Europe, it being a question of dead roots that are not part of the present identity.' Anyone can embrace Europe's new identity by embracing its humanistic (and religiously non-specific) value system. And in terms of membership, the EU will embrace any nation that can embrace these values:

> Only the norms and contents of the Enlightenment culture will be able to determine Europe's identity and, consequently, every state that makes these criteria its own will be able to belong to Europe. It does not matter, in the end, on what plot of roots this culture of freedom and democracy is implanted.[18]

Turkey – the only Muslim country in NATO, and an early member of the Council of Europe – has been a secular democracy since Atatürk's reforms of the 1920s. Yet for Ratzinger, Turkey cannot escape its Muslim roots:

> It is a question of a state, or perhaps better, a cultural realm, which does not have Christian roots, but which was influenced by Islamic culture. Then, Atatürk tried to transform Turkey into a secular state, attempting to implant in Muslim terrain the secularism that had matured in the Christian world of Europe. We can ask ourselves if that is possible.[19]

While European amnesia or denial of its own Christian cultural underpinnings would allow the admission of Turkey to the EU, Ratzinger implies that proper integration would be impossible, because Europe remains culturally Christian just as Turkey remains culturally Islamic:

> [T]he question must be asked, if this secular Enlightenment culture is really the culture ... that can give a common cause to all men; a culture that should have access from everywhere, even though it is on a humus that is historically and culturally differentiated. And we also ask ourselves if it is really complete in itself, to the degree that it has no need of a root outside itself.[20]

In November 2006, following the embarrassment caused by the injudicious remarks of his Regensburg lecture, Ratzinger – now Pope Benedict – visited Turkey to mend some bridges, but his belief in Europe's special relationship with Christianity has not gone away and, for Benedict, this determines just how inclusive (Christian) Europe can afford to be.

What's in a name?

It is no coincidence that the patron saint of Benedict's papacy is Benedict of Nursia, who was declared patron saint of Europe by Paul VI. St Benedict is of symbolic importance to this debate because he allows his papal namesake to construct a story of Europe's Christianization through the spread of monasticism. Pope Benedict describes him as 'a fundamental reference point for European unity and a powerful reminder of the indispensable Christian roots of its culture and civilization'.[21] St Benedict's achievement, according to this reading of history, is to save Europe from the social and moral decline that threatened it following the collapse of the Roman Empire and the onset of hostile invasions. The social fabric was strengthened through the proliferation of monasteries, and Christianity took root. This highly successful movement filled a potential moral vacuum, giving a unifying shape to moral and social life.

Let us leave aside historical questions concerning the political factors that might also have cemented Christianity's success in Europe, such as the role played by the expansion of the Frankish kingdom, because the point, of course, is to draw a parallel between the moral crisis in Europe at the time of Benedict of Nursia and that of our own era. Christians today 'need men like Benedict of Norcia, who at a time of dissipation and decadence ... gathered together the forces from which a new world was formed. In this way Benedict, like Abraham, became the father of many nations.'[22] Today's Europeans are at a moral turning point and living in a continent once more in need of Christian evangelization, according to Pope Benedict:

> Today, Europe – deeply wounded during the last century by two world wars and the collapse of great ideologies now revealed as tragic utopias – is searching for its own identity. A strong political, economic and legal framework is undoubtedly important in creating a new, unified and lasting state, but we also need to renew ethical and spiritual values that draw on the Christian roots of the Continent, otherwise we cannot construct a new Europe.[23]

Whose ethics? Which values?

For John Paul and Benedict, Christianity contains the moral nourishment necessary to enrich a post-Enlightenment secular Europe. Secularity breeds a form of tolerance that, in Pope Benedict's words, can degenerate 'into an indifference with no reference to permanent values'.[24] By contrast, Catholic social teaching, according to Pope John Paul, 'contains points of reference which make it possible to defend the moral structure of freedom, so as to protect European culture and society ... from the utopia of "freedom without truth" which goes hand in hand with a false concept of "tolerance"'.[25] Paradoxically, such licence leads not to unlimited freedom for all, but to constraint. Thus, argues Cardinal Ratzinger, laws prohibiting discrimination can threaten the freedoms of others:

> The concept of discrimination is ever more extended, and so the prohibition of discrimination can be increasingly transformed into a limitation of the freedom of opinion and religious liberty. Very soon it will not be possible to state that homosexuality, as the Catholic Church teaches, is an objective disorder in the structuring of human existence.[26]

In this view, Europe's moral vision is flawed. The values with which the EU intends to fashion a new Europe are not the positive marks of civilization but rather are a symptom of the more fundamental wounds that afflict it. Not surprisingly, therefore, certain legislative proposals put forward by the EU that are seen to promote 'freedom without truth' have met with strong Catholic opposition. The Church's most vehement response has been to legislative efforts within Europe to extend the civil rights of lesbian and gay people, and it is in this regard that we see the sharpest contrast between the EU's politics of inclusion and Catholicism's ecclesiology of exclusion.

Europe's making or undoing? Legal rights for lesbian and gay people

Across Europe there is greater openness about and acceptance of sexual diversity than at any other time, and this is reflected in unprecedented levels of legal protection for gay and lesbian people. Consenting same-sex intercourse between adults has been decriminalized. Workplace-based sexual orientation discrimination is illegal within the EU. Many – though by no means all – European countries now permit lesbian and gay people to serve openly in the armed forces. A score of nations legally recognize gay partnerships, and the issue is under consideration in Italy, Greece and Ireland. The Netherlands, Belgium and Spain have legalized same-sex marriage. Nine of the European countries that extend marriage or partnership rights to same-sex couples allow such couples legally to adopt children.

Nonetheless, the picture remains mixed. Attitudes vary across the European nations. Eastern Europe, in particular, is less tolerant of alternative lifestyles. In all European nations, prejudice, discrimination and hate crimes against gay people continue to occur. Europe is far from a safe space to be gay, but there are growing regions of security, toleration and respectful coexistence. The various EU institutions have been instrumental in transforming the legal frameworks of the Member States. The unacceptability of discrimination on the grounds of sexual orientation was first given explicit mention in Article 13 of the EU's *Treaty of Amsterdam* (1997). Since then there has been a gradual though by no means identical legal implementation of this vision across Europe.

Legislation recently enacted in the United Kingdom provides a useful example of the extension of legal rights to gay people. Since 2000 gay people may openly serve in the military. In 2001 the age of consent was equalized. The *Adoption and Children Act 2002* allows same-sex couples to jointly adopt children. In 2003 the *Employment Equality (Sexual Orientation) Regulations* extended protections in the workplace. The *Civil Partnership Act 2004* confers on same-sex couples that register their union the same rights and responsibilities as marriage (some 27,000 couples have registered their unions since December 2005).[27] The *Equality Act 2006* ensures equal treatment in the provision of goods, facilities and services.

This proliferation of legal protections for gay people in Europe stands in sharp contrast to legal provision worldwide. Same-sex acts remain illegal in 72 countries, and may be punishable by death in ten of these. Seen through this wider lens of global attitudes to gay rights it is uncontroversial to state that, as a continent, Europe is furthest advanced in seeking to establish a political community where gay citizens can participate in, contribute to and benefit from the goods of civil life on a par with their neighbours. For some this represents a substantial moral achievement in a continent where, just decades earlier, gay identity was sufficient grounds for human extermination, alongside other identifiers such as ethnicity and religion. For others, including the official Roman Catholic Church, it signals any number of concerns, including the further erosion of Europe's moral character, a damaging attack on appropriate patterns of human existence as reflected in the basic institutions of social life, a confirmation of the waning of Europe's Christian identity, and a rejection of God's will for humanity.

Catholicism's problem with homosexuality

Roman Catholicism proclaims the equal dignity in the eyes of God of all women and men, including lesbian and gay people; homosexuals 'must be accepted with respect, compassion and sensitivity. Every sign of unjust discrimination in their regard should be avoided.'[28] Yet when the Church moves from this general statement to the particulars of how Church and society should guarantee the dignity of homosexual persons, the emphasis shifts dramatically from concerns about how gay and lesbian people might wrongly be subject to negative discriminatory treatment towards assertions of how certain legal restrictions on access to social goods are both morally justifiable and politically necessary. 'Sexual orientation', according to Vatican teaching, 'does not constitute a quality comparable to race, ethnic background, etc. in respect to non-discrimination. Unlike these, homosexual orientation is an objective disorder and evokes moral concern.'[29] Legislation that makes discrimination on the grounds of sexual orientation illegal could have 'a negative impact on the family and society' and should be rejected.[30] According to the Vatican's Doctrinal Note on Catholic participation in political life, such laws 'ignore the principles of natural ethics' and promote freedom of choice 'as if every possible outlook on life were of equal value'.[31] For these reasons, the Church defends the right to discriminate on grounds of sexual orientation.[32]

With regard to civil partnerships, 'the *family* needs to be safeguarded and promoted, based on monogamous marriage between a man and a woman ... in no way can other forms of co-habitation be placed on the same level as marriage, nor can they receive legal recognition as such'.[33] John Paul dismissed attempts 'to accept a definition of the couple in which difference of sex is not considered essential', as one of the many modern threats to marriage and family life that 'jeopardize the truth and dignity of the human person'.[34] In 2003, in a document devoted to the subject, the CDF reiterated that 'the principles of respect and non-discrimination cannot be invoked to support legal recognition of homosexual unions'.[35] On the contrary, 'clear and emphatic opposition is a duty. One must refrain from any kind of formal cooperation in the enactment or application of such gravely unjust laws and, as far as possible, from material cooperation on the level of their application.'[36]

In so saying, the Vatican has placed Catholic hierarchies across Europe on a collision course with their national governments. Bishops must judge how far the Church can become associated with state laws and legalized behaviour of which the Church disapproves without undermining its Christian witness and causing scandal while taking into account what the political ramifications of non-cooperation might be. As legal provisions for gay people begin to impinge on the practices of Catholics (such as fostering and adoption agencies), hierarchies are identifying their national churches as discriminated parties and appealing to conscience in order to assert the right to religious belief and to defend differential treatment. Across Europe and beyond, legal provisions for gay people are creating newly antagonistic church–state relations. In the secularized platform of the EU, Catholicism finds itself increasingly marginalized: one among any number of potentially competing voices with no power of veto, and offering a vision of life that appears increasingly unappealing to Europe's citizens.

Catholicism's identity crisis and the ecclesiology of exclusion

Since the end of the Second World War, Europe has set itself the task of forging a community of nations united by common interests and shared values that transcend but do not eradicate religious, cultural and regional particularity. This politics of inclusion remains a work in progress. Many Catholics have contributed to the rebuilding of Europe, convinced of the compatibility between the goals of the EU and the vision of social life found within their religious tradition. However, in its exclusivist tendencies, Catholicism represents the antithesis to the European Project.

The Catholic Church and the EU both share a desire to build in Europe a truly moral civilization. Both proclaim their commitment to the construction of a just political order based on the equal dignity of each, in which everyone can participate and flourish to the fullness of their potential. Yet deep differences in understanding exist about how these values should be promoted in practice. For the leadership of the Catholic Church, Europe's values make no sense apart from the meaning conferred on them by their Christian underpinnings. Strategies that deny or dilute that influence risk creating not a community based on shared values but a zone of coexistence based on relativistic tolerance and a right to non-interference. We may all recognize this tendency and the dangers inherent in it. But in this world of diversity and difference a corresponding tendency exists in Churches overly concerned with questions of belonging and identity. They erect boundaries to form exclusive communities by division and separation. Such ecclesiologies of exclusion are found throughout Christianity. They offer a fragile security for their membership but embody an inability to live with plurality and therefore risk the same political instability that comes from the opposite extreme of indifferentism.

Catholicism's exclusivist position is deeply problematic for the European Project of finding common ground amid plurality and difference, and it creates a version of Christianity that many Christians do not wish to own. The spirit of Christianity in Europe is not to be celebrated by way of its insertion into the text of a Constitution to the exclusion of other religions. Neither will Christianity have the power to convince if it attempts to do so by appeal to a version of the past that neglects the ambivalence of its own history. The Christian character of Europe is not to be enhanced but only deformed by excluding Turkey on the grounds of its non-Christian identity. Such separatist experiments have been tried before in Christianity's name and have given rise to some of the most shameful aspects of European and world history. And Christians who proclaim God's equal love for all, while invoking a Christian opt-out from equality laws, undermine their witness and shame their God. Another way of being church is possible and must be allowed to flourish; one based not on ecclesiologies of exclusion but on community building that prefigures that inclusive community of God's Holy Polity.

Notes

1. Jacques Maritain, 'Introduction', in UNESCO (ed.), *Human Rights: Comments and Interpretations* (London: Allan Wingate, 1949), 9–17, at 9.
2. The full text of the Schuman Declaration of 9 May 1950 is available at the portal of the European Union: http://europa.eu/abc/symbols/9–may/decl_en.htm (accessed 15 July 2008).
3. The text of the Treaty of Lisbon is available at: http://europa.eu/lisbon_treaty/index_en.htm (accessed 15 July 2008).
4. Conference of the Representatives of the Governments of the Member States, *Draft Treaty Amending the Treaty on European Union and the Treaty Establishing the European Community* (CIG 1/1/07 REV 1), Brussels, 5 October 2007, article 2.
5. Pope John Paul II, Post-synodal Apostolic Exhortation, *Ecclesia in Europa*, 2003, n. 12.
6. Ibid., n. 105.
7. Ibid., n. 98.
8. Ibid., n. 114.
9. Ibid., n. 108.
10. Here discussion will be confined to Cardinal Ratzinger's lecture entitled 'On Europe's Crisis of Culture', delivered at Saint Scolastica, Subiaco, Italy, on having been awarded the St Benedict Award for the promotion of life and the family in Europe, 1 April 2005, the eve of John Paul's death. The text (pages unnumbered) is available at the website of the Catholic Education Resource Center under the title 'Cardinal Ratzinger on Europe's Crisis of Culture': http://www.catholicedu-cation.org/articles/politics/pg0143.html (accessed 15 July 2008).
11. Cf. Ratzinger, 'On Europe's Crisis of Culture'.
12. *Ecclesia in Europa*, n. 9.
13. Cf. Ratzinger, 'On Europe's Crisis of Culture'.
14. Hilaire Belloc, *Europe and the Faith* (London: Constable, 1920).
15. John Milbank, *Theology and Social Theory: Beyond Secular Reason* (Oxford: Blackwell, 1990), 9.
16. *Ecclesia in Europa*, n. 57.
17. Sophie de Ravinel, Interview with Cardinal Josef Ratzinger, *Le Figaro*, 13 August 2004.

18. Ratzinger, 'On Europe's Crisis of Culture'.
19. Ibid.
20. Ibid.
21. Pope Benedict XVI, 'Reflection on the Name Chosen: Benedict XVI', General Audience, 27 April 2005.
22. Ratzinger, 'On Europe's Crisis of Culture'.
23. Pope Benedict XVI, 'Saint Benedict of Norcia', General Audience, 9 April 2008.
24. Pope Benedict XVI, 'Address to Austrian Politicians', Vienna, 8 September 2007.
25. *Ecclesia in Europa*, n. 98.
26. Ratzinger, 'On Europe's Crisis of Culture'.
27. Cf. National Statistics online: http://www.statistics.gov.uk/cci/nugget.asp?id=1685.
28. *Catechism of the Catholic Church*, rev. edn, 1997, n. 2358.
29. Congregation for the Doctrine of the Faith (CDF), 'Some Considerations Concerning the Response to Legislative Proposals on the Non-Discrimination of Homosexual Persons', 1992, n. 10.
30. 'Some Considerations Concerning the Response to Legislative Proposals ...', Foreword.
31. CDF, 'Doctrinal Note on Some Questions Regarding the Participation of Catholics in Political Life', 2002, n. 2.
32. 'Some Considerations Concerning the Response to Legislative Proposals ...', n. 11.
33. 'Doctrinal Note on Some Questions Regarding the Participation of Catholics in Political Life', n. 4.
34. *Ecclesia in Europa*, n. 90.
35. CDF, 'Considerations regarding proposals to give legal recognition to unions between homosexual persons', 2003, n. 8.
36. Ibid., n. 5.

Chapter 13

INSTRUMENTS OF FAITH AND UNITY IN CANON LAW: THE CHURCH OF NIGERIA CONSTITUTIONAL REVISION OF 2005[1]

Evan F. Kuehn

From the beginning, the Archbishop of Canterbury, both in his person and his office, has been the pivotal instrument and focus of unity; and relationship to him became a touchstone of what it was to be Anglican. [2]

Within Anglicanism, scripture has always been recognized as the Church's supreme authority, and as such ought to be seen as a focus and means of unity.[3]

Introduction

On 14 September 2005 the Church of Nigeria revised its constitution, shifting the explicit basis of ecclesial unity from the See of Canterbury to the authority of scripture and historic doctrinal statements.[4] This chapter examines the structural reforms made in the revision as they relate to the Anglican 'instruments of faith'[5] and 'instruments of unity'.[6]

While both the historic Chicago-Lambeth Quadrilateral and the more recent 'instruments of unity' have played a significant role in Anglican ecclesiology, the current conflict over human sexuality as it relates to ordination and ecclesial blessing has revealed a paucity of reflection upon these principles in anything but the most ideal terms and circumstances.[7] Actions of disunity have challenged the assumption that canonical bases of faith and unity mutually support each other,[8] and deeper investigation into the relationship between 'faith' and 'unity' must occur in order to find an advisable way forward.

In Section I, I will identify the 2005 revision as canonical reform, a neglected acknowledgement amidst the theo-political tension that has resulted from the crisis over ordination of practising homosexual persons and the blessing of same-sex unions. In Section II, I will outline the constructive nature of the revision as it relates to the Anglican episcopate and the current dialogue on *communio* as an issue of canon law. In Section III, I will conclude by highlighting the implications of this canonical structure for inter-Anglican and ecumenical unity.

Section I

The 2005 canon law change was neither significant nor unique in itself;[9] in light of the current situation of the Anglican Communion, however, the Nigerian revision has raised serious concerns about unilateral provincial action,[10] the bypassing of conventional instruments of ecclesial unity[11] and the question of impaired communion more generally.[12]

The canon law revision addresses ecclesiastical questions: the terms of inter-Anglican communion and episcopal oversight of 'like-minded faithful'[13] in 'non-geographic' convocation.[14] However, its impetus in the crisis of communion over issues of human sexuality has indelibly marked its reception. The Church of Nigeria's call to discipline ECUSA (now TEC),[15] its declaration of broken ties,[16] and its eventual declaration with 12 other provinces that ECUSA 'has separated itself from the remainder of the Anglican Communion and the wider Christian family'[17] have all tended to substantiate interpretations of the constitutional revision as yet another response to the actions of ECUSA rather than as a reform of ecclesiastical structures. Amidst this atmosphere, it is difficult to view the canonical revision without recourse to its wider theological context. There is, however, a distinction between the purposes of canon law and theology,[18] and this division of labour allows for an assessment of canonical structures that is connected to, yet independent from, theological consideration. Archbishop Akinola stated in a press conference on the revision, 'in Onitsha we took a number of actions to clarify our commitment to the apostolic faith. One of the things we did to strengthen this position was to amend our constitution.'[19] Only by considering the constitutional amendment as a structural revision may we be able to assess its relevance for a theological 'commitment to the apostolic faith' as it has been expressed through ecclesial actions.

Canonical revision is appropriate and expected in accordance with the edification of the body of Christ. '[I]nstructive criticism and suggestion are normal tasks of the science of canon law',[20] and in themselves represent a renewal of polity rather than a reversion into politics. Theology and theological conflict does inform canon law, though canon law does not lose its juridical mandate because of its theological source:

The scientific study of the Church's reality in all its aspects is the function of the exegete, the patrologist, the historian, the theologian, the moralist, the liturgist, the sociologist, the missiologist, etc. The canonist is concerned only with the various ways in which this reality can be given a certain order by means of authorized regulations.[21]

In 2003, Archbishop Akinola commissioned, with Archbishops Gomez and Venables, a study of recent actions taken by ECUSA, intending to demonstrate 'the case against the Episcopal Church (USA)'. Examination of subsequent canonical actions of the Church of Nigeria should refer back to this and other earlier statements, which laid the foundation for later canonical action. Legal precedent supporting Lambeth 1998 resolution I.10 is cited in *Claiming our Anglican Identity*, including 'English Canon Law and Common Law since the Middle Ages' and under Elizabeth I, '[s]ubsequent local, provincial, and national British synods and councils' and 'numerous non-British and international Anglican synods'; mentioned specifically among these are 'ECUSA's House of Bishops in 1977' and '[t]he 66th General Convention [ECUSA] in 1979'. It is also noted that neither of these final two interpretations had been repealed by ECUSA.[22] Ecclesial and pastoral procedure concerning the ordination of practising homosexual persons and the blessing of same-sex unions is therefore established as a matter of authoritative resolution,[23] and non-compliance with these statements introduces an ecclesial conflict requiring discipline based upon established theological standards rather than ecclesial diversity resulting from theological *adiaphora*.[24] In fact, there is no canonically recognized 'diversity' on the matter, as the report seeks to emphasize that ECUSA's regulatory instruments[25] were themselves ignored in the consecration of Gene Robinson and exploration of rites of ecclesial blessing for homosexual persons.[26]

The 2005 revision concerning the terms of inter-Anglican communion, however, has nothing directly to do with the Church of Nigeria's status of impaired communion with TEC. What has changed is the focus of the multipartite form of canonical communion,[27] which has in all other aspects been preserved. While the Church of Nigeria previously established communion based upon the communal focus of the See of Canterbury, the revision has established the focus of the still multipartite communion as 'the Historic Faith, Doctrine, Sacrament and Discipline of the one Holy, Catholic, and Apostolic Church',[28] properly given in the scriptures and received in historic statements of the church. Based upon previous statements made by Archbishop Akinola this should be understood to encompass previous condemnations of TEC; however, the canon law revision itself seeks to reform provincial ecclesiological structures of relation to the See of Canterbury.[29]

Section II

Canon law and Anglican episcope

The 2005 canon law revision followed the 2004 impairment of communion, a disciplinary instrument[30] directed towards those provinces that had disregarded canonical statements wherein standards of faith had been defined for the Communion.[31] The revision was not a disciplinary action itself; rather it sought to reform canonical structures in response to the current crisis. In 2006, the Council of Anglican Provinces in Africa (CAPA) released *The Road to Lambeth*, presenting the dilemma affecting Anglican instruments of both faith and unity:

> The current situation is a twofold crisis for the Anglican Communion: a crisis of doctrine and a crisis of leadership, in which the failure of the 'Instruments' of the Communion to exercise discipline has called into question the viability of the Anglican Communion as a united Christian body under a common foundation of faith, as is supposed by the Chicago-Lambeth Quadrilateral.[32]

This statement presents the relationship of these instruments such that the instruments of faith 'suppose' the instruments of unity, and the instruments of unity have a responsibility to exercise appropriate discipline[33] in order to safeguard the more foundational instruments of faith.[34] While all authoritative Anglican bodies are held to account in this report (including the African bishops themselves) a certain focus is directed towards the Archbishop of Canterbury: 'So far as we can see, the Archbishop of Canterbury as Primate of All England has failed to oppose this compromising position [the Civil Partnerships Act] and hence cannot speak clearly to and for the whole Communion.'[35] This duty of speaking 'to and for the whole Communion' is consonant with *The Windsor Report*, paragraph 109, but beyond this the bishops of CAPA clarify that standards of faith and order have been established within global authoritative statements as well as provincial canon law and must be the source from which the Archbishop of Canterbury speaks 'to and for the whole Communion', especially in cases of dispute.[36] These canonical standards are the same ones as those cited in response to ECUSA; CAPA simply insists that the Archbishop of Canterbury be mindful of the disciplinary function to which the entire episcopate is called, and the See of Canterbury all the more so because of its role as the focus of unity.[37] This duty is understood to fall within the confines of 'moral authority' and so may result in measures of discipline appropriate to episcopal authority.[38]

The Church of England's response of 25 July 2005[39] to the Civil Partnership Act[40] appears to have factored heavily into the Archbishop of Nigeria's explanation of the September 2005 canon law revision concerning the See of Canterbury. Archbishop Akinola personally stated in a letter of August 2005: 'While I have great affection and respect for the historic role that the Church of England has played in all of our lives, no church can ignore the teaching of the Bible with impunity and no church is beyond discipline.'[41] Adherence to biblical teaching may be read as shorthand for the 'instruments of faith'; the 'historic role' of the Church of England is more particularly the role of its primate as 'instrument' and indeed 'focus' of unity.[42] Yet the Church of Nigeria did not seek to abandon one for the other; indeed, one of the 'instruments of faith' is itself a 'principle of unity'.[43] Rather, disunity was perceived already in the body of Christ, and a canonical response was deemed necessary to re-establish unity. The canon law revision of 2005 located this unity foundationally in scripture, but did not thus exclude the episcopate insofar as the bishop is implied by reference to 'Anglican Churches[,] Dioceses and Provinces'.[44] What has changed is a re-emphasis on the necessary 'evangelicity of the episcopate'. This principle is already present in the Chicago-Lambeth Quadrilateral but has been more recently established in ecumenical discussion between ECUSA and the Evangelical Lutheran Church in America.[45] Evangelical unity buttresses the episcopate as a sign of the apostolic continuity of ecclesial unity:

> The significance of the episcopate as a mark of apostolic continuity with the gospel ... is not given antecedently and then visibly manifested in the church; the sign is also reconstructed over and over again by its concrete service to the gospel (which is its evangelical character). The episcopate as a sign receives its significance from the historical dimension of its apostolic succession, yet also from the authenticity of its contemporary acts of service and proclamation.[46]

Having established the proclamation of the gospel as essential to the episcopal claim to apostolic unity, as well as the Church of Nigeria's identification of and response to episcopal disunity in its canon law revision, I will examine the constructive nature of this revision as it relates to ecclesiological communion.

Canon law and Anglican Communion

Communio ecclesiology has held distinct canonical significance in Roman Catholicism since the publication of *Lumen Gentium*.[47] In Roman

Catholicism, a balance tends to be sought between *communio* and *societas*[48] or *concilium*[49] ecclesiology, while in Anglicanism balance exists with ecclesial 'autonomy'.[50] *Communio*, however, relativizes any ecclesiological atomism by its call to evangelical unity: 'The essence of the principle of *communio* consists in the fact of postulating the *total immanence, and the inseparability, of all the elements that make up the Church*.'[51] Diversity is not simply autonomy, rather, '[d]iversity is seen here as constitutive of unity and not a hindrance to it'.[52] The basis of unity, again, 'involves sharing the same faith, partaking the same sacraments, and loyalty and obedience to the bishops'.[53] In Anglicanism these bases are reflected in the instruments of faith which through mention of the historic (and necessarily evangelical) episcopate form the basis of the focus and instruments of unity.

The global order of a communion is not juridical, but rather a moral order.[54] The moral interdependence of Anglican provinces has been described in terms of 'bonds of affection' or 'an implicit understanding of belonging together'.[55] Unfortunately, the moral order of communion is often contrasted to provincial juridical structures in a way that renders it impotent. The moral order displays 'a high level of generality' and is 'not binding' and 'unenforceable'.[56] It is likely because of this perceived deficiency that a more coherent global structure of faith and order is being pursued, the two most prominent proposals of which are an Anglican *ius commune*[57] and covenant.[58]

Proposals for a global canonical order are understood to codify pre-existing provincial canons, or inter-provincial conventions. This being the case, however, the question is begged whether current communal structures are, in fact, inadequately suited to fulfil the needs of Anglican communion. Numerous difficulties arise when the 'bonds' of affection are described as 'non-binding', even if only a lack of legal obligation is intended, because this observation undercuts the non-legal foundation upon which communion is structured. While the instruments of unity are at most 'quasi-legal',[59] communion ecclesiology has always retained this form and claimed its authority nonetheless.[60] The non-legal character of ecclesial communion does not disallow authoritative reading of, and disciplinary action based upon, holy scripture:

> The existence of Communion is precisely what provides for the possibility of a genuine reading of Scripture in unified diversity. The notion of mutually contradictory readings of Scripture as requiring equal respect and coexisting integrity derives from a lack of a comprehension of and respect for Christian communion itself ... through which the Holy Spirit works and leads.[61]

When such contradictory readings occur, communal authorities have an obligation to discipline erring members.[62] While the Archbishop of Canterbury has recognized that repudiation of the interpretation provided by LC 1998 resolution I.10 would constitute a threat to Anglican Communion,[63] disciplinary action has not been forthcoming from the instruments of unity out of respect for provincial autonomy[64] and perceived limits of jurisdiction in the global moral order.[65] As a result, the Church of Nigeria has exercised its own autonomy[66] towards the goal of communal unity,[67] and has done so by means of canon law.

Section III

I will conclude by discussing the implications of the 2005 revision for ecumenical and inter-Anglican unity. These considerations are central to informed amendment of canonical structures because of the ecumenical character of ecclesiological bases of Anglican canon law.[68] A communion in dialogue with others must consider not only its own legal structure, but also those of other Christian communions.[69]

Canon law and ecumenical unity

The current Anglican crisis over issues of sexuality has been as detrimental to ecumenical relationships as it has been to bonds of unity within the Communion itself. In its 2003 meeting, the Inter Anglican Standing Commission on Ecumenical Relations (IASCER) recognized the damage done to ecumenical dialogue, noting in particular 'impairment of the work' with the Roman Catholic (IARCCUM) and Oriental Orthodox commissions, as well as the Russian Orthodox Church's severing of ties with ECUSA.[70]

Consultation with the Roman Catholic Church has, in particular, provided valuable insight into the development of the current Anglican crisis and how it has affected the canonical structures of communion. In July 2004, the IARCCUM *ad hoc* sub-commission submitted its reflections to Archbishop Rowan Williams and Cardinal Walter Kasper. The report commented on the effects of Anglican provincial disregard for global authoritative statements:

> The fact that the New Hampshire Consecration took place in opposition to Resolution 1.10 passed by the bishops at the Lambeth Conference, to Resolution 34 of ACC 12, to the statement of the Primates' Meeting in October 2003, and to a public statement of the Archbishop of Canterbury,

would seem to call into question the processes of discernment in communion, and *in particular the place of the episcopate and the ministry of primacy in their respective responsibilities for the maintenance of unity in the Anglican Communion.* When individual dioceses and provinces act autonomously against the recommendations of the Communion's instruments of unity, at what cost is this done?[71]

The heart of the report's critique is a failure of the 'processes of discernment in communion' which should safeguard the continually emphasized 'basic moral values' necessary for ecclesial communion.[72] Rejection of these 'basic moral values' has put in question both the state of the Anglican Communion and the Anglican–Roman Catholic dialogue. Towards the end of this document, the possibility is left open for further dialogue if Anglican structures of communion are mended appropriately:

> If you choose to strengthen the authority structures and instruments of unity within the Anglican Communion and find an effective means of addressing the tendency towards divergence on matters of faith and doctrine, we would clearly see this as enhancing the possibility of meaningful and fruitful dialogue in the search for Christian unity, and of an increasing commitment to shared witness and mission.[73]

These critiques were revisited in December 2004, in Cardinal Walter Kasper's invited letter to Archbishop Rowan Williams giving his thoughts on *The Windsor Report*. Kasper raised two concerns: the lack of a clearer articulation of 'the importance of being in communion with the faith of the Church through the ages' and 'the moral questions at the heart of the current controversy'.[74] The inadequacy of *The Windsor Report* in considering both of these issues was presented as an obstacle to ecumenical unity, although the report as a whole was recognized as helpful and in line with previous work of the ARCIC.[75]

The concerns of ecumenical partners have been expressed by the Church of Nigeria as well, and the resulting canon law revision was intended to be a provisional answer to the failure of communal structures of moral order. The similar tone of response between the Church of Nigeria and other Christian communions to Anglican disunity suggests that subsequent canonical actions of the Church of Nigeria may contribute to the satisfaction of ecumenical concerns. The canon law revision is both consciously provisional as an Anglican structure and convergent with the ecclesiastical status of other Christian bodies.[76]

Canon law and inter-Anglican unity

The Lambeth Conference of 1998 stated its commitment to dialogue and reconciliation with 'continuing Anglican churches' that have broken away from the Anglican Communion while acknowledging an association with historic Anglicanism.[77] Unfortunately, the current crisis over sexuality has not only hindered this process of reunion; it has, in fact, instigated a larger exodus of parishes and dioceses out of the Anglican Communion.[78] These continuing churches are committed to the historic moral standards outlined by the instruments of faith, and in principle to the instruments of unity,[79] properly exercised.

The Church of Nigeria has been able to pursue the goals of LC 1998 resolution IV.11 more effectively than TEC or other provinces of the Anglican Communion, largely because of its canonical efforts to maintain ecclesiastical balance between the instruments of faith and unity. While the Anglican Provinces in America (APA) and the Reformed Episcopal Church (REC) entered into recognized dialogue with ECUSA in 2003,[80] these efforts were 'mutually suspended' due to 'the present instability in the Anglican Communion'.[81] The Church of Nigeria, on the other hand, has entered into a *Covenant of Union of Anglican Churches in Concordat* with the APA and REC, drafted in December 2004 and approved on 12 November 2005. The *Covenant of Union* demonstrates one aspect of the effects of the 2005 canonical revision upon inter-Anglican communal structure. Documents of unity and intercommunion among other 'continuing' Anglican Churches[82] suggest that the extent of the 2005 *Covenant of Union* may anticipate further acts of reunion among Anglican churches that are presently not in communion with the See of Canterbury. The condition of inter-Anglican communion based fundamentally upon adherence to the instruments of faith is consistently emphasized by the continuing Anglican churches, and reflected in the Nigerian canon law revision of 2005.

Conclusion

While the 2005 canon law revision of the Church of Nigeria has remained controversial as a response to current structures of Anglican unity, it should be recognized as a legitimate revision of ecclesiastical law. The new canonical formulation affects the terms of inter-Anglican and ecumenical unity primarily by its structuring of the 'instruments of faith' as a fundamental principle of unity rather than the Anglican episcopate as represented in the See of Canterbury. The revision has acted both as a response to the current ecclesiastical crisis in the Anglican Communion and as an instrument of future Anglican and ecumenical unity.

Notes

1. This chapter, which has been revised and updated, first appeared in the *Ecclesiastical Law Journal* 10 (2008), 161–73. It is reproduced with permission.
2. 'The Lambeth Commission on Communion', *The Windsor Report* (London: The Anglican Communion Office, 2004), para. 99.
3. *The Windsor Report*, para. 53.
4. I will examine only the revision of chapter 1(3):

    (1)The Church of Nigeria (Anglican Communion) ... shall be in full communion with all Anglican Churches[,] Dioceses and Provinces that hold and maintain the Historic Faith, Doctrine, Sacrament and Discipline of the one Holy, Catholic, and Apostolic Church as the Lord has commanded in His holy word and as the same are received as taught in the *Book of Common Prayer* and the ordinal of 1662 and in the *Thirty-Nine Articles of Religion*.
    (2) In the interpretation of the aforementioned formularies and in all questions of Faith, Doctrine and Discipline, the decisions of the Ecclesiastical tribunals of the Church of Nigeria shall be final. The Revd Canon AkinTunde Popoola, 'Church of Nigeria Redefines Anglican Communion', Church of Nigeria, http://www.anglican-nig.org/Onitsha2005_pressls2.htm (accessed 27 September 2008).

5. Norman Doe, 'Communion and Autonomy in Anglicanism: Nature and Maintenance', 15–16, http://www.anglicancommunion.org/commission/process/lc_commission/docs/autonomy.pdf (accessed 27 September 2008). Identifying the constituent elements of the Chicago-Lambeth Quadrilateral as 'instruments of faith' helpfully allows juxtaposition with the 'instruments of unity'.
6. Represented, in particular, by the See of Canterbury as the episcopal focus of Anglican unity. John Rees, 'The Anglican Communion: Does it Exist?', *The Ecclesiastical Law Journal* 5 (1998), 15, and John Paterson, 'Structural Changes in the Anglican Communion', *Journal of Anglican Studies* 4, 2 (2006), 254.
7. *The Windsor Report*, para. 97.
8. *The Windsor Report*, para. 123.
9. 'On a canonical level, the laws of most churches make no explicit reference, in their provisions on self-identity, to the See of Canterbury.' Australia, Japan and Melanesia are mentioned in particular. Norman Doe, 'Communion and Autonomy in Anglicanism', 8.
10. *The Windsor Report*, para. 29(1).
11. Robin Eames, 'Where Now for World Anglicanism?', ACNS 4048, 14 October 2005, http://www.anglicancommunion.org/acns/news.cfm/2005/10/14/ACNS4048 (accessed 27 September 2008):

    Acceptance of an individual Province's view of orthodoxy becomes the basis for relationship. Further the revision of its Constitution states that in all questions of interpretation of faith and doctrine the decision of the Church of Nigeria shall be final.
    As a Primate of the Anglican Communion I find the implications of this

revision most serious. Am I alone in interpreting such wording as the removal of established bonds of communion and their replacement by a Provincial-only wide authority which will set its own criteria for whoever or whatever it considers worthy of a communion relationship?

12. '[W]hat does such a rupture of relationships mean to other Provinces if broken communion refers to the See of Canterbury? The commutations for ecclesiology in such instances are immense. They underline again that "bonds of affection" based on fraternal gestures alone were never geared to meet the challenge of division.' Robin Eames, 'The Anglican Communion: A Growing Reality', ACNS 4041, 5 October 2005, http://www.anglicancommunion.org/acns/news.cfm/2005/10/5/ACNS4041 (accessed 27 September 2008).

13. The Church of Nigeria, *Constitution of the Church of Nigeria*, http://www.anglican-nig.org/constitutions.pdf (accessed 27 September 2008), chapter 9(39)(c).

14. *Constitution of the Church of Nigeria*, chapter 16(75)(8).

15. Ephraim Radner *et al*, *Claiming our Anglican Identity: The Case against the Episcopal Church, USA* (Colorado Springs, CO: The Anglican Communion Institute, 2003), IV(a). ECUSA will be used to refer to the Episcopal Church in the United States of America when discussing events preceding its name change to The Episcopal Church (TEC).

16. Jan Nunley, 'Anglican Provinces Declare "Impaired" or "Broken" Relationship with ECUSA', ACNS 3703, 9 December 2003, http://www.anglicancommunion.org/acns/news.cfm/2003/12/9/ACNS3703 (accessed 27 September 2008).

17. 'Thirteen Global Primates State ECUSA has separated itself', ACNS 3773, 9 February 2004, http://www.anglicancommunion.org/acns/news.cfm/2004/2/9/ACNS3773 (accessed 27 September 2008).

18. Theodore Urresti, 'Canon Law and Theology: Two Different Sciences', in *Concilium: Renewal and Reform of Canon Law*, ed. N. Edelby, T. Urresti and P. Huizing (New York: Paulist Press, 1967), 17–26.

19. http://www.anglican-nig.org/primate's_pressbrief.htm (accessed 2 December 2007).

20. Peter Huizing, 'The Reform of Canon Law', in *Concilium: Pastoral Reform in Church Government*, ed. T. Urresti and N. Edelby (New York: Paulist Press, 1965), 118.

21. Huizing, 'The Reform of Canon Law', 120.

22. *Claiming our Anglican Identity*, II(3).

23. Lambeth resolutions and the ecclesiastical law of other provinces do not technically constitute a canonical law which is in any way legally binding upon a province; however, they certainly take on a canonical form based upon moral authority, which in the context of ecclesial communion is a real authority. See Norman Doe, *Canon Law in the Anglican Communion* (Oxford: Oxford University Press, 1998), 339–40 and John Rees, 'Primates Meeting, October 2003: Some Legal and Constitutional Considerations', 2(1), 3(1)(3), http://www.anglicancommunion.org/commission/process/lc_commission/docs/200310johnrees.pdf (accessed 28 September 2008).

24. It should be noted that while *The Windsor Report* seems to interpret the 'listening process' as a call to re-examine these canonical structures (paras 135, 146), the exclusive focus of the Lambeth resolutions detailing the 'listening process' (1978 res. 10(3), 1988 res. 64, 1998 res. I.10(c)) has consistently been upon the 'pastoral

care' and 'moral direction' of homosexual persons rather than a re-examination of ecclesiastical law or other statements concerning homosexuality as a theological question. Listening towards this end is requested in accordance with authoritative statements on homosexuality.

25. Norman Doe, 'Canon Law and Communion', *The Ecclesiastical Law Journal* 6 (2002), 247. '[I]n ECUSA ... episcopal policy ... allows ordination of practicing homosexuals.' While *Stanton v. Righter* (1996) may be an appropriate precedent for Doe's statement, ECUSA (now TEC), canon III(4)(1) says nothing about homosexual *practice* but rather *orientation*. It should also be noted that 'episcopal policy', as established in *Stanton v. Righter*, stands in acknowledged disagreement with resolution 1979–A053 of the 66th General Convention: 'we believe it is not appropriate for this Church to ordain a practicing homosexual'. This act of repudiation is often unjustifiably overshadowed by focus upon the non-legal nature of General Convention recommendations. See Section II for a discussion of the limits of scriptural interpretation within ecclesial communion and the authority of non-legal ecclesial structures in setting these limits.

26. *Claiming our Anglican Identity*, II(6)–(7).

27. Doe, 'Communion and Autonomy in Anglicanism', 8–9.

28. Constitution of the Church of Nigeria, chapter 1(3). Robin Eames misinterprets the revision by failing to acknowledge its canonically multipartite and indeed catholic aspects. See note 10.

29. Doe, 'Communion and Autonomy in Anglicanism', 22: 'If, as is the case for very many churches, the relationship of full communion is embodied in the law of the church, then it might be that alteration of that relationship must be effected by altering the law, in accordance with procedures necessary for amendment.'

30. 'After the Robinson election, many provinces chose the only instrument of discipline available: declaration of impaired or broken Communion.' CAPA, *The Road to Lambeth*, http://www.globalsouthanglican.org/index.php/comments/the_road_to_lambeth_presented_at_capa/ (accessed 28 September 2008).

31. *The Road to Lambeth*:

> The importance of [LC 1998, res. I.10] cannot be overstated. By using the phrase 'contrary to Scripture,' the bishops indicated that homosexual practice violates the first principle of the Communion's Quadrilateral and indeed the fundamental basis of Anglican Christianity (as expressed in Articles VI and XX). They were saying: 'Here is an issue on which we cannot compromise without losing our identity as a Christian body.'

32. *The Road to Lambeth*.

33. '[Provincial changes in faith and order are] liable to revision by any synod of the Anglican Communion in which the said province shall be represented.' LC 1867, resolution 8, http://www.lambethconference.org/resolutions/1867/1867–8.cfm (accessed 28 September 2008).

34. 'A church becomes a member of the Anglican Communion when it displays loyalty to the instruments of faith, and a practical expression of membership is participation by a church in the work of the institutional instruments of the Anglican Communion.' Doe, 'Canon Law and Communion', 245.

35. *The Road to Lambeth*.

36. For an extended discussion of the relationship between communion ecclesiology and the accountability of the episcopate to the faithful, see Robert Kaslyn,

'Accountability of Diocesan Bishops: A Significant Aspect of Ecclesial Communion', *The Jurist* 67 (2007), 109–52.

37. LC 1930, res. 49; LC 1998, res. III.6(e). David Hamid notes that '[t]he right to speak on behalf of Anglicanism is not necessarily a charism inherent simply in being the incumbent of the See of Canterbury'. ('Church, Communion of Churches and the Anglican Communion', *The Ecclesiastical Law Journal* 31 (2002), 365.) While this is true, the See of Canterbury does hold a moral authority within the Anglican Communion.

38. 'The apostle Paul never invoked law for his churches (indeed there was no canon law at that time), but he nevertheless exhorted them to be of one mind with him and to conform their lives to apostolic tradition (2 Thess. 2: 15).' 15 November 2005 letter from Global South Primates to Archbishop Rowan Williams, http://www.globalsouthanglican.org/index.php/article/global_south_primates_respon-se_to_archbishop_rowan_williams/ (accessed 28 September 2008). See also *The Windsor Report*, para. 65.

39. 'House of Bishops Issues Pastoral Statement on Civil Partnerships', http://www.cofe.anglican.org/news/pr5605.html (accessed 28 September 2008).

40. http://www.parliament.the-stationery-office.co.uk/pa/ld200304/ldbills/053/2004053.htm (accessed 28 September 2008).

41. 'A Statement by the Primate of All Nigeria', ACNS 4017, 8 August 2005, http://www.anglicancommunion.org/acns/news.cfm/2005/8/8/ACNS4017 (accessed 30 September 2008).

42. Hamid, 363: '[The Archbishop of Canterbury] has a primacy within England itself and by extension throughout the Anglican Communion.'

43. That is, the historic episcopate. Joseph Britton, 'The Evangelicity of the Episcopate', *Anglican Theological Review* 85 (2003), 610.

44. Constitution of the Church of Nigeria, chapter 1(3).

45. *Called to Common Mission*, http://archive.elca.org/ecumenical/fullcommunion/episcopal/ccmresources/text.html (accessed 3 October 2008), para. 12.

46. Britton, 616.

47. Robert Kaslyn, *'Communio with the Church' and the Code of Canon Law* (Lewiston, NY: Edwin Mellen, 1994), 13–22. The centrality of communion ecclesiology to post-conciliar thought may be more accurately traced to the Extraordinary Synod of 1985, which synthesized the message of *Lumen Gentium* in terms of 'communion'.

48. Eugenio Corecco, 'Ecclesiological Bases of the Code', in *Concilium: Canon Law–Church Reality*, ed. J. Provost and K. Wulf (Edinburgh: T&T Clark, 1986), 3–13.

49. For a description of *communio* with brief reference to *concilium*, see J. Ratzinger, 'Communio: A Project' (1992), 19 *Communio: International Catholic Review*, 436–49.

50. See LC 1930, res. 48 and Doe, 'Communion and Autonomy in Anglicanism'.

51. Corecco, 7, emphasis in original. See also *Lumen Gentium* 3(23): 'in and from these particular churches there exists the one unique catholic church'. *Decrees of the Ecumenical Councils*, ed. Norman Tanner (Washington, DC: Georgetown University Press, 1990), 867. The passage from *Lumen Gentium* is noted in Kaslyn, *'Communio with the Church' and the Code of Canon Law*, 23.

52. Kaslyn, *'Communio with the Church' and the Code of Canon Law*, 23.

53. John Renken, '*"Duc in Altum!"* Communio: Source and Summit of Church Law', *The Jurist* 63, 1 (2003), 55.

54. See Doe, 'Canon Law and Communion', 243–6.
55. The Anglican Consultative Council, *The Virginia Report*, http://www.lambeth-conference.org/1998/documents/report-1.pdf (accessed 3 October 2008), chapter 3(28).
56. Doe, 'Canon Law and Communion', 246.
57. *The Windsor Report*, para. 113. See also Norman Doe, 'The Common Law of the Anglican Communion', *International Journal for the Study of the Christian Church* 5, 3 (2005), 242–55, and 'The Contribution of Common Principles of Canon Law to Ecclesial Communion in Anglicanism', *The Ecclesiastical Law Journal* 10, 1 (2008), 71–91.
58. *The Windsor Report*, paras 118–20. See also 'An Anglican Covenant: St Andrew's Draft Text', http://www.anglicancommunion.org/commission/covenant/st_andrews/draft_text.cfm (accessed 3 October 2008).
59. See Norman Doe, 'Ecclesiastical Quasi-legislation', in *English Canon Law*, ed. N. Doe, M. Hill and R. Ombres (Cardiff: University of Wales Press, 1998), 93–103; and Doe, *Canon Law in the Anglican Communion*, 339–40.
60. The distinction between 'covenantal' and 'contractual' relations helpfully parallels the 'moral' and 'juridical' order of Anglican Communion. 'Covenantal systems rest on the creation of a compliance structure such that reflection by the participants will produce the conclusion that noncompliance to expectations constitutes a breakdown in their own moral essences' (David Bromley and Bruce Busching, 'Understanding the Structure of Contractual and Covenantal Social Relations: Implications for the Sociology of Religion', *Sociological Analysis* 49 (1988), 22S). See Edwin van Driel's chapter in this volume for another perspective on covenantal aspects of communion.
61. *Claiming our Anglican Identity*, II(2). See also *The Windsor Report*, para. 86.
62. Disciplinary protocol is much more established within Anglican provinces than on a global scale; nonetheless, something like 'admonition' or 'rebuke' may be found in *The Windsor Report*, para. 144. For descriptions of these terms, see Doe, *Canon Law in the Anglican Communion*, 88–9.
63. 'I accept that any individual diocese or even province that officially overturns or repudiates this resolution poses a substantial problem for the sacramental unity of the Communion.' Archbishop Rowan Williams, Letter to the Primates, 23 July 2002, quoted from *The Windsor Report*, para. 25 n. 9.
64. *The Anglican Communion Primates' Meeting Communiqué, February 2005*, para. 13. ACNS 3948, http://www.anglicancommunion.org/acns/news.cfm/2005/2/24/ACNS3948 (accessed 3 October 2008).
65. Doe, *Canon Law in the Anglican Communion*, 339: 'There is no formal Anglican canon law globally applicable to and binding upon member churches of the Communion. No central institution exists with competence to create such a body of law.'
66. Constitution of the Church of Nigeria, chapter 1(3)(2).
67. Press briefing by Archbishop Akinola, 29 September 2005: 'Our earnest desire is to see the fabric of our beloved Anglican Communion restored and our bonds of affection renewed through our common commitment to God's Word written as expressed in Article XX of our common Articles of Religion.' Archbishop Peter Akinola, Press Briefing, http://www.anglican-nig.org/primate's_pressbrief.htm (accessed 3 October 2008).
68. Doe, *Canon Law in the Anglican Communion*, 354–5.

69. See Robert Ombres, 'Ecclesiology, Ecumenism and Canon Law', in *English Canon Law*, ed. N. Doe, M. Hill and R. Ombres (Cardiff: University of Wales Press, 1998), 48–59.

70. IASCER 2003, Resolutions Arising from the 2003 Meeting, http://www. anglicancommunion.org/ministry/ecumenical/commissions/iascer/docs/2003resolutions.cfm (accessed 3 October 2008), res. 1.03. The terms of the Russian Orthodox Church's declaration are quoted as, 'wanting to maintain contacts and co-operation with the members of the Episcopal Church in the USA who clearly declared their loyalty to the moral teaching of the Holy Gospel and the Ancient Undivided Church'. This provision has also been clearly laid out by various provinces of the Anglican Communion that have otherwise declared impaired communion with TEC.

71. *Ad hoc* sub-commission of IARCCUM, *Ecclesiological Reflections on the Current Situation in the Anglican Communion in the Light of ARCIC*, http://www. prounione.urbe.it/dia-int/iarccum/doc/e_iarccum_2004.html (accessed 3 October 2008), para. 35, emphasis added.

72. Ibid., paras 25, 38 and 41.

73. Ibid., para. 48.

74. See Walter Cardinal Kasper, Letter to Rowan Williams, 17 December 2004, http://www.vatican.va/roman_curia/pontifical_councils/chrstuni/card-kasper-docs/rc_pc_chrstuni_doc_20041217_kasper-arch-canterbury_en.html (accessed 3 October 2008).

75. 'The text stands in line with our ARCIC documents, though there are other elements of ARCIC's work which we believe deserve further attention.' Kasper, Letter to Rowan Williams, 17 December 2004.

76. See Ombres, 'Ecclesiology, Ecumenism and Canon Law', 48–59.

77. LC 1998, res. IV.11.

78. The Church of Nigeria is involved in reconciliation with these groups as well through its controversial oversight of CANA. While discussion of this involvement is important, the issue of actual primatial oversight is beyond the scope of this chapter, as it requires consideration of the revisions to chapters 9 and 16 of the *Constitution of the Church of Nigeria*.

79. A bewildering array of communions, usually with established constitutions, makes it difficult to give an exhaustive citation of this claim. Continuing Anglican Churches are, however, generally characterized by a stated commitment to the Lambeth Quadrilateral and the apostolic episcopate. For further information, see http://www.anglicansonline.org/communion/nic.html (accessed 3 October 2008).

80. The Episcopal Church, USA, General Convention Resolutions 2003–B006, 2000–D047, http://www.episcopalarchives.org/cgi-bin/acts/acts_search.pl (accessed 3 October 2008).

81. Action on Resolutions Referred by the 74th General Convention, 2003–B006, http://episcopalarchives.org/e-archives/bluebook/15.html (accessed 3 October 2008).

82. For an example, see the *Articles of Ecclesiastical Fellowship* of the Bartonville Agreement of 1999, http://anglicanprovince.org/ccef.html (accessed 3 October 2008).

Chapter 14

SACRAL AUTHORITY AND PASTORAL MINISTRY: A SHAMANISTIC INCULTURATION OF THE PROTESTANT CHURCH IN KOREA

Hak Joon Lee

Introduction

This chapter discusses the nature and dynamics of sacral spiritual practices and pastoral ministry of Korean Protestant churches. Korean Protestant churches have been well known for their spiritual fervour, evangelical passion, and missionary zeal for the gospel. They have become one of the strongest and most active Protestant churches in the world since the first two Protestant missionaries landed in Korea 120 years ago. Almost all of the churches hold an early morning service every day around 5.00 a.m. (some even at 4.00 a.m.). More than half of the world's ten largest congregations are now located in Korea. The Protestant population has reached about a quarter of its total population. Korea is now second only to the USA in the number of missionaries it sends overseas. Those who travel to Korea immediately notice the numerous red-neon-signed crosses that light the sky of South Korea.

Yet Korean Protestant Christianity, now at the pinnacle of its power and influence, is, ironically, experiencing an unprecedented crisis. This is not a crisis imposed by outside forces, such as political oppression or religious persecution. It is an internal crisis mostly due to the deficiency of its moral credibility and public trust. The symptoms of the current crisis and malaise are found in several areas: the stagnation or even the decline of the once explosive numerical growth of the Korean Protestant churches; the silent exodus of young people and the greying of congregations; the implication and conviction of several prominent Christian lay leaders in national corruption scandals; inter-denominational conflicts and schisms; and so on. At the centre of this public distrust are the church's negligence of public responsibility and the underdevelopment of Christian social ethics.

How can we explain the unprecedented growth and sudden crisis of Korean Protestant Christianity? Are the two phenomena interrelated or unrelated? In addition, how should we understand the unique spiritual practices of Korean churches, such as early dawn services, fasting, passion for overseas missionary activities, and people's extraordinary financial commitment to the church? How are these practices related to the growth of the church? What ethical orientations, psychological motivations and sociological concerns underlie these spiritual practices?[1]

It is not easy to define the nature of Korean Protestant Christianity in a word. For Korean Protestant Christianity is already a complex religious entity with diverse denominational and theological expressions and practices. Nevertheless, Korean Protestant Christianity, despite its denominational differences and theological variations, demonstrates a distinctive characteristic which is quite unique from its Western counterpart – namely, a highly sacral nature as exhibited through various spiritual practices, such as the daily early dawn service, and a high respect for sanctuary and clergy. This is quite a dramatic characteristic given the fact that Protestantism is anti-sacral in nature.

Before we move further, I want briefly to define the word 'sacral' as used in this chapter. The sacral means a perceived or experienced sense of the numinous or the holy manifested through particular objects or practices. According to Paul Tillich, the sacral or the sacramental is a ubiquitous aspect of every religion. Every religion has some concrete media (sacraments) which its followers believe manifest the deity. Through sacral objects, believers experience the sense of the numinous, the sense of awe, respect and fear. A strict separation is usually required between sacral and profane objects.

The Protestant Reformation began as an anti-sacral movement to reform the church, in particular the ecclesiastical authority of the Roman Catholic Church which was extensively supported by various elaborate sacral practices, such as icons, statues, saints, stained glass, and sacraments. Iconoclastic movements reflected the zeal of Protestants to abolish these sacral practices of the church that espoused the transmission and manifestation of the magical power of God through icons, stained glass, and sculptures. Similarly, the Reformation slogan of *sola scriptura* intended to eliminate all the sacrally oriented ecclesiastical practices that did not have any scriptural basis.[2]

Like Western Protestant Churches, Korean Protestant Churches also started with strong iconoclastic, anti-sacral energy and orientation. They strictly prohibited any participation in traditional ancestor worship, or Buddhist and shamanistic sacral practices. They demanded that their members remove all the charms and icons associated with shamanism,

Buddhism or Taoism. Protestant Churches in Korea prohibited the construction of any visible human forms and statues because of the danger of idolatry. However, despite their formal doctrinal stances against sacraments, the content of their pastoral ministry is ironically sacral.

I contend that this sacral orientation is the source of both its explosive growth and current malaise and trouble. The sacral nature of Korean Protestant Christianity is the consequence of its indigenization of traditional Korean religions, most notably shamanism:[3] it results from its adoption of the sacral orientation, modality, and distinctive spiritual practices of shamanism. By striking a popular shamanistic spiritual chord in Korean people, the sacral orientation of Korean Protestant ministry has helped the churches to grow explosively with strong spiritual fervour, while, at the same time, ironically serving as a major cause of current problems.

The challenge for Korean Protestant Christianity is to determine how critically to balance its sacral spiritual practices with the moral and prophetic demands of the gospel in a rapidly changing society. It is a task that goes beyond minor adjustment of liturgical and pastoral methods, or management styles of the churches, but that demands the reconstruction of its theological and ecclesiological paradigm.

Inculturation of Korean Protestant Christianity

Korean shamanism

As the oldest folk religion in Korea, shamanism has constituted the most distinctive and resilient undercurrent of Korean popular religiosity. It has survived even extreme suppression and harsh persecution by so-called high religions, such as Buddhism and Confucianism, and the ruling elite class of Korea. If traditional elite classes resorted to the metaphysics and moral teachings of Buddhism and Confucianism to justify their governance and ruling, the Korean masses followed shamanism to meet their basic religious and psychological needs. Korean shamanism was rarely publicly or formally acknowledged by ruling classes and other organized religions. It has been dismissed as a religion of uneducated and lower-class people. However, according to Korean religious scholar Ryu Dong Shik, shamanism, rather than withering away, has exercised its resilience by subtly transforming the very nature of dominant religions. Anchored in the deepest psyche of primal human desires, wishes and anxieties, it repeatedly appears in disguise in the rituals, ceremonies and spiritual practices of established religions. Korean Buddhism and Christianity are shamanistic in their content to a certain extent, as they have been internally changed by shamanism.[4]

Broadly speaking, shamanism is a primitive sacral polytheism or polydemonism. It is a sort of animism which believes that every object has an indwelling spirit or soul, thus is sacral.[5] In Korea, shamanism is called *sinkyo*, meaning spirit worship. It believes that the human realm and nature are permeated by various kinds of spirits. Every human event is under the control and influence of spirits. The universe is inhabited and controlled by these spirits of the living and the dead, and inanimate objects. Human misfortunes and calamities are the results of the manipulation of discontented, malicious spirits. A shaman's role is to appease the malice of evil spirits and to enlist them to the service of human well-being.[6] *Kut* is performed to appease and control malignant spirits. The participants of *Kut* are required to purify themselves with ascetic ritualistic activities, such as washing and temperance.

Since shamanism is a religion of pan-demonism, it takes a highly sacral nature. Every object or entity where a spirit dwells becomes sacral. This pervasive sacral orientation is couched in a popular Korean phrase, *bujung tanda*, meaning impurity or contamination may happen. The phrase is used when one fears that something ominous might occur as a sacred object or an entity (where one believes a spirit dwells) is contaminated. This shamanistic idea of purity/impurity is the expression of sacralism. It is based on the belief that spirits dwell in certain entities, and that proximity to these sacral entities means proximity to them. Therefore, these entities, where spirits are believed to dwell, must be treated with extreme care and respect. When they are properly treated and respected, they bring blessing to a person; otherwise, a curse.

In most aspects, shamanism shows a highly utilitarian character in its ethical orientation. The chief goal of a religious practice is to secure fortune, happiness, material prosperity, and psychological peace. The relationship between gods and humans is understood in contractual terms. It is based on the transaction of benefits and rewards – human beings give respect, homage and tributes to gods, and gods in return provide them with material blessings and protection.[7]

Although shamanism has played a substantial pastoral function for *minjung* (a Korean word for ordinary or oppressed people), it should be noted that it has never developed a methodology of ethics or political practices that are critical of the oppressive system of patriarchy and feudal class. (We have never heard of revolts or rebellions initiated or organized by shamans.) Rather, shamanism takes a dominant social system for granted. Shamanism functions within the circumscribed boundary of the status quo. Its focus is therapeutic in helping people to adjust to a given situation. By providing a channel or outlet to express *han* (unresolved and accumulated feelings of oppression and injustice) in a way that is non-destructive to a dominant social structure, shamanism has rather contributed to maintaining the status quo. This provides one sociological explanation for why the ruling class or regime has tolerated shamanism at the margin and often used it for its own political purpose.

Korean Protestantism and shamanism: affinities and collusions

The association and similarity between shamanism and Korean Protestantism is found in several aspects of Korean Protestant spirituality and practices: sacral practices, spiritualism, experientialism, and therapeutic emphasis.

Sacral practices of Korean Protestantism

Korean Protestantism has taken on a strong sacral nature. It emphasizes a strict separation of several sacral objects from other profane or mundane ones. A sacral nature is discovered in the fact that proximity to these sacral entities means proximity to God, thus access to more divine favour and blessing.[8] When these sacred objects are offended or violated, one is warned that something ominous might happen (in a popular Korean phrase, *bujung tanda*, as aforementioned).[9] When they are properly treated and respected, they bring blessing to a person. In particular, sacralization is found in the consecration of a particular time (early dawn; Sabbath), space (sanctuary) and person (clergy), which are closely associated with indigenous Korean shamanism.

Sacralization *of time:*

The early dawn service (held every morning around 5.00 a.m.; for some churches, 4.30 a.m.) is a unique Korean Protestant religious practice. It has its liturgical root in a folk religious practice. When there was a family emergency or crisis, Koreans went to a shrine at dawn to pray about it to the spirit. Dawn is the time of hierophany, that is 'something sacred shows itself to us'.[10] In Korean Protestant Christianity, like the Sabbath, this time is consecrated as a specially designated, sacred time. Borrowing from a Taoist–shamanist cosmogonic understanding of dawn, many Korean Christian pastors believe that, unlike ordinary times of a day, this early dawn time has a numinous power and efficacy in experiencing God's grace. Since the dawn is the beginning of the day, it has a cosmogonic power. By participating ritually in this time, a person is born anew. Just as 'New Year' is the moment of rebirth and purification, dawn is the time of the cosmogony of a day.[11] A day is reborn and purified at dawn. The old day is finally abolished, and a new day begins.[12] Clergy emphasize that prayer and worship in the early dawn time have a special healing and regenerative (transformative) power for one's life and family. The usual suggestion of Korean clergies is: 'If you have some trouble in your personal, family or business life, start to attend early dawn service.' To accommodate the needs of members, some churches have three or four official early dawn services.

Korean Protestant Christians support the significance (sacral nature) of the early dawn service through reference to several biblical passages:

1. They believe that Jesus Christ practised the early dawn prayer. 'In the morning, while it was still very dark, he got up and went out to a deserted place, and there he prayed' (Mk 1.35).
2. A Psalmist praises God's answer and response to his or her prayers at dawn. 'Awake, O harp and lyre! I will awake the *dawn*' (Ps. 108.2). 'Awake, my soul! Awake, O harp and lyre! I will awake the *dawn*' (Ps. 57.8). 'I rise before *dawn* and cry for help; I put my hope in your words' (Ps. 119.147).
3. Women disciples heard the good news of resurrection at dawn of the day. 'After the sabbath, as the first day of the week was *dawning*, Mary Magdalene and the other Mary went to see the tomb' (Mt. 28.1).

Sacralization *of space:*

For the Korean Protestants, the church sanctuary takes on a similar sacral nature. The sanctuary or religious places are believed to be in communication with the divine, spiritual world, as contrasted against a human, profane world. Biblically, the Korean Protestant respect for a sanctuary has a basis in the Old Testament idea of the temple. The Temple is a special place of divine dwelling and manifestation. Korean Protestant Christians have an extraordinary passion for erecting church buildings. They believe that a sanctuary has a sacral power as the place of divine dwelling. Korean Protestant Christians believe that the temple (a sanctuary) is a special space opened upward, thus one where a communication with the divine is ritually possible.[13] A sanctuary offers a higher degree of access to the presence of God. Hence, worship and prayer in the sanctuary have a higher spiritual efficacy than other ordinary places. Many Korean pastors encourage their members to live in close proximity to the sanctuary. It is an unstated rule and general expectation that core and active members and church officers live in the immediate vicinity of the church. According to Eliade, humans tend to believe that the true world is at the centre, and the temple constitutes that centre spatially on earth. A universe is born and developed from the centre, and reaches out to other realms.[14] Therefore, living nearer to the church and worshipping there as frequently as possible have a direct relationship with rebirth and the renewal of one's life in every aspect. For life is renewed from the centre, namely, the sanctuary.

Sacralization *of person:*

Similarly, a sacral aspect is found in Korean Protestant Christians' view of a cleric. The respect and unconditional moral support for a cleric is often emphasized not only as the duty of the members but also as a source to bring a blessing to one's family. Criticism of a cleric was equated with inevitable recourse to divine judgement. Even in their various moral deficiencies and misdeeds, a cleric should not be disobeyed, nor publicly criticized. Numerous biblical stories and passages are cited in support of this belief (e.g. 1 Sam. 1 (Hannah's obedience to Eli); (David's refusal to kill Saul as God's anointed king)).

A cleric is perceived (or required) to be a spiritual mediator, standing between God and the congregation. Members of the congregation expect ministers to supplicate or intercede for the well-being of their family, business, career, children and so forth. They perceive a cleric as a charismatic figure. The authority of clergy resides in his or her spiritual power to solve a problem.[15] This spiritual orientation is found in various ministry practices, such as visitation, spiritual healing, and deliverance. Especially, attending the opening ceremony for a new business is an obligation that a minister should not miss, it being believed that the minister's presence and intercession will bring a blessing to the business. Such a view of clergy is resonant with the shamanistic idea of a religious mediator, a shaman.

In shamanism, access to the invisible world of spirits is privileged to shamans. The shaman's authority is charismatic in nature; their authority comes from their intimate relationship with the spiritual realm. They know the secret plans and intentions of the gods and spirits which are blocked to ordinary people. In short, shamans take on a sacramental characteristic towards others. By mediating the spiritual and the mundane realms – namely, through their sacramental persona – shamans exercise a priestly function.

Compared to their Western counterparts, Korean clergies command a much higher spiritual and moral authority. These religious characteristics are commonly found across various Protestant denominations.[16]

Spiritualism Korean Protestantism shows a similarity with shamanism in terms of its strong spiritualism. Koreans do not have any difficulty in accepting the actuality of the spirits and the supreme deity, whom Korean shamanism and Taoism call *Hananim*.[17] In particular, Korean Protestant

Christians show extraordinary interest in and concern for the agents in the spiritual realm, such as demons, ghosts and evil spirits – their work and influence on human affairs and destinies. The biblical world of demons, evil spirits, ghosts and the Supreme God is not alien to the ears of Korean people. This religious preference made Koreans receptive to Protestant Christian ministry, which gives more extensive and serious attention to the Holy Spirit than Catholicism. This point is validated by the fact that, more than any other Protestant denomination, the Pentecostal Church, which gives the most extensive and fervent ministerial attention to the works of the Spirit, has been the fastest-growing denomination in Korea. Pentecostal ministerial practices strongly resonate with indigenous Korean shamanism in terms of their beliefs in and emphasis on spiritual healing, spiritual prophecy, spiritual trance, exorcism, and various spirit-related phenomena such as trembling, shaking and spirit possession. For example, the shamanistic idea of spirit possession (or trance) has a strong resonance in Korean Pentecostalism, namely, possession by the Holy Spirit.

Experientialism   Like shamanism, Korean Protestantism emphasizes the importance of a religious experience for being Christian. Being an authentic Christian means to have a certain religious experience of God rather than relying on information and knowledge of the Bible. Despite its doctrinal underdevelopment, the person and the work of the Holy Spirit have received an inordinate degree of attention in Korean Protestantism through various practices and events, such as prayer, fasting and revivalism.

Religious experience is closely associated with the Spirit. To be religious means to be filled with, or possessed by, a spirit. The Holy Spirit is understood as the immanent power of God who cures and works miracles, often manifested in speaking in tongues, shaking, shouting, trance, and so forth. This understanding of the spiritual led to a belief that the efficacy of a religious practice should be assessed by the consequences it produces for the well-being of a person.

Spiritualism and experientialism in Korean popular religiosity provide a rich and favourable condition for the development of sacral practices. Spiritualism and experientialism are ritualistically practised through the sacralization of a particular time (such as dawn), space (such as a particular mountain, or shrine), and person (such as a shaman, or clergy). These sacral objects are understood as the media of divine manifestation and presence.

Therapeutic orientation

A further notable evidence of a shamanistic influence on Korean Protestantism is the latter's emphasis on a pastoral rather than prophetic dimension of ministry. Shamanism, by virtue of its harmonic tendency and utilitarian orientation, is overtly therapeutic and pastoral. As we have seen previously, it is primarily oriented towards the service of the interests and concerns of clients. Its primary goal is the well-being and self-interest of its clients. This overwhelmingly pastoral emphasis is also reflected in Korean Protestant ministries. Most Korean Protestant churches are rarely prophetic; the ministerial practices of Korean Protestantism are mostly governed by personal concerns, such as health, success and blessing in this life. The prominent example is Revd Cho's theology of 'Three Fold Blessings', which on the basis of 3 Jn 1.2 emphasizes God's blessings in three areas: spiritual (soul), physical (health), and all matters of life.[18]

The therapeutic orientation of Korean Protestant ministry has to do with the class background of Korean Protestant Christians. Unlike Protestant churches in Japan, Korean Protestant churches were built from below. Churches proselytized most of their converts from the under or lower class and women – those whose popular religiosity was predominantly influenced by shamanism. In approaching and offering pastoral care for these poor and marginalized people, pastors used spiritual methods, forms and words that were familiar to them. In a word, Korean Protestant Christianity offered the kind of therapeutic pastoral service that shamanism has traditionally done for *minjung*.

Historical-cultural factors for sacralization

When and how did this sacralization process take place? How did a once prophetic and socially active Protestantism become a sacral-experiential one? Although indigenization is usually a long, natural, historical process involving continuous evolution and transmutation, I argue that in Korea several crucial historical events and cultural conditions were especially conducive towards such a sacral development in Korea.

Since its first introduction to Korea in 1885, Korean Protestant Christianity was a socially engaging, politically active, prophetically oriented religion. Despite its small membership, it exercised its leadership in national independence movements from Japan, various social reform movements – including the advocacy of women's and children's rights – popular education, and so on. Missionaries and early Korean Protestant church leaders were active in establishing schools, hospitals, newspapers and publishing companies to promote democracy and human rights through education and civic organizations. For example, many prominent Korean private colleges and schools were established by Protestants, and a disproportionately large number of early political and social leaders were Protestants.

However, several significant historical events and social forces have contributed to the apoliticization, and consequently the sacralization, of Korean Protestant Christianity.

1. Historically, apoliticization resulted from a distressing political and social situation of Korea in the early twentieth century under Japanese colonialism. Facing oppressive Japanese colonialism, Korean Protestant Christianity increasingly took on a more other-worldly, mystical form, thus ahistorical and asocial, distancing itself from social and historical issues and problems. The historical oppressive force of colonialism pushed Korean Protestant Christianity in the direction of apoliticization, thus making it vulnerable to the influence of indigenous popular religiosity. This ahistorical and asocial attitude has a great deal of affinity with the spiritual orientations of the indigenous religions of Korea. Over time, it caused Protestant Christianity to fit nicely into, and become easily adaptable to, the sacral and mystical modalities and ethos of the indigenous religions.

2. Western missionaries' protective concern for the church also made an impact. They had profound concerns about the political participation and activism of Korean Protestant Christianity under Japanese domination, so intentionally steered the church away from political engagements, emphasizing the separation of church and state. Their primary concern was for the survival of young fledgling churches which they had newly implanted. This concern coincided with the political interest of Japanese colonial power, which vehemently wanted to domesticate and control Korean Protestant Christianity so that it would not become the source of political protest and unrest. The missionary control of theology, theological education and ecclesiastical bodies effectively blocked the expression of spiritual energies and ministry engagement in the public social realms. It diverted and deferred Christian energy to a mystical otherworldly realm or the eschatological future.

3. The 1907 spiritual awakening played a formative influence in the shaping of Korean Protestant Christianity's spirituality in the direction of the mystical, experiential, and apolitical on a popular and massive level. It would not be an exaggeration to say that the

tone, colour and ethos of Korean Protestant Christianity were shaped by the 1907 movement and the theology of its leaders.

One should notice that the popularization of the early dawn service coincided with the apoliticization of Korean Protestant Christianity. Korean church historians identify the Revd Kil Sun Joo as the Korean pastor who started the early dawn service. With a deep and extensive Taoist background, he played a formative and leading role in the 1907 Great Awakening in Korea, which took place two years after Korea became the Protectorate of Japan. This was a grim and desolate time in Korean history. The original reforming and transformative social energy and ethos of Korean Protestant Christianity began to dissipate, to be replaced by a personal and interiorized spirituality. The goal of the movement was spiritual purity, but it was profoundly apolitical in nature.

Through the interplay of these internal, external and institutional forces, Korean Protestant Christianity was transmuted into an apolitical, mystical, sacral religion, gradually dissipating its early political activism, prophetic spirit, and transformative energy and zeal. Eschatology became a favourite subject of revival meetings and Bible expository meetings. Christ was understood as the sacrificial lamb, the perfection of self-sacrifice. Under the harsh repression of Japanese colonialism, after-life rewards and blessings were emphasized over this-worldly struggles and services. Personal ascetic piety and self-sacrifice were the dominant virtues of Christian ministers.[19]

If apoliticization effectively tamed the prophetic passion of Korean Protestantism, then grassroots pastoral needs opened up and facilitated a more extensive assimilation into shamanistic religiosity. From the early twentieth century to recent times, Korean Christians have collectively undergone a series of enormous traumatic experiences, such as Japanese colonialism, persecution, war, poverty, displacement, and radical transition from agricultural to industrial society. In such situations, pastoral and therapeutic needs are huge and naturally came to the forefront of the church's ministry. Churches were forced to respond to this collective demand for care and healing. And in the process of responding to people's growing needs for therapeutic care and support, the ministry of Korean Protestant churches has become pastoral in nature and more explicitly assimilated into a dominant shamanistic religious orientation, form and pattern which are familiar to the ordinary people of Korea.[20] Churches responded to the therapeutic needs of people using the categories, thought patterns and spiritual methods that are familiar to *minjung*, namely, those of shamanism.

Later, the Korean Protestant churches' penchant for church growth facilitated a further assimilation into a shamanistic religiosity. Shamanistic influence has become more dominant since the mid-1960s, which coincided with the major capitalistic development of Korea. Even during this historic time (1965–87), a strong external political reality, such as anti-communism and suppression of human rights by military governments, discouraged the political participation of most Korean Protestant churches. Intimidated by political suppression, yet having already grown accustomed to compromise with and acquiescence to a political power, Korean Protestant Christianity discovered the economy as a relevant realm of its participation and activity. Riding on this capitalistic tide sweeping Korean society, Korean Protestant Christianity actively espoused and advocated the sacral, this-worldly form of Christianity that emphasizes the material blessings and comfort of capitalism. This materialistic orientation found a home in a shamanistic religiosity. Christian faith was blatantly espoused as the most effective means to achieve wealth, health, fame and power. The previous ascetic, otherworldly form of Christianity was discarded as defeatism. The primary christological image has shifted from Jesus as the ascetic, sacrificial lamb to the triumphant shaman. This-worldly reward and blessing were emphasized. Although poverty was not condemned as a vice, wealth and power were emphatically upheld as the signs of divine blessing for obedient Christians. Korean Protestant Christianity grew explosively. Mega-churches mushroomed together with conglomerates (*chae-bols*).

The Revd David Yonggi Cho of Yoido Full Gospel Church was a popularizer of this gospel of wealth and blessing. In a sense, his ministry was typically Korean; he has built the largest church in the world by starting his ministry in a poor neighbourhood using the message of prosperity, healing and success, securitized with Korean shamanistic spirituality. One should not underestimate the impact of the phenomenal growth of the Full Gospel Church and of the Revd Cho's theology on Korean Protestant Christianity between the 1960s and 80s. Many churches adopted his model of ministry – the most explicit form of a shamanistic Christianity – as they sought for similar success. His theology of blessing has exerted enormous influence upon the direction and spread of this spiritual orientation. At the forefront of the church's pastoral care and ministry, and driven by church growth, pastors have been responsive to effective methods of ministry, evangelism, preaching and therapeutic healing, which appeal to and mobilize people. Many adopted Cho's ministry methods.

In sum, Korean Protestant Christianity, which had begun as a vibrant, socially active and reformative religion in Korea, has increasingly transformed into an apolitical, asocial, sacral religion, negatively through the pressure of the oppressive political realities, and positively through its response to the therapeutic-pastoral needs of people experiencing suffering and trauma. In the process of responding to these external and internal pressures, Korean Protestant Christianity naturally adopted and utilized indigenous shamanism, which was constitutive of Korean people's religiosity.

Evaluation

The inculturation of Korean Protestantism into shamanism is not necessarily negative, because, as preaching is a communication of the gospel, any communication cannot disregard the operating values, entrenched habits and shared ethos of the audience. In other words, a cultural translation of the gospel is an inevitable aspect of Christian ministry. However, a serious problem occurs when this translation process compromises the essential truths of the gospel.

Sacralization is an indispensable aspect of any human world-making activity. Human beings construct their symbolic world through the distinction of the sacred and the profane. In this respect, one may say that the sacralization of early dawn, sanctuary, and clergy is a unique cosmological construction of Korean Protestant Christians imbued with indigenous shamanistic religiosity. The sacral categories of time, space and person constitute the matrix of the Korean Protestant symbolic universe. The idea of Sabbath as the centre/beginning of a week, early dawn as the centre/beginning of a day, and sanctuary as the centre/axis of space is extensively taught and preached in Korean Protestant Christianity. Respect for the sacral nature of these temporal, spatial and anthropological entities is considered the basic requirement for any dedicated Christian. These sacral objects function to provide a point of reference and orientation for many Korean Protestant Christians. Their experiences are interpreted and organized around such categories. By fixing focuses and demarcating boundaries, sacral objects have helped establish order in the lives of Christians.

The sacral objects outlined have provided pragmatic anchorage points for Korean Protestant Christians in taming and controlling often alien, harsh and uncertain realities created by rapid social change and structural transformations. During the last four decades, Korea has been one of the most dramatically changing societies in the world. Literally every realm of the society – from the political system, to the economy, the family and mass culture – has experienced a radical transformation. As one can easily imagine, this transformation has generated enormous anxiety, expectation, uncertainty and confusion among people. More urgently than at any other time of their history, Koreans have needed spiritual guidance and orientation to hold their lives together.

For example, the establishment of the early dawn service and its popular ritualization was partly a response to the enormous pastoral needs experienced by lay Christians. People needed a spiritual outlet to express their frustration, despair and hopelessness. Lay Christians could not be left unattended until the next Sunday service – the time in between is simply too long for many of them. This is especially true for those living in highly unfavourable environments – rejected and even persecuted by their families due to their conversion to Christianity, or facing economic difficulties, or struggling to cope with the challenge of rapid social change. More immediate pastoral care and spiritual guidance have been required, and thus Korean Protestant Christianity has used early dawn services as a spiritual triage (a spiritual emergency room) to provide daily opportunities for spiritual care, many receiving pastoral counsel immediately after such services.

Many of them conveniently located in cities, Protestant churches have used daily dawn services and cell group meetings to make pastoral care accessible to their members, successfully meeting their needs and equipping them with spiritual energy and personal discipline. Many Korean Protestant Christians literally begin their day with an early dawn service. They organize their daily schedules in relation to this, going to bed early in order to attend the service. This means exercising an enormous degree of self-control and self-restraint in their social lives. They cannot watch late-night TV or movies, nor go to a bar nor spend time with friends into the small hours.[21]

Korean Christianity was able to grow explosively by virtue of its exploitation of and appeal to an inherited shamanistic religiosity, and through providing the sort of therapeutic pastoral service that shamanism has traditionally performed for *minjung*. According to David Kwang Suh, 'Korean Christianity has its deepest roots in ... *mudang* [meaning shamanistic] religion, and thereby, Christianity put down roots in the minds of the *minjung*. Thus, Korean Christianity has been able to grow in numbers, and become one of the most powerful and dynamic religions in Korea.'[22]

In particular, Korean Protestant Christianity, by and large, has met two sociological requirements that Harvey Cox suggests every religious institution needs for its numerical growth:

> [F]or any religion to grow in today's world, it must possess two capabilities: it must be able to include and transform at least certain elements of preexisting religions which still retain a strong grip on the cultural subconsciousness. It must also equip people to live in rapidly changing societies where personal

responsibility and inventiveness, skills associated with a democratic polity and an entrepreneurial economy, are indispensable.[23]

Korean Protestant churches effectively tapped into the deep and vibrant religious and cultural subconsciousness of Korean people through its sacral, therapeutic pastoral ministry, which offered healing of wounds, release from stress and anxiety, and ecstatic religious experiences. It also provided individuals with a structure and form of personal discipline and responsibility that assisted the ordering and stability of their personal and social lives remarkably well in a hugely turbulent, modern social life.

Suggestion

Despite all the above, today a shamanistic sacral Protestantism is increasingly losing its vitality and efficacy, failing to respond to the various new and complex demands and needs of a highly industrial society. Cultural subconsciousness, such as shamanistic religiosity, and personal needs and values do not remain intact. They alter not only as time goes by but also as the economic status of people, institutional structures, social expectations and norms change. The change is more explicit and extensive among young people.

Deeply integrated into the global economy and media – with the thirteenth largest economy in the world, producing world-class cell phones and electronics, and computer chips in auto vehicles – Korean people are familiar with highly impersonal and rational organizational structures, including sophisticated managerial systems that demand objective analysis and public accountability. They no longer rise and go to bed by nature's rhythms and tempos. Through a successful democratic transition and the rise of a strong civil society, Korean mass media, intellectuals and citizens appreciate and promote critical thinking, democratic processes and transparency, and dialogical partnership, rather than uncritical indoctrination, hierarchical structures and authoritarian leadership. Sacral Christianity thus finds itself in deep dissonance and conflict with democratic society. This raises a challenge for Korean Protestant Christianity, the pastoral ministry and authority of which is built upon sacralism. As a recent series of investigative reports of Korean Protestant Christianity by major Korean TV networks has revealed, Korean society is highly critical of its sacral practices.

How should Korean Protestant Christianity respond to these challenges and criticism? Its problem is that, although sacral objects are instrumental in orienting people's lives, producing a cosmos out of chaos, such objects are interpreted too narrowly through a shamanistic religious periscope. One cannot deny that shamanism provided a significant modality/pattern of religious experiences and interpretation for Korean Protestant Christians. By channelling and interpreting religious energies and experiences, a modality could affect the content of such experiences. Modalities in religious experiences exercise a selective and discriminative power over the content as the latter is appropriated and interpreted through the former. The shamanistic religious modality selectively chooses certain aspects of the Christian gospel over other aspects. In many cases, the significance of these sacral entities is emphasized primarily for the sake of personal blessings rather than for sanctification or for public justice and righteousness. The inculturation of Korean Protestantism into shamanism requires its critical and extensive re-evaluation. Sometimes, it can barely be distinguished whether Christianity has absorbed shamanism, or the other way around. In many cases, the boundary and content of the moral life constituted by such sacral entities turn out to be not so different from those of shamanism. Without constant and rigorous theological scrutiny and ethical examination of their content, spiritual practices will continue their compromises with a pseudo-shamanistic cultural ethos and its values. Korean Protestant churches need to examine the primary goal of their ministry: whether it is the kingdom of God or their own institutional-numerical success. Assimilation has gone unnoticed because Korean Protestant Christianity, preoccupied with church growth, has failed to critically examine the theological and moral presuppositions of its ministry, and their dangerous similarity to those of shamanism.

In order to cope with the challenges of public credibility and the demands for elaborate ethical guidance, Korean Protestant Christianity needs to restore a prophetic and public dimension of the gospel in balance with sacral-pastoral dimensions. This implies that the free-giving, unconditional grace of God in Jesus Christ (the ultimate) must be combined with the care of the poor and the body (the penultimate). As Korean Christianity looks for a plausible moral framework that can guide its leadership and exercise of stewardship, it must retrieve a Reformed Protestant spirit that embraces every realm of human existence and activity as the realm of God's dominion; a spirit that empowers individuals in their worldly vocations for the service of the kingdom rather than confining their Christian activities to the church. In short, it needs to develop a contextually grounded public theology that maintains a creative balance between public and private, historical and mystical, evangelism and social activism. By doing so, Korean Protestant Christianity will continue to be a culture-shaping power in Korea, just as it was in the past.

Notes

1. The analysis of spiritual practices is crucial for the understanding of the nature and characteristics of the Korean Protestant Church and its ministry; it provides clues to Korean Protestant Christians' religious dispositions, ethical predilections and cultural preferences. My premise is that the primary object of analysis and observation of ecclesiological practices is not confessional documents or theological doctrines but spiritual practices. As the medium through which hidden popular religiosity is disclosed, spiritual practices reflect people's deep meaning structure, unspoken values, and metaphysical understandings which are often in disparity with the formal doctrines and beliefs of the church.

2. For example, out of this anti-sacral concern, the Reformers reduced seven sacraments to two, baptism and the Eucharist, according to the rule of the scriptures.

3. Shamanism is not the only religion that is amalgamated into Korean Protestant Christianity. Confucianism, with its emphasis on harmony, respect for authority, virtue ethics, and differentiation of sex roles and age, has also left indelible marks on the institutional structures of Korean Protestant Christianity. One can also trace the influences of other religions, such as Taoism and Buddhism, more often than not in a way quite indistinguishable from each other, as Korean society has been religiously syncretistic for many centuries.

4. One typical structure of Korean Buddhist temples is the conjoining of a shamanistic shrine right next to the main temple. This implies that Korean Buddhism already has a shamanistic ethos and spirituality.

5. Pan-demonism implies that in shamanism there is no strict duality between human beings and gods, life and death, the sacred and the secular (Young Chan Ro, 'Ancestor Worship: From the Perspective of Korean Tradition', in *Ancestor Worship and Christianity in Korea*, ed. Jung Young Lee (Lewiston, NY: Edwin Mellen Press, 1988), 11.

6. Ibid.

7. The utilitarian and this-worldly nature of shamanism is manifested in the names and nature of *kuts* as they are regularly performed in Korean society: good harvest *kut*, good fishing *kut*, village *kut*, Sungju *kut*, Chukwon *kut*, Jaesu *kut* – all have to do with luck, fortune and wealth.

8. Cf. Mircea Eliade, *The Sacred and the Profane: The Nature of Religion* (New York: Harcourt, 1959), 14.

9. Strong Korean temperance practices (prohibition of alcohol, tobacco and dance) also sometimes take a sacral tendency, although they were first initiated by early Western missionaries.

10. Eliade, *The Sacred and the Profane*, 11.

11. Ibid., 78.

12. Its cosmogonic power could be explained by a religious anthropological notion, namely liminality. As a betwixt between night and day, chaos and cosmos, darkness and light, it has a liminal and self-renewing power.

13. Eliade, *The Sacred and the Profane*, 43.

14. Ibid., 44.

15. This dimension becomes the source of conflict and trouble for a congregation when lay members believe that they have more spiritual powers than a pastor.

Hence, Korean Protestantism in its religious practice finds it hard to embrace the Protestant idea of the priesthood of all believers.

16. However, the shamanistic influence on the process of the sacralization of Korean Protestant Christianity does not imply the reduction of all ministry practices to shamanistic origins. Early dawn, sanctuary and clergy are not worshipped as the holy itself, although they are certainly treated as sacral objects. The spiritual practices are also enacted on the biblical basis, although they have not been critically reflected in coherent theological terms.

17. *Hananim* literally means 'the only one' or 'the highest one'. Korean Christianity, both Catholic and Protestant, has adopted this particular noun in referring to God.

18. 3 Jn 1.2 says, 'Beloved, I pray that all may go well with you and that you may be in good health, just as it is well with your soul.'

19. In my observation, during this period (1907–45), a Taoistic and Buddhistic orientation was more prominent than a shamanistic one.

20. This approach is visible today among many seeker-oriented mega-churches across the world.

21. One could easily see to it that this daily ascetic practice could play a positive role for the formation of a capitalistic work ethic.

22. David Kwang Sun Suh, 'Korean Shamanism: The Religion of Han', in *Essays on Korean Heritage and Christianity*, ed. Sang H. Lee (Princeton Junction: Association of Korean Christian Scholars in North America, Inc, 1984), 84.

23. Harvey Cox, *Fire from Heaven: The Rise of Pentecostal Spirituality and the Reshaping of Religion in the Twenty-first Century* (Mass.: Addison-Wesley Pub., 1995), 219.

Chapter 15

CONFUCIANISM, INTERNATIONALISM, PATRIOTISM AND
PROTESTANTISM: The ECCLESIOLOGICAL MATRIX OF JAPANESE
CHRISTIAN ACTIVISTS IN JAPAN AND THE US DIASPORA

Madeline Duntley

From 1890 to 1935 Japanese Christian leaders provided the US Japanese
diaspora with a missionary model of internationalist ecclesiology that
merged and harmonized ideas and initiatives from both East and West.
From the Japanese religious milieu missionaries combined Confucian
moral remonstrance and Samurai loyalty ethic with Western internationalist peacemaking and vice reform activism. Japanese Christians created an
ecclesiological model of an ecumenically oriented 'Church of the Pacific
Era' that transected existing racial, national, gender, denominational and
inter-religious boundaries. The influence of these Japanese leaders upon the
diaspora community in Seattle, Washington, is most apparent in the
establishment of the *Domei* or Church Federation League established in
1912 and surviving into the twenty-first century. This ecumenical league
consists of six [sic] historic Japanese ethnic congregations (Methodist,
Baptist, Presbyterian, Episcopal and Congregational) all of which are over a
century old.[1]

This chapter will examine the native Japanese mission heritage that
shaped this diaspora community, and will utilize *Shiatoru Nihonjin Kirisuto
Kyokai Domei* (a little-known Japanese-language mission history of this six-
church interdenominational confederation). The Japanese diaspora in
Seattle did not merely recreate ethnic versions of American denominations,
but implemented a uniquely Japanese Christian vision that set the stage for
twentieth-century ecumenism and activism in Seattle's Japanese American
community.

Evidence of the influence of the native Japanese missionaries can be seen
at many junctures in the history of Seattle's Japanese Christian community.
Perhaps the most striking example is the interfaith ecumenism practised by
Seattle's Japanese Americans during their wartime incarceration in

internment camps and relocation centres. The wartime story of Tsutomu
'Tom' Fukuyama is emblematic of the ecumenist sensibility inherited from
Japanese Christian missionaries.[2] One cold, spring day in April 1942, 26-
year-old Fukuyama was hastily ushered into the sanctuary of Seattle's
largest ethnic congregation, the Japanese Baptist Church. As the rain pelted
noisily against the arched glass windows, a small band of determined
Baptists sang hymns and performed the brief, age-old service that would
ordain Fukuyama into the gospel ministry. It was an anxious time in
Seattle's Japanese community. Within three weeks, all of Seattle's 7.000
Japanese Americans would be evacuated to nearby Puyallup Assembly
Center for a four-month incarceration before final transfer to Minidoka
Relocation Center in Hunt, Idaho. The rushed ordination ensured that
Fukuyama would be fully qualified to lead the church in captivity.
Fukuyama felt that the providence of God guided his ordination that
stormy day, and was struck by the irony of a Bible verse a former teacher
had recently mailed him: 'Who knoweth whether thou art not come to the
kingdom for such a time as this?' (Esther 4.14b).

Eight months later, Tom Fukuyama stood in his barracks offices at
Minidoka Relocation Center cranking an old mimeograph to print his
1942 Christmas card. Fukuyama's Christmas letter framed the Second
World War incarceration and exile of the Japanese American community
within a wider global context of injustice and oppression. 'After all, we are
only an insignificant part of exiles at Christmas time', he wrote, and
mentioned the downtrodden in Burma, China, and the homeless of all
lands. Then he spoke in startling ecumenical visionary terms of Minidoka
as

> ... an experiment in communal living, progressive education, and religious
> cooperation which [has] challenging possibilities. All class barriers which
> existed among the Japanese before have been completely obliterated ... This
> extends into the realm of religion, and we are enjoying the creative challenge
> of working across denominational lines ... And we have gotten rid of the old
> antagonisms between Christians and Buddhists. I have a hope that the faiths
> represented on the project: Catholic, Protestant, and Buddhist can come
> together to draw up a statement of faith to which all can subscribe.[3]

Fukuyama believed that wartime incarceration must not be merely one of
the 'dark tragedies of American history'. Rather, he sought to transform this
disorienting exile into an opportunity to forge cross-religious connections
and understanding.

The interfaith work that Fukuyama was referring to is one of the most
striking features of Japanese American religious life during their wartime

incarceration. Buddhists, Protestants and Catholics participated in interfaith public worship services at Minidoka Relocation Center. At this time in the 1940s, it was highly unusual for Protestants and Catholics to gather in interdenominational worship, as it was rare for Buddhists to cross sectarian lines. Yet several Buddhists cooperated with many denominations of Protestants as well as with Catholic Christians in a variety of interfaith gatherings. Buddhists and Protestants even cooperated in sponsoring a Vacation Church School in the summer months. For the first time, Catholics, Protestants and Buddhists were able to see each other's rites publicly celebrated. For some residents, this time in Minidoka was a time of unparalleled religious discovery and experimentation. Minidoka residents often commented on how, despite the injustice and dispossession of the experience, the relocation experience did allow Buddhists and Christians unprecedented opportunities for social contact and intellectual exchange.[4]

This wartime ministry that Tom Fukuyama embarked upon in 1942 proved to be a crucible for his spiritual identity. Fukuyama regarded the war years as a refining time: a purifying and purging experience. He emerged from Minidoka with new religious vision and insight that he credits to the unique ecumenical experiences and interdenominational work he engaged in there. Fukuyama embarked upon a postwar career marked by a firm resolve to promote interracial and interreligious harmony and understanding, and with a determination to construct innovative religious communities that could both promote and model civil rights and social justice. After the war, Tom Fukuyama became a co-director of Brotherhood House, a revolutionary interracial and interreligious residential and fellowship centre committed to implementing interethnic, global Christian fellowship. Later in his career he served parishes again in Washington state (even serving a brief stint at Seattle's Japanese Baptist Church) and became a well-known Pacific Northwest Civil Rights activist in the 1960s and a tireless campaigner for urban renewal in the 1970s.

Tom Fukuyama's ecumenical programme at Minidoka was possible because the groundwork for this vision had been laid decades before by Japanese missionaries to the diaspora. From 1890 to 1937 Japanese Christian leaders exported to Seattle their missionary model of 'internationalist ecclesiology'. Japanese American Christian missions in Seattle were staffed and nurtured in the nineteenth and twentieth centuries by large numbers of male and female native Japanese missionaries and visiting evangelists. Even the Japanese religious leaders who were trained in America credit Japan for the crucial formation of their religious thought and careers. Japanese native missionaries arriving for sojourns in Seattle during the first three decades of the twentieth century brought to Seattle's

Protestant diaspora their intellectual, ethical and religio-political ideas, as well as Japanese mission strategies, books and newspapers.[5]

Studies of Christianity in the US Japanese diaspora largely ignore the influence of Japan and native Japanese missionaries and are hampered by the conceptual vocabulary of assimilation or nationalism: i.e. the idea that religious choice is an expression of either Americanist accommodationism or Japanese nationalism. Similarly, religious choice for the diaspora in America is often seen as either preserving ethnic identity, or fostering assimilation. As Adam McKeown notes, too often immigrants are forced into 'binary conception(s) of identity' and 'are seen as either here or there, and no room is left for more complex orientations and circulation'.[6] This chapter reconceptualizes the Seattle Japanese missions by tracing the internationalist mission matrix of its male and female Japanese missionary leaders. The Protestantism embodied and taught by native teachers to Seattle's Japanese community reflected a multi-tiered cultural identity that was more fluid and interactive across cultural and national boundaries than is normally supposed.[7]

Both Japanese and American church historians have tried to categorize and organize the variety of foundational theological approaches to Christianity in Japan. Historian Tomonobu Yanagita uses five subheadings to classify Japanese Protestant theologians who served Japan and its diaspora in the first decades of the twentieth century. First is the 'sub-orthodox school', which included mainline Protestant theologians who argued against the infallibility of scripture, such as Masahisa Uemura and Kajinosuke Ibuka. Second is the 'syncretized Christianity school', which ranged from radical theologians who wanted to merge Buddhist and Christian forms, to theologians who argued that Christianity was the greatest but not the only valid religion. Scholars usually place Danjo Ebina, Hiromichi Kozaki, Tokio Yoko and Tasuku Harada in this category. Third is the 'social work school'. These are members of the YMCA and WCTU, such as Utako Hayashi, Gunpei Yamamuro, Hideotoya Wada, Fumiko Ando and Kaji Yajima. Fourth is 'Christian socialism' – a broad category including internationalists, peacemakers and environmentalists, such as Kanzo Uchimura, Isowo Abe, Yoichi Honda, Saichira Kanda and Michi Kawai. Lastly is the 'Non-Church movement', or *Mukyukai*. The *Mukyukai* movement is what most scholars refer to when they use the term 'Japanese Christianity'. Yet 'Japanese Christianity' as a category should not be limited to the *Mukyukai* efforts to indigenize the church in a para-denominational fashion. For this chapter, Japanese Christianity refers to the wider indigenous matrix of Christianity, the agendas and concerns of which ranged well beyond those of Kanzo Uchimura and his movement.[8]

The theological currents within the Christianity of Japan were in many ways unique to the modernizing country and its challenges. And although the Japanese religious milieu is difficult to categorize, what remains constant throughout this period is the conviction that the Protestant Christianity these Japanese missionaries brought to the diaspora in Seattle was seen as a distinctly 'Japanese religion'. Not only was this position clearly articulated by native Japanese missionaries, but Caucasian missionaries and historians of religion in Japan also conceded this point: 'Christianity has ceased to be a hothouse plant, has become naturalized upon Japanese soil, and has sunk its roots deep into that soil.'[9] Even the architectural style of worship spaces reflected the Japanese spirit of independence from American Christianity. The Okayama Congregational Church in Japan, organized in 1880, paid the mortgage within five years through the congregation's sale of the sacred material culture from their pre-Christian lives: samurai swords, Buddhist icons, and domestic shrines. There were no pews, but people 'crowded together on the soft mats' on the floor. On the wall beside the preaching platform was a large, white paper frame where leading Chinese scholars of the province had written the Beatitudes in Chinese, and beside that hung a painting of the Road to Emmaus from the gospel story.[10]

Caucasian missionaries and historians often agreed that Japanese Christianity conformed to Japanese needs and values, not American ones. And it was not only missionaries who saw Christianity as Japanized: non-Christian Japanese leaders like Count Shigenobu Okuma also could make this concession: '[the Japanese] collect what is good, what is true, and what is beautiful, from all quarters of the earth. In a good sense, we Japanized Confucianism and Buddhism, and are Japanizing Christianity.'[11]

Japanese Christians were much less inclined to internalize and institutionalize American values than is normally presumed.[12] What Japanese missionaries disliked most of all was the accusation that they were engaged in mere imitation of American forms. Kanzo Uchimura cleverly remarked that too often Westerners tried to impose 'Americanianity' rather than preach true Christianity. Uchimura warned against the imitation of Western theologies, ecclesiastical structures and mission strategies, noting that 'aping is hypocrisy, and no good comes out of it'.[13] One way in which this hesitancy to imitate Americanist Christianity is clearly apparent is in the critique of the religious hypocrisy of American materialism. Frank assessments of American Christian culture abound in Japanese Christian writings:

As to religion, [Americans] consent to pay their pew-tax, and to be bored by an occasional sermon on Sunday, for appearance sake; but their real churches are their counting-houses, their real bible their ledger, and last of all, their real god is not Almighty God, but the 'almighty dollar'.[14]

This refusal merely to imitate Western forms and values is also strikingly demonstrated in publications by prominent Japanese Christians who theologized about how best to inlay non-Christian Japanese religions into the missionary message of Christian revelation. Tasuku Harada is typical of those who found many 'points of contact' between Christianity, Buddhism and Confucianism.

> Anyone who wishes to commend Christianity to thoughtful Japanese must certainly give the most careful attention to the relation of Christianity to non-Christian religions ... [I]f Christianity is the absolute religion, do we thereby declare that there is no truth whatsoever in other religions? ... For my part it is inconceivable that any one who has impartially studied the history of religion can fail to admit the universality of the activity of the Spirit of God, and the consequent embodiment of a degree of truth in all faiths.[15]

The Japanese Christianity brought to the diaspora in Seattle was in many ways internationalist, interreligious, and ecumenical years before these trends were common in the United States.[16] Japanese Christian missionaries who established the first US missions were well versed in interreligious contact. These missionaries were in active dialogue with a Buddhist religious community in Japan that was on the defensive. Buddhism had been weighed and found wanting as a 'traditional Japanese religion' because it had originally come to Japan from China and India.[17] Early in the Meiji era (1868–1912), Buddhism lost its quasi-established status, and many temples were dissolved, their statues and temple artefacts destroyed in an iconoclastic purge that sought to institute as the national religion of Japan a form of Shinto that was purified of all Buddhist syncretism. Ironically, Christians and Buddhists were both engaging in similar mission goals: how best to convince people that their message constituted a *bona fide* 'Japanese' religion. Both Christian and Buddhist groups argued that their religion could serve as the truest culture-bearer for Japan: as the religion that could best transmit and preserve the finest cultural traits of the Japanese in terms of ethics, loyalty, spirituality and patriotism. Thus, it is important to realize that Japanese native missionaries were bringing to early-twentieth-century Seattle a Christianity that was the product of the ecumenical and interreligious milieu of a rapidly modernizing Japan.[18]

Japanese missionaries integrated the indigenous concepts of *Bushido* and *Yamato Damashii* (the Japanese spirit) into their patriotic construction of Christianity. *Bushido* was an eighteenth-century Samurai loyalty ethic that had been adopted by Christians in the late nineteenth and early twentieth centuries to show how the Samurai concept of fealty to feudal lord that transcended filial loyalty could be transferred and perfected in loyalty to the Christian Lord. [19]

> *Bushido* ... is no longer the spirit of a class or portion of the people ... It is *Yamato Damashii*, the soul of Japan ... The element for its preservation is ... its new alliance with Christianity [which] has possibilities of development into something far more exalted than Japan has yet experienced.[20]

The Japanese concept of *kokutai* (fundamental character) was popular with Christian leaders because it served to moralize, and thus transform acquisitive nationalistic imperialist aims. The 'spirit of tolerance and freedom, is our *kokutai*, our imperialism, our ancestors' principle, and the anthem of our country'. One of the most marked and important differences between the various versions of Japanese Christianity's sacred patriotism and Japanese secular patriotism was Christians' complete disavowal of the idea of the racial superiority and uniqueness of the Japanese race. As a rule, Japanese Christians were highly critical of all forms of racial prejudice – in fact, one of their most consistent criticisms was the failure of American Christians to eradicate racism in the United States – a multicultural tolerance and openness that would later be a crucial factor shaping diaspora Christian identity.[21]

Openness to new types of women's leadership was another point of originality that the native Japanese Christian mission bequeathed to the diaspora. Japanese Protestant Christians constructed notions of women's leadership that both integrated yet transcended prevailing Eastern and Western norms. This model of Christian women's leadership utilized American norms of the single and married female missionary, but also co-opted the Neo-Confucian model of the 'good wife'. From 1887 to 1937, Japanese Christian women had only two pre-existing social models to choose from in pursuing a career in Christian social reform work. They could perform a leadership role in conjunction with their Christian husbands and/or children or other kin (brothers, sisters, etc.) and still fulfil the Japanese normative role of 'good wife/wise mother' (*ryosai kenbo*) or they could remain unmarried Christian workers. To these existing models Japanese Christians added a third: they could choose to leave their children and non-Christian husbands behind in pursuit of a higher calling they referred to as 'holy ambition'.[22]

Women at this time in Japan had a limited sphere for leadership in any capacity. Wives in particular were expected to be involved in philanthropic and patriotic activities, but all women were excluded from political meetings until 1922. The state's claims on the home 'preempted the women's claims to the state'. Thus, female political activists were arrested and their publications banned. Yet Christian leadership was protected by religious liberty clauses included as part of US/Japanese trade agreements. Thus Christian work provided a loophole for women to be social reformists under the auspices of legally acceptable philanthropy and religion.[23]

Three women missionaries important to the Seattle diaspora community exemplify the three models of women's leadership: Fumiko Ando, the Confucian/Christian 'good wife' leader; Michi Kawai, the unmarried woman leader who devoted her life to promoting peace, education reform, and internationalism; and Kaji Yajima, the divorced temperance leader who left family for the higher calling of 'holy ambition'. [24] These Japanese Christian women were not simply Western Christians in kimonos. In particular, Confucian ideals of moral self-cultivation and a woman's right to moral remonstrance helped to justify the leadership role of Japanese Christian missionaries in a nation and diaspora that had no pre-existing ideal of women's role as a public leader.

The story of Fumiko Ando is wonderfully preserved in the pages of a previously untranslated Japanese-language source from the Seattle Japanese diaspora. The six-church confederation or *Domei* founded in Seattle in 1912 published a Japanese language history for its 60th anniversary in 1972. It opens with the history of the Japanese Christian mission to the diaspora by telling the story of a woman leader, Fumiko Ando. This intemperate woman's temperance story, called 'The Sake Barrel Smashing Incident', occurs in December 1887. Not only does it use a story about a female leader to constitute the very origins of Christianity in the Japanese diaspora, but the tale provides us with information how typical it was for these Christians to see their faith as encompassing and perfecting Confucian ideals and norms.

The Sake barrel smashing incident

In the beginning [in] December, 1887 [the] president of the *Nihon Yusen* Corporation sent two barrels of Japanese sake to the then Consul General of Hawaii, Taro Ando. His wife [Fumiko Ando] was concerned. [But her husband] ... saw no harm in the Japanese population in Hawaii enjoying drinking ... Having come to a decision, the wife ordered her footman to carry the barrels to the back yard while the Consul General was out, and then destroyed the two barrels. The husband, stunned at the situation when he returned home, was given an ultimatum by his wife. Upon hearing her words, the Consul General felt empathy for his wife's position, and then decided to ban alcohol. In June, 1888, Consul General Ando and ten others were baptized by Admiral Harris ... The change of heart in these leaders represented a major first step towards a new way of living for people in Hawaii and on the mainland.[25]

The Fumiko Ando of the Sake Barrel Smashing Incident is much more than simply a Japanese caricature of Carrie Nation, axe-in-hand, smashing the sake barrel. The shock value of Fumiko Ando's conduct is not what one might presume. She does not directly violate late nineteenth-century Japanese moral norms of women's sphere of obedience and propriety. When viewed through the lens of Neo-Confucian teachings on moral remonstrance, Fumiko Ando can be seen as *exemplifying* Japanese gender ideals. In the Confucian text, *Classic of Filiality for Women*, there are guidelines for the concept of remonstrance, or 'demonstrating and expostulating'. 'If a husband has a remonstrating wife, then he won't fall into evil ways. Therefore, if a husband transgresses against the Way, you must correct him. How could it be that to obey your husband in everything would make you a virtuous person?'

Also, from the *Analects for Women*: 'Listen carefully to and obey whatever your husband tells you. If he does something wrong, gently correct him. Don't be like those women who not only do not correct their husbands but actually lead them into indecent ways ...'[26] Thus, this Sake Barrel Smashing tale and its literary role as the origin story for the diaspora mission in this Seattle six-church ecumenical history reveals that the moral ideal of Confucian good wife was no longer a relatively unattainable goal for most Japanese women. Instead, it was co-opted into the normative missionary model of the effective female Christian leader.[27]

The climax of the Sake Barrel Smashing incident is not in the spilling of the barrels, but in the stirring speech Ando gave to her no doubt stunned and probably angry diplomat husband. In the story, Fumiko Ando's convincing rhetoric and her responsible moral action sway her husband to become a temperance reformer. Up to this time, Taro Ando as Consul General had been publicly advocating temperance as good for the working-class labourer for it inspired thrift, efficiency and respectability. Yet prior to 1887, he had not yet taken the temperance pledge himself. This is precisely the moment when Christian Fumiko Ando acted as the Confucian good wife: by destroying the sake and exhorting her husband. Together, her actions and speech convinced Taro Ando of his hypocrisy. He realized that he too must personally and professionally enact the values of temperance. The story that begins the Seattle *Domei* church league history ends with Taro Ando becoming a leader of the transnational Japanese temperance movement and eventual publisher of its signature magazine, *Light of the World*. For Seattle's Japanese readers, Fumiko Ando in the Sake Barrel

Smashing Incident was playing the role of the ideal Japanese Christian female leader: she set her husband Taro Ando on the path of moral responsibility.[28]

Another Japanese female leader who greatly influenced women's moral reform work in the diaspora was Kaji Yajima (1832–1925). She co-founded the Japanese WCTU in 1886 and served as its president for many years. She divorced her alcoholic husband and became a Christian temperance reformer and peace activist at age 45. Her work to reform gender roles in Japan was also accomplished in part through an intellectual and ethical synthesis of Neo-Confucian and Christian teachings.[29]

For Kaji Yajima, gender reform could be possible through the Japanese WCTU (Women's Christian Temperance Union) platform of the 'three Ps': world purity, world prohibition and world peace. For Japanese Christians, temperance and anti-prostitution work was much more than mere vice reform. It constituted a direct route to redefining gender roles in Japan through the 'radical reform of the ideals of family life'. If men and women were to be equal partners, they must be willing to practise sobriety and sexual fidelity. Her peacemaking activism, culminating in her speech at age 89 before the World Disarmament Conference in Washington, DC, in 1921, was also directly connected to gender reform in Japan. There she presented 10,000 signatures from Japanese women calling for an end to all wars. The petition was 100 yards long, on Japanese rice-paper parchment.[30] The women signing this document were directly challenging (and by signing, subject to retaliation) the imperialist exemplar of motherhood that was actively taught in schools to fuel rising Japanese imperialist and military designs:

> The government's idea of the ideal Japanese mother, disseminated through school education, was a paragon of moral rectitude, who would stoically accept the entire burden of housework and totally dedicate herself to the service of her husband, in-laws, and children. That was supposed to be the way a mother would raise her children, who in turn would become loyal subjects of Imperial Japan. When the nation was at war, so the official propaganda went, a mother should readily surrender her children for the good of the state without a word of complaint ... The government stepped up propaganda campaigns extolling its version of maternal virtues such as self-effacement and self-sacrifice ... the only public activities women were allowed to take up were those aimed at supporting the war effort.[31]

Thus gender reform in both early twentieth-century Japan and Seattle necessitated a three-part social reform programme that included temperance, anti-prostitution campaigns, and global peacemaking efforts.

Michi Kawai (1878–1953) was an educational reformer influential in the diaspora who in the 1920s and 1930s worked on a woman-centred peacemaking and internationalist agenda during the difficult period of Japan's mounting imperialist phase. Her books *Japanese Women Speak*, *My Lantern* and *Sliding Doors* were widely read in the US. Several chapters of *Japanese Women Speak* are devoted to describing the internationalist and disarmament activity of Japanese Christian women. Japanese women were especially critical of the Japanese invasion of Manchuria (1931).

> Morally speaking we cannot say Japan is all wrong, but religiously speaking we must acknowledge and confess we are wrong. There ought to have been some other means. We must take one step at a time, depending on God. It is at least clear that three hundred thousand Christians in Japan ought to speak out clearly against the war. We must all be ready to sacrifice ourselves, one by one.[32]

Peacemaking and temperance were part of a radical religio-political platform that was inspired both by Neo-Confucian ethics and Western Christianity. For Michi Kawai, education was a precursor to social action.[33] Michi Kawai conceptualized education primarily in terms of Confucian vocabulary: as the moral 'self-cultivation' of the individual. As such, it was an essential foundation and precursor to any kind of personal and communal engagement in social gospel-type charity work in hospitals, tenements, prisons and orphanages, or to political work for any kind of significant internationalist or peacemaking programmes. '[T]he Japanese concept of peace ... becomes entwined with the Confucian idea that inner moral rectitude contributes to good social and cosmic order ... the emphasis [is] placed on individual moral cultivation.'[34]

The *Domei*, or interdenominational league of Seattle's six Japanese American ethnic congregations, celebrated its sixtieth anniversary by preserving stories of men and women who worked tirelessly in ecumenical coalitions to accomplish many of the ecclesiological goals and agendas of the Japanese Christian missionaries. These Seattle Japanese-American diaspora churches raised money to send delegates to world disarmament conferences. They worked to reform abuses to the picture bride system, and worked to reform gender role and relations by sponsoring anti-vice and anti-drinking campaigns. They established church day-care centres, kindergartens and English-language classes. After the Second World War, they sponsored several postwar peace initiatives, including 'Hiroshima Houses' – rebuilding campaigns to assist war-ravaged Japan. During the 1960s they provided a nucleus of leadership for Seattle's Asian American Civil Rights movement. During the 1970s they sponsored

Southeast Asian refuges and built greenhouses to supply Laotian refugee immigrants with seedlings for their hillside community gardens.[35]

Even during the racial-ethnic identity power movements of the 1960s and 1970s, the foundational internationalist and ecumenical sensibilities of Seattle's native Japanese missionaries made it possible for Japanese American Christians in Seattle to approach 'ethnicity with a prophetic eye'. As Fumitaka Matsuoka notes: '[E]thnicities provide the framework and perspective to enable us to see the reality of life clearly and to motivate us to engage in the civic life in the society. The celebration of ethnicity creates a doorway into the world rather than an escape out of the world.'[36]

Native Japanese missionaries taught the Seattle Christian diaspora 'to understand the gospel anew for the sake of mutuality, reconciled diversity, and community building among the estranged'. The internationalist, ecumenical, Confucianist spirit of Christianity brought to the mission field in Seattle provided a spiritual rationale and motivation for the six-church ecumenical federation to form a network of compassion and cooperation that extended beyond the ethnic enclave to reach many oppressed and marginalized peoples of this diverse Pacific Rim city. Missionaries from Japan brought to the city of Seattle their ecclesiological vision of the internationalist 'Church of the Pacific Era' – a model of ecumenism which continues to shape the institutional structures and agendas of Seattle's historic Japanese American churches.

Notes

1. The Japanese diaspora congregations in Seattle, with the dates of their foundings, are: Japanese Baptist (1899); Blaine Memorial Methodist – formerly Japanese Methodist (1904); Japanese Presbyterian (1907); Japanese Congregational (1907); St Peter's Episcopal (1908). All Japanese names used in this chapter follow the Americanized pattern of proper name, surname. The Japanese style is surname, proper name.

2. Tsutomu Tom Fukuyama (1915–88) was born in Winslow, Washington, and grew up in the Bainbridge Island Japanese American community. He joined his mother and sister in Seattle in 1942, and thus was incarcerated in Minidoka. His archives are included in his wife Betty's papers, donated to the University of Washington in 1993. The information is from a typescript document entitled: 'A Report of My Work at Minidoka': 2. Betty Fukuyama Papers, Acc. #4411, Box 7, used with permission, University of Washington Libraries.

3. Mimeographed Christmas Letter from Tsutomu Tom Fukuyama, dated 16 December 1942. Found in the Revd Emery Andrews Papers, Acc. #1908, Box 1, used with permission, University of Washington Libraries.

4. The camp newspaper, *The Minidoka Irrigator*, abounds with information about cross-religious exchange. See also, 'Japanese Americans in Idaho' by Robert Sims,

in *Japanese Americans: From Relocation to Redress*, ed. Roger Daniels *et al* (Seattle, Washington: University of Washington Press, 1986), 103–11.

5. There was a brisk traffic in Christian books and literature in the Meiji period. As one missionary noted in 1896, 'A large, independent Christian literature, including more than forty periodicals, all in the vernacular, is in constant circulation.' See James L. Barton, *The Japan Mission and Its Problems* (n.p., 1896), 10.

6. Adam McKeown's 'Chinese Migration in Global Perspective', in *Chinese Migrant Networks and Cultural Change, Peru, Chicago, Hawaii, 1900–1936* (Chicago: University of Chicago Press, 2001), 10–11. He discusses the overuse of binary oppositions and suggests ways better to integrate globalization theory and transnationalism into diaspora studies. Although he does not incorporate religion into his analysis, his suggestion that diaspora be seen in terms of cultural hybridity and multiplicity is useful here. Ann Laura Stoler's work, 'Rethinking Colonial Categories: European Communities and the Boundaries of Rule', in *Colonialism and Culture*, ed. Nicholas B. Dirks (Ann Arbor: University of Michigan Press, 1992), 321 is also helpful. Her caution against using the dichotomy of colonizer/colonized can be used here to challenge the common dichotomy of missionary/immigrant and missionary/native. To study Japanese-native Christian missionaries challenges the applicability of such theoretical categories.

7. Bryan Hayashi's *'For the Sake of Our Japanese Brethren': Assimilation, Nationalism and Protestantism Among the Japanese of Los Angeles, 1895–1942* (Stanford, CA: Stanford University Press, 1995) shows how Protestantism can serve pro-Japan nationalism as easily as pro-American nationalism, yet it does not explore the theological context of Meiji-era Japanese Christianity much outside of the Caucasian mission.

8. Tomonobu Yanagita, *A Short History of Christianity in Japan* (Sendai: Seisho Tosho Kankokai, 1957), 53–7. What is curiously missing from this list is any mention of an 'orthodox' school.

9. See *Fragments of Fifty Years: Some Lights and Shadows of the Work of the Japan Mission of the American Board, 1868–1919* (American Board of Commission for Foreign Mission – Japan Mission, n.p. 1919), 28.

10. Chinese language was high culture in nineteenth-century Japan, and Japanese first read the Bible in Chinese as it was not translated into Japanese until late in the century. See M. L. Gordon, *Thirty Eventful Years: The Story of the American Board Mission in Japan 1869–1899* (Boston: American Board Commission for Foreign Missions, n.p., 1901), 61.

11. Count Shigenobu Okuma, 'Our National Mission', in *Japan's Message to America: A Symposium by Representative Japanese on Japan and American–Japanese Relations*, ed. Naoichi Masaoka (Tokyo: n.p., 1914), 4.

12. The accommodationist thesis is quite common, as Rumi Yasutake writes: 'Internalizing Protestant American middle-class moral values (103) ... Japanese women and men interpreted and accommodated American Protestant middle-class gender ideology and their methods of activism to the ... jingoistic sociohistorical conditions of Meiji Japan' (108). See 'Transnational Women's Activism: The Woman's Christian Temperance Union in Japan and the United States', in *Women and Twentieth-Century Protestantism*, ed. Margaret Lamberts Bendroth and Virginia Lieson Brereton (Urbana: University of Illinois Press, 2002), 93–112.

13. Kanzo Uchimura, *Diary of a Japanese Convert* (New York: Fleming H. Revell Co., 1895), 205, 183.

14. E. R. Inouye, 'The Practical Americans', in *The Japanese in America*, ed. Charles Lanman (New York: University Publishing Co., 1872), 70. This book is a collection of essays by Christian and non-Christian Japanese after their sojourns in the US.

15. Tasuku Harada, *The Faith of Japan* (New York: Macmillan Co., 1914), 180–1.

16. Japanese Christians were internationalist several decades before the term became popular in post-First-World-War Wilsonian liberal internationalism. See Tomoko Akami, *Internationalizing the Pacific: The United States, Japan and the Institute of Pacific Relations in War and Peace, 1919–56* (New York: Routledge, 2002).

17. Hideo Kishimoto has a useful discussion of the 'nationalistic rejection' of Buddhism 'as a foreign faith', in *Japanese Religion in the Meiji Era*, trans. John F. Howes (Tokyo: Obunsha, 1956), 51.

18. See James Edward Ketelaar, *Of Heretics and Martyrs in Meiji Japan: Buddhism and Its Persecution* (Princeton, NJ: Princeton University Press, 1990).

19. The most well-known popularizer of the conflation of Bushido with Christianity was Inazo Nitobe, a Christian internationalist who served as Under-Secretary General of the League of Nations from 1919 to 26. See *Bushido: The Soul of Japan* (Philadelphia: The Leeds and Biddle Co., [1899] 1900).

20. Tasuku Harada, *The Faith of Japan* (New York: Macmillan, 1914). For many years Harada was president of Doshisha University, a Christian university, in Kyoto.

21. Yamaji Aizan is here quoted in Graham Squires' introductory essay in *Yamaji Aizan, Essays on the Modern Japanese Church: Christianity in Meiji Japan*, trans. Graham Squires (Ann Arbor: Center for Japanese Studies, University of Michigan, 1999), 22. *Kokutai* was used by non-Christians as well, and meant 'the fundamental character of our Empire'. For more on *Kokutai*, see John Paul Reed, *Kokutai: A Study of Certain Sacred and Secular Aspects of Japanese Nationalism* (Chicago: University of Chicago, 1937), 207ff.

22. Essays on Christian womanhood extol the virtues of 'ladies, unmarried as well as married . . . leaving home and kindred and country to teach and help their sisters of another race and nation. How insensibly and powerful this fact has wrought upon their ideals of womanhood . . . [in] how many girls has it awakened high and holy ambition.' See 'Christian Womanhood' from M. L. Gordon, *An American Missionary in Japan* (Boston: Houghton, Mifflin and Co., 1892), 180. For Michi Kawai's views on how women could have 'brilliant professional careers' in the church see *Japanese Women Speak* (Boston: The Central Committee of Foreign Missions, 1933), 132.

23. See Sharon H. Nolte and Sally Ann Hastings, 'The Meiji States' Policy Toward Women', in *Recreated Japanese Women, 1600–1945*, ed. Gail Lee Bernstein (Berkeley, CA: University of California Press, 1991), 151–74 and Kathleen S. Uno, *Passages to Modernity: Motherhood, Childhood and Social Reform in Early Twentieth Century Japan* (Honolulu: University of Hawaii Press, 1999).

24. This phenomenon of the maternal absence of women missionaries is not new or unique to Japan, however. See *Unbecoming Mothers: The Social Production of Maternal Absence*, ed. Diana L. Gustafson (London: Haworth Clinical Practice Press, 2005), 123–40.

25. Juhei C. Kono, (ed.), *Shiatoru Nihonjin Kirisuto Kyokai Domei Rokuju Shunen Kinenshi* [In Commemoration of the 60th Anniversary of the Seattle Japanese Church Federation, 60th Anniversary History] (Matsuyama City, Japan: Matsuyama Printing Limited, 1974), 6–7. Selection translated by Roger Chriss.

26. Women who received any education or cultural training in Japan were exposed to Neo-Confucianism in their youth. Included in the Confucian Classics would have been the great Neo-Confucian reformer Wang Yang Ming, 1472–1529. In addition to Wang Yang Ming, Japanese girls could be exposed to a set of 'Confucian classics for women' developed and compiled, to correspond to the canonical four Confucian classics taught to men including *The Analects, Mencius, Doctrine of the Mean*, and *Great Learning*. For women, there was: Pan Zhao's (Han Dynasty) work *Admonitions for Women*; the Tang Dynasty texts *Classic of Filiality for Women* and *Analects for Women*, and *Instructions for the Inner Quarters*.

27. For the historical chain of events, see the chapter 'Religion', in Yukiko Kimura's *Issei: Japanese Immigrants in Hawaii* (Honolulu: University of Hawaii Press), 158–9. For Taro Ando's own views, see *Account of My Conversion in Hawaii*, Hon. Taro Ando, trans. K. Yabuuchi (Tokyo: Methodist Publishing House, 1907), 1–8. His widely read pamphlet was popular in his time, but rare today. (The only US copy is in Columbia University Library.)

28. William T. De Bary *et al.*, *Sources of Japanese Tradition*, vol. 1, 2nd edn (New York: Columbia University Press, 2001), 827, 830.

29. This training, while by no means the norm, still was not unique to Kaji Yajima. See William T. De Bary *et al*, *Sources of Japanese Tradition*, 399, where it notes that 'women [in Japan] had available not only a considerable body of classical literature but also … *Classics of Filiality and Admonitions for Women* … and *Analects for Women* …'

30. *The New York Times*, 1 November 1921, 16. This article mistakenly lists her age as 90.

31. Mari Yamamoto sets the connection here between statism, pacifism and gender in early twentieth-century Japan. See *Grassroots Pacifism in Post-War Japan* (London: Routledge Curzon, 2004), 127–8.

32. Address by Ochimi Kobushiro, quoted in Michi Kawai, *Japanese Women Speak* (Boston, MA: Central Committee on the United Study of Foreign Missions, n.p., 1934), 173.

33. One such education reformer was Naomi Tamura (Naomi is not to be confused with the biblical female name; it is here a Japanese male name). He campaigned for the Christian education of the child as a way to convert Japan. He saw this educational reform not as implementing Horace Bushnell's ideals, but as an innovative Japanese reform of American methods based on his 25-years' experience in the parish. See *The Child the Center of Christianity* (Tokyo: Taishio Kindergarten Publishing Dept., 1926).

34. Robert Kisala, *Prophets of Peace: Pacificism and Cultural Identity in Japan's New Religions* (Honolulu: University of Hawaii Press, 1999), 18.

35. These activities are all carefully outlined in the various congregational histories and reports throughout the pages of the Domei history. See Juhei C. Kono (ed.), *Shiatoru Nihonjin Kirisuto Kyokai Domei Rokuju Shunen Kinenshi* [In Commemoration of the 60th Anniversary of the Seattle Japanese Church Federation, 60th Anniversary History] (Matsuyama City, Japan: Matsuyama Printing Limited, 1974). Select translations by Roger Chriss were funded through a Luce Foundation Grant, College of Wooster, Ohio. For a case study of how one of these Seattle congregations implemented this vision of ecumenicity and multicultural outreach, see Madeline Duntley, 'Heritage, Ritual and Translation',

INDEX